ECHOES
of the MOON

ECHOES

of the MOON

Kathryn Clark

Sryos – New York

This is a work of non-fiction. The events are as I experienced them and are only my perceptions. Names have been changed.

ISBN-13: 978-1469904337
ISBN-10: 1469904330

We kindly thank the publishers for permission to reprint the following:

Page 1: Roethke, Theodore; *Straw For The Fire*, Random House

Page 47, 416: Nagy, Gregory; *The Best Of The Achaeans: Concepts Of The Hero In Archaic Greek Poetry*, © 1980, 1997 The Johns Hopkins University Press. Reprinted by permission of the author.

Page 67: Excerpt from *The Throne Of Labdacus: A Poem* by Gjertrud Schnackenberg. Copyright © 2001 by Gjertrud Schnackenberg. Reprinted by permission of Farrar, Straus and Giroux, LLC.

Page 110: Keeley, Edmund; *C.P. Cavafy*, © 1975 by Edmund Keeley and Philip Sherrard Reprinted by permission of Princeton University Press.

Page 180: "[Ignorant before the heavens of my life]", from *Ahead Of All Parting* by Rainer Maria Rilke, translated by Stephen Mitchell, translation copyright © 1995 by Stephen Mitchell. Used by permission of Modern Library, a division of Random House, Inc.

Page 266: Burkert, Walter; *Greek Religion*, translated by John Raffan, Cambridge, Mass.: Harvard University Press, pp 326, 327, Copyright @ 1985 by Basil Blackwell Publisher and Harvard University Press. Reprinted by permission of the publisher.

Page 296: Greenbaum, Norman; *Spirit In The Sky* © 1969 Reprinted by permission of Great Honesty Music, Inc.

To all of us who experience life

"I am nothing but what I remember"
Theodore Roethke

April 2007: "How do you do it?" A tall woman wearing a long black dress coat and a black fur pillbox hat, golden hair spilling down to her shoulders, stood on the sidewalk inches away from me. I was in our front yard, cleaning out the winter debris from the flowerbed under the magnolia tree, preparing to plant seeds, my knees cold and damp as the moisture from the ground seeped through my torn jeans. At first, I thought she was referring to cleaning the flowerbed. "I mean with your husband?" she continued.

I slowly rose, taking off my soiled garden gloves, rubbing the dirt from my sweatshirt and looked into her piercing blue eyes inquisitively.

I responded the only way I knew, "One step in front of another."

She stepped onto the grass while her massive black lab sniffed the ground, straining against his red collar. She slowly told me of her husband's battle with lung cancer and now with a rare form of leukemia. She told me that his sister had already died of this type of leukemia just last year. She thought her husband would only live for two more years. She looked my age and I wondered how old her husband was. We spoke for awhile. She told me that all her husband wanted was another dog: to be exact, a chocolate lab puppy. They had attended the National Westminster Dog Show in New York City to interview breeders and had chosen an excellent one in Connecticut, about three hours away. They had visited the breeder twice and had selected the puppy. They would pick her up in June. I wished her the best as she walked away with the largest black lab I had ever seen.

———⬥———

Let me explain. I have lived in this house on this street for the past fourteen years and she has lived in her house, across the street and three houses down for the last twenty-seven. I had never spoken to her before now. I remember seeing her one or two times before. I knew that she lived there and I knew her name. Her name was Dorothy. How did I do it, she wanted to know.

How did I do it? I never really thought about how I did it. Now, reconsidering the past seven years, the events my family and I experienced could be the story of any one of us. Maybe not in such a condensed time period, but all of us experience life and this is a story about life.

WINTER
2000 – 2001

My husband came home from work one evening in late November, briefcase in hand. He walked over to the stove where I was cooking and kissed me on the cheek. As he washed his hands at the kitchen sink with his back towards me, I looked over to him and noticed a large blood stain on the back of his yellow dress shirt.

I asked, "What happened to your back?"

"Oh, it's just a mole that got a scab on it," he replied.

My husband had fair skin, a light complexion with brown hair that used to turn bleach blond in the Southern California sun where he grew up. He turned to help finish the salad, adding the celery and onion. He was actually the cook in the family, not me, but on weekdays I did the routine cooking and the kids endured it. He began cooking when he was in elementary school when his mother was sick. He was never afraid to experiment with ingredients and portions and consistently concocted masterpieces. Me, I stayed the course and followed the recipe to the nth degree and the result was usually edible.

I suggested that a dermatologist should look at it and he agreed. Because of our insurance, he saw a dermatologist not at the leading medical center where he worked, but a dermatologist in a suburb north of us. A few days later, he told me a biopsy had been taken and the doctor wanted to take a wait and see approach. He didn't say anything else. I didn't even know the dermatologist's name.

He knew that I was taking my dad to radiation treatment five days a week for the next six weeks, a herculean feat for my mother and myself. This entailed my mother driving an hour from their country home to our house. Then I drove them in their car the half hour, depending on traffic, into the city. I dropped them at the medical center, parked and joined them at the radiation center. After my dad's radiation treatment was completed for the day, we reversed course, stopping at a local diner for a late lunch.

———

My father was diagnosed with glioblastoma phase four in early August. Glioblastoma is an aggressive brain cancer. He had a craniotomy in late August to remove as much of the cancer as possible, but glioblastoma is like a jellyfish. If you try to remove all the tentacles, you remove most of the brain. The idea is to remove the biggest chunk of cancer and give the patient quality of life for whatever life remains. It is the speed at which the tentacles grow that will determine the length of your life. This is what I know now. Not what I knew then.

———

Then I began the never-ending research of how to cure glioblastoma, to find clinical trials that were at the cutting edge, that were closest to the cure. I rationally knew this was a death sentence. I know I did because I came back early from our annual family sailing cruise on Cape Cod, leaving my husband and our three children stranded to visit Plymouth Plantation for the day and keep the boat moored. While I had never been the captain on our sailing cruises, I was a solid first mate who intervened at critical times alleviating potential disasters. My husband had reluctantly agreed but I knew he was not happy. But I wanted to be with my father in the doctor's office where he would be given the definitive diagnosis and I didn't want to even think about the possibility of something happening to my family, sailing without me.

While I didn't want to hear the doctor mutter the words, more importantly, I didn't want my dad to be alone, with only my mother. My dad was now walking with a cane and his large frame depended on it. He sat in the chair in front of the neurologist's massive mahogany desk. From behind the desk, the neurologist explained glioblastoma to him in detail. At the end, my father stood up, bent over the desk and shook the physician's hand and thanked him.

"You're welcome. We like to be honest so that you can get your affairs in order," the neurologist said.

I felt those words slam into my gut and I gasped silently for air. The three of us walked out of the neurologist's office slowly without saying a word to each other and I left to get the car. Walking to the car, I thought *I want to take those words out of history. Those words should not exist. They should be permanently removed.*

And still seven years later, I feel the same way. The first death, maybe like the first birth – every memory, every feeling, is etched in stone in your heart. Every pulsating passion is felt throughout your entire body. In this case, anguish.

From 1993 to 2000, this was the man I talked with on a regular basis. Every morning, we talked on the phone for about an hour after the kids got to school, my husband to work, the dog walked, the laundry started. He bought me a headset so I could continue to do the household chores while we spoke on the phone. This was the man who taught me everything I know about stocks, the Street, capital gains and losses, bonds, mutual funds, how to compute detailed tax forms B, C and D, not to mention the 1040.

This was the man who drove an hour almost every day to repair our house for years. My husband and I had bought a foreclosure and the previous owners had trashed the house. Live electrical wires, broken windows, closets without shelves, graffiti sprayed on walls. This was our house. Simply trashed, but he came in with his tools and worked. He stopped when the kids came home from school and sat and chatted with them at the kitchen table as they ate their snack.

This was the man who, in the midst of painting upstairs, would yell out "B-flat" to my oldest daughter, Rebecca, practicing the piano. By the third missed note, his ears hurting, he would put down his paintbrush and run down the stairs to the piano and hit the B-flat for her. Rebecca had begun piano lessons when she was six years old and diligently practiced everyday.

When my five-year-old son complained that he couldn't put his toys away on his closet's top shelf, my dad built a ladder inside his closet so he could climb to the top shelves and put his toys away. He was that type of a guy. He solved problems.

This was the man who traveled to Greece with us year after year. The first exploratory trip was with my mother, him and me. Then, the seven of us, four adults and three children, traipsed from Crete to Delphi each May. And each year, my dad and I would begin our planning in January in preparation for the annual May trip. From January through April, we would talk about details, leaving no stone unturned and our trips were always perfect, fun stuff for the kids and those out-of-the-way, remote archeological sites for me.

This was the man who, if the statistics were right, would be dead in less than a year.

Every weeknight, I drove my eleven-year-old son, William, and my thirteen-year-old daughter, Heather, to swim practice about thirty minutes away from our home. Heather began competitively swimming when she was six years old and William had followed her lead. They loved not only swimming, but the friendships they developed there. Me, I never was a typical swim club parent. I didn't hang out in the bleachers with the rest of the parents watching swim practice, talking about how their kid took off 2.75 seconds in the 500 freestyle last swim meet or how they didn't like the coach's technique. This was what inevitably caused junior to add on seconds to his swim race. I dropped the kids off in front of the swim club and found a place to park. I brought my green tea and latest research on clinical trial information on glioblastoma. I pored over the material with a fine-tooth comb, trying to glean any amount of help. It seemed like the rare hope lay with the holistic approach. I researched western doctors who combined both approaches. I settled on an oncologist at a different leading medical school's hospital from where my dad was receiving his current radiation treatment and as soon as radiation stopped, my dad would be transferred there. I thought *this is a plan: a plan with hope.*

Early December, immersed in learning how shark cartilage could stave off the growth of glioblastoma, sipping green tea and holding the flashlight in the car, William startled me when he appeared in the window, sobbing, holding his hand with dangling fingers. His fingers appeared unconnected to the palm. I immediately opened the passenger side door and he climbed in, holding his swollen fingers. We drove to a local pizzeria, a block away, and I ran in and asked for a bag of ice to stop the swelling.

Once I applied the ice, I asked, "What happened?"

Through tears, he sobbed "Before practice, I was running on the deck and smacked my hand on the sign on the pole."

"The sign that reads, 'No Running on the Pool Deck'?" I smiled and asked.

At that moment, Heather opened the sliding door of the van and climbed in and we took off for the emergency room. She had left swim practice, knowing her brother had smashed his hand. I called their father from the car to tell him what had happened. He had just arrived home from work and was heating up his dinner, but he agreed to meet us in the local hospital. Waiting to be seen, I watched my husband enter the waiting room. He walked over to his son and took his son's hand in his own. He carefully inspected each of his son's fingers.

"The third, fourth and fifth fingers are dislocated," he informed us. "No worries, they can easily be relocated into their proper sockets." My husband, the ex-football player, the ex-swimmer from Southern California had seen much worse in his day. He was right. The orthopedist used a pencil to relocate William's fingers and all was well.

The next morning, in the front yard, preparing to take our golden retriever for his ritual walk, I greeted my husband as he came out to drive to work. Instead of getting into his car to drive to work, he put his briefcase down by the car and walked slowly over to me. "I received the results of the biopsy from the mole on my back yesterday."

I thought *this result is not going to be bad. This is going to be a blip on the radar screen. This is not going to be a problem. My dad is the problem. One problem, one problem like this is all I can take. This result is not going to be a problem.*

He interrupted my thought process and said, "The result is melanoma."

My mind swirled. I thought *okay. We can beat melanoma. This is not a death sentence like glioblastoma. This is melanoma. We can handle this. This is not a problem. People don't die from melanoma.*

Again, he interrupted my thoughts, "The dermatologist wants to take a wait-and-see approach. I found out yesterday, but I didn't think it was a good idea to bring it up last night. You looked upset about William's fingers."

I appreciated his discretion and consideration, but I forgot to thank him.

———

William's fingers relocated, my dad's radiation treatment almost completed, I arranged for my dad's new treatment plan at the other medical center. It was now time to research melanoma. It was nearing Christmas and I should have been decorating our house for the season, but I wanted to read up on melanoma.

Melanoma is the most serious kind of skin cancer. The thicker the tumor is, the more serious the disease. If the mole is ulcerated, the prognosis is not as good. To see if the disease has spread, the patient should have a sentinel node biopsy. Dye is injected in the area where the melanoma was removed. The dye flows to the nearby lymph nodes. The first lymph nodes to take up the dye are removed and tested for cancer. If these (sentinel lymph nodes) are cancer free, there is a good chance that the melanoma has not spread beyond the area, where it was first discovered.

I stopped reading and dashed downstairs to the basement and entered my husband's office. Shuffling through an array of papers, I found his pathology report. I read that his tumor was thick and ulcerated. I thought *no question about it. My husband must have the sentinel node biopsy. We need to know that the melanoma has not spread. We need to know this is not a problem. But his doctor wanted to take a wait and see approach. That must mean he thinks the disease has not spread. This must mean he is cancer free. This is not a problem.*

⟶•⟵

Each Christmas before this one, all five of us – my husband, the three kids and me with our golden retriever – would bundle up in our winter gear, pile into the station wagon and drive out to the country in search of the perfect Christmas tree. Equipped with rope, saw and canvas, we would drive to the grandparents' house, pick them up and then continue on to a country Christmas tree farm. Invariably, after much mulling and discussion, we would find the fullest, most robust tree to adorn our home and we would find a smaller, lovely one for the grandparents. We would take our time in cutting the tree down, wrapping it in canvas and securing it to the roof rack. Gramma would bring hot chocolate in thermoses and afterwards, sitting in the car, the hot chocolate would warm our insides.

This year, William and I drove out alone to the grandparents. My father was in no position to cut down a Christmas tree and no one else in my family was in the mood for this adventure. It was a bleak, gray, overcast day, typical of the northeast in December. William and I made small talk during the drive, but we both know we were beginning a new Christmas ritual: a ritual we weren't so sure about. We stopped at a local nursery where pre-cut small, but fresh Christmas trees were aligned in rows in buckets. William selected a very small, but full tree. He tossed it in the backseat of our van and we set out for the grandparents' home. My dad, at this point, still retained his happy disposition, but he admitted to me that he ends up in a room and can't remember why he came into it. The tentacles were growing. Unable to walk by himself, he walked with a cane or sometimes a walker. William located the tree holder in the garage and installed the Christmas tree in their living room by the baby grand piano and the large windows that overlooked the hill in their rolling backyard.

———◆———

Rebecca's seventeenth birthday was in mid-January. To celebrate, we invited the grandparents for a dinner party at our house. All my life, my father had done the driving. The joke had been that my mother was allowed to drive for thirty minutes when they were first married. My mother drove and was a good driver, but this was the way it had always been. When they were together, my father drove. In Greece, he and my husband took turns. One day, my husband drove. The next day, my dad would. Neither my mother nor I ever drove in Greece. On my daughter's seventeenth birthday, my mother drove from the country into our house. My father sat in the passenger seat. I worried about her driving since the days were short, the roads were icy and the dark country roads remote at night.

Before dinner, we congregated in the living room to enjoy our cocktails and hors d'oeuvres. My dad reclined in the leather easy chair across from the piano and my mother nestled herself into the white fluffy couch. I noticed how my dad's left eyelid drooped and how his skin looked red and blotchy. I sat on the piano bench with my birthday girl, who sat slightly in front of me. My dad took an envelope from his jacket's inner pocket and I held my breath. Customarily, enclosed would be a generous check, but tonight somehow I doubted it would be a check for the birthday girl. He slowly opened the envelope and took out a letter. He put on his reading glasses and read:

January, 2001

Dear Granddaughter,

Happy Birthday! The years roll by and your birthdays keep on coming. Let's keep up with that habit.

I believe I have told you the story about my Baldwin piano but I will repeat some of it here.

My mother and father wanted to give a major gift to each of the three sons when they were young. They thought a piano was appropriate for me since, like you, I had practiced long and hard on my mother's old upright. So one day the three of us went to Denver to the Baldwin Piano Company. We looked and played on every piano in the showroom. I picked out one with very good tone and action but not too big. (It had to fit in our house.) My parents agreed and the purchase was made. The piano was delivered to my parent's home in Boulder. After high school and the start of World War II, all three boys left home for military service. But before I left in 1943, my parents told me that when I returned home and had a home of my own I could have the piano as my own. I did return home, completed four years of university, married a beautiful young girl and bought our home in Aurora, Colorado.

Guess what was the first thing we did after moving into our new home. You're right. I called the moving van to move the piano to our new home.

I want to do the same thing for you. When you have your first home and are reasonably established, call the moving van for your piano. It's yours. Happy Seventeenth Birthday! I believe there are many more good years in this piano and I know there are many good years left in your musical life to develop your skills and enjoy good music.

We hope you enjoy the piano over the years to come as much as we have. Perhaps a smile might appear sometime as you approach the piano in your own home.

Much love,

Grandfather

Yes, my dad was a consummate pianist. It was his ear. His piano was his most prized possession. And now, it would be my daughter's. She walked over to him and gave him the biggest bear hug her petite arms could muster. I thought *how is it possible to be elated and devastated at the same time. But that's what Rebecca must be.* He gave no other possession away before his death. I admired his courage to look death squarely in the face and say, "I know I'm going to die soon, but I'm still going to do what is important to me."

SPRING – SUMMER
2001

In late March, my husband agreed to the sentinel node biopsy. I was relieved. The other shoe was not going to drop. We drove together to his appointment at the medical center where he worked and located the procedure room. It was a small room with a huge leather exam table. Behind it huge black screens hung on the walls and many high tech medical machines stood beside the table. My husband changed into a hospital gown and sat facing the screen. The technician opened the gown to expose his back. He took a long needle with a tube at the end of it and stuck the needle into the site where the ulcerated mole had been removed. I watched as the fluid flowed into my husband's back and then looked at the lit black screen that would display where the dye would travel as it traced the path where the melanoma had metastasized. The technician told me that this would take upwards of an hour and I should sit in the waiting room. My husband had been given a sedative. He would doze during the procedure.

I left the room and discovered a chair in the hallway beside the door. I had grabbed the *Smithsonian* magazine before I had left the house and I picked it up. I scanned the table of contents. An article about Cape Cod whalers caught my attention. My husband's great-great uncle had been killed off of Harwich Port in a whaling accident. When we had first moved to this area, we had driven to Harwich Port and had located the local small library. The librarian had assisted us in finding the actual newspaper article written about the uncle. I had gained a deep respect for whalers that day. The sperm whale had violently snapped his whaling dory in two and the uncle drowned. I had wondered if the coldness of the November Atlantic water anesthetized him before his lungs filled up with the briny salt water. I flipped to the article and read.

An hour or so later, the technician found me. The test was completed and the radiologist would be here shortly to interpret the test. I reentered the exam room and saw my husband asleep. I stared at the black screen trying to figure out what all the scattered red and blue lines represented, but it was hopeless. I couldn't tell if the lines indicated the metastases. It was like a jigsaw puzzle.

The radiologist walked in and introduced himself. He shook my hand and reviewed the black screen.

"The melanoma has not metastasized to any lymph node. You can assume your husband has a clean bill of health," he informed us.

At that moment, my husband woke up and we both heard these words together. We smiled at each other. I thought *I should not be so harsh on suburban doctors. Now we know for sure that our lives will continue in our normal pattern. Our routines will stay the same.* That evening, we treated the kids to our favorite Japanese restaurant in celebration of the life affirming news.

———◆◆———

Rebecca, who attended boarding school outside of Boston, was home for spring break. She had hated our town's high school. In ninth grade, when she continuingly asked "why" in her math class and kept receiving the response, "It just is.", she pleaded to go to a different school. My husband and I agreed. She transferred her sophomore year to the girls boarding school I had attended years before. She thrived in her academics and began fencing with a passion. This year, she qualified for the World Cup and her fencing coach had registered her for the competition in New Hampshire. My husband couldn't take the time off from work, so we decided that I would accompany her. Rebecca and I packed the Sienna van and drove four hours to the outskirts of Boston so she could practice with her coach before driving the last two-hour stretch up to New Hampshire. The competition was scheduled for the following day. It was late in the afternoon and the sky threatened snow when we arrived.

I dropped her at the fencing club and searched for a local diner to have coffee and to listen to the weather report. Greeks owned most of the diners in this area and their food and coffee were consistently good. I sat at the counter, sipping a large coffee, hazelnut, milk and sugar, nibbling on sesame biscuits. I listened to the television behind the counter. Snow was predicted to accumulate eight to ten inches by midnight for the greater Boston area. A storm warning was in effect for the greater metropolitan area.

I finished and returned to the fencing club. I was anxious to begin driving, but her coach was in the middle of instructing her on the mat. Both of them were dressed in full fencing attire. I leaned against the wall, watching them. It was the World Cup, I reminded myself. Finally, she left the mat and went into the locker room to change. As we drove around the city of Boston, snow began to fall. Driving north along the coast, the northeaster picked up and I remembered the northeasters I had lived through as a child sixty miles south of here. In preparation, my dad would have had the Coleman stove with gas, kerosene lamps, flashlights, matches, and a battery operated radio ready. My mother would have had our pantry stocked with canned goods, dried beans and rice. When the electrical wires went down, our house became the neighborhood center. We fed anyone and everyone, first from the refrigerator, then the freezer, then from the pantry.

The drive became treacherous and I felt the anti-lock brakes working beneath my feet. Three and a half hours later in the pitch of darkness, we located our hotel as the snow came down horizontally and the slush piled up along the windswept highway. We climbed out of the van and were nearly blown away by the frigid, howling wind. We were exhausted and starving.

The hotel dining room would close in fifteen minutes and I dare say, we were not going to venture out again that night. We found our room, but before we went down to eat, I insisted that we call the grandparents to let them know we made it. Our multigenerational family rule: when traveling, once at your destination, notify your parents that you're safe. Some things do not change, no matter how old you are. I called and while the call was being connected, I thought *this might be the last time I call him while traveling. Shake off this empty feeling before you hear his voice. Do not let him hear your sadness. Be cheerful.*

It was another typical bitter gray morning as we waited for the doors to open for the World Cup. The fencing girls were verbally assaulting one another, trying to undermine each other's confidence. I eased past the girls dressed in thick white canvas fencing suits and took my seat in the bleachers. Rebecca went to prepare. She was the only fencer from her school and I was slightly concerned for her. I breathed a sigh of relief when I saw her advisor, a wonderfully warm woman, climb the bleacher with her husband. They took their seats right next to me and we exchanged pleasantries.

Never having been to a fencing meet, only swim meets prior to this, I tried to determine who was winning and who was losing by the scoreboard. It was hopeless to figure it out by the competitors. They moved their sabers with lightning speed. We saw my daughter walk onto the mat to compete. I thought *wow, this is my daughter and this is a World Cup. But, something is not right. She doesn't look right. I don't know what is the matter. Something is wrong. What is it?*

She didn't score a point. Her advisor, who had seen her compete several times, agreed with me. I couldn't see her face behind the mask, but her body was betraying her. It was as if each movement was in slow motion. The duel was over. I climbed down from the bleachers and found her in the vast expo. She looked terrible. She was sweating from every pore of her body. Her eyes were glazed. I felt her forehead. It was on fire. She thought she had the flu. I didn't know what she had. I only knew we were going home. I would make an appointment with her doctor for the next day. We drove home in a record of six hours on the snow-crusted highways.

The next day, at the doctor's office, the doctor examined Rebecca and gave her the monospot test. The results indicated she had the Epstein Barr Virus: mononucleosis. She would be fine in a few weeks, her doctor assured her. Three weeks of rest, fluids, nutritional food and all would be well. For three weeks, she stayed home moping around the house, watching a kindergarten TV show. She was not fine. Here was an above-average student, taking three Advanced Placement Courses her junior year of high school and was now watching a man on TV teaching children how to tie their shoes. No, this was not right. I began my research on Epstein Barr Virus.

> Neurological syndromes due to EBV infectious mononucleosis include optic neuritis, transverse myelitis, aseptic, meningitis, encephalitis, meningoencephalitis, cranial nerve (CN) palsies (particularly CN VII, and Guillain-Barre syndrome.

> Fatigue resolves itself in three months. Some patients experience prolonged fatigue with neurological complications.

I called her doctor and explained my daughter's symptoms and requested a referral to an infectious disease specialist. The infectious disease specialist confirmed that this virus could cause neurological deficits, although this was rare. Only time could heal her. I inquired how long the healing process would take. The specialist answered that it might involve several months of rest and a low activity level. It was then that we decided she would take a leave of absence from school since this was the end of April. I thought *she and her grandfather can commiserate together. Both of them are neurologically impaired.*

In April, my father's brother came from Iowa to visit him. I met him at the airport and drove him to my parent's house in the country. This was the first of the visitors to pay their last respects. I didn't know how people knew this was near the end. Maybe they had done their research, too. Maybe we all had a new-found respect for medical statistics.

We had a delicious dinner and the two men traded stories about growing up in the mountains of Colorado. Lots of laughter, love and camaraderie filled the dining room that evening. After dinner, sitting in the living room, I saw the tiredness in my father's face and I suggested it was time to leave. We began our farewells and as I started the car, I saw my father standing on the front porch, holding onto his walker, waving goodbye. He had lost so much weight. I thought *I am looking at a dead man walking. I am looking at my father. He is not going to be alive for very long. No, the tears may not come. Not now. You must be strong for your father's brother. Think what he is feeling. No, tears, no.*

As we departed, my uncle began a conversation about his kids. When he finished talking about his kids, he moved on to the activities of his grandkids. After he finished with his last grandchild, we drove down the hill on the two-lane road, ready to merge onto the interstate highway. He slowly turned to me and in his deep western voice told me that my dad was his very best friend. He had never had such a best friend as he. This was the beginning of my silent tears slipping down my cheeks while driving.

My dad's stepsister was the next to arrive from Colorado. She was in her nineties, but quite lively and down to earth. Their grandmother had been a full-blooded Cherokee Native American and her granddaughter, my dad's stepsister, was just like her. She had woven a beautiful blanket for my father to warm his lap while napping in the afternoon. She stayed for several days and gave my mother a respite from the nursing care.

By mid-June, the doctor's visits became less frequent since my father was on the established chemotherapy track along with all the holistic herbs and pills. He was mostly confined to a wheelchair to maneuver around the house, which his stepsister navigated with ease. Sometimes he held a conversation, but mostly he was tired and preferred to sleep.

———◆◆———

The following days are reconstructed by my journal, as my body went into overdrive and my mind into automatic pilot.

My Journal:

25th of June 2001

I brought my brother to see our father. My father wanted to know who would take of mother. My brother comforted him by saying I would take care of my mother after he left.

My Journal:

29th of June 2001

My father is dying, lying in a hospital bed in his bedroom, reduced to nothing except his strength. He held my hand and my fingers were almost squashed. When I returned home, I wanted a private word with Rebecca. I was concerned about her priorities and school. My husband told me I was being rude. I read somewhere the narrowing of the lips red margin is the most reliable physical sign to depict how angry a person is: my husband's lips. I couldn't take his anger. I didn't know why he was angry. I didn't ask. I left to spend the night in a hotel.

My Journal:

July 8th, 2001

My father died at 11:05 on July 2, 2001, a Monday. I had not planned on driving out that day, but my mother called me early in the morning and said he didn't recognize her. I drove out immediately. I called to let her know I was only ten minutes away – only to hear my mother say, "He's gone." I called the children's father and my brother from the car. When I arrived, I went directly to my father and gave

him a kiss and then hugged my mother. We
waited for the visiting nurse to pronounce him
dead. Then the funeral workers came to take his
body. I was grateful that my mother's back was
to the door as the two funeral men struggled
to carry my father out in a black body bag. He
had been a strong, large man. Afterwards, my
mother said, "I can't believe he's gone. If I hadn't
gone into the kitchen to get a cookie, he may not
have died."

The funeral service, widely attended, was conventional and
held in the local Episcopal church. There was nothing personal
about it except the copious flower arrangements sent by his many
friends. It was a large church with wooden pews, built in 1878.
A substitute minister performed the service as the presiding
minister was on vacation. The substitute minister, not knowing
my dad, commented that he must have been a very decent man
because of the large number of people in the congregation.
Sitting on the hard wooden pew, I thought *the number of people
here does not constitute my father's decency. His character defined
his decency. I want someone who knew my dad to be talking, not
this minister who never met him. How can you talk about my
father like this? You never even shook hands with him. It's your
loss, too. He was a great man.*

The substitute minister asked the congregation to approach
the altar and kneel to take communion. My mother in all the
years I could remember had never taken communion and she
remained seated. She had said she was Methodist and it would
be a sin. I had never taken communion before either, but today I
thought *maybe if I take communion, somehow, part of my dad will
stay with me.* I walked up, knelt down and cupped my hands to
receive the wafer. I thought *the ancient Greeks never kneeled to
worship. They stood with their arms raised to their gods. They were
embracing life and giving thanks to their gods. We are kneeling
in front of a strange minister who is going to have us drink grape
juice and chew a wafer, a minister who never met my father.* After

I drank the juice and put the wafer in my mouth, I returned to my seat next to my husband. I took a kleenex from my bag and spit the wafer into it and put the kleenex back in my bag. I thought *what is wrong with you? Why did you take communion? Communion is between you and god, not between you and your father. Where is your logic?* My brother sat in the pew in front of us and cried the entire service. Tears cascaded down his cheeks and I kept handing him kleenex during the remainder of the service.

After the service, while people were milling about, I approached the flower arrangements to write down who had given each one. I knew my mother would want to write thank you notes to each and everyone of them. I came across a tall exotic palm tree and read the card. It was from a woman's educational organization that my mother belonged to,. My father had helped them by organizing and publishing their directory each year. All the little ladies had loved him. I thought *how unusual, a palm tree. I remember the palm tree on the island of Delos where Leto gave birth to Apollo and Artemis. Zeus's wife, Hera, was furious at Leto for her husband, Zeus, had sired Leto's twins, Apollo and Artemis. Hera decreed that Leto could not deliver her twins in any place where the sun shone. But there on the island of Delos, protected between an olive tree and a palm tree, Leto gave birth to Apollo, the god of healing Trees epitomize both beauty and continuity across generations for the Greeks. Here was a palm tree for my dad. How wonderful. I'll research how much water she needs and how much sunlight. We'll place her in a perfect location.*

Touching my elbow, my husband snapped me out of my daydreaming. Sternly, he instructed me to go to the reception area and to stand in the receiving line with my mother. I obeyed and found my mother. I stood by her as we kissed and hugged each guest, listening to their individual stories of how they would remember and miss my father.

Later, chartered buses drove the guests to my house where I had arranged a catered supper. It was a warm early evening and people gathered on the deck and in the living room. On the deck, I saw several of the ladies who had given the palm tree and made my way over to them and thanked them. One woman with bleach white hair and the deepest blue eyes hugged me closely and told me what a wonderful memorial service it had been. She had particularly been impressed by the minister. She knew my father would have been honored. She continued that this minister presided over the church every July while the regular minister took vacation. She said that she always made it a point to attend every Sunday in July. I looked into her blue eyes and thought *really?*

The doorbell kept ringing as my neighbors kept coming by. They felt that my dad was part of their neighborhood as well. He had been to our house so often fixing it up during the last seven years that even the hardware store owner dropped by to say how much he would miss talking with him.

In the middle of the festivity, I began feeling emotionally drained and physically tired. My feet hurt from standing in high heels for so long. My stomach growled, but I did not feed it. I knew I would get sick if I did. My head throbbed from the afternoon wine. I went outside on the front porch, away from all the guests and sat on the stairs. A florist's truck pulled up in the driveway. The driver climbed out and went to the back of his white truck and took out a large, beautiful basket of sprawling summer wildflowers and brought it to the porch. He placed it next to me, smiled and left. I breathed in their fragrances. I had never seen anything as beautiful. I searched for a card, but I didn't find one. I should call to find out who sent this beautiful arrangement, but I had not noticed the name of the florist company on the truck. Touching the flowers with my fingers, the purple asters and the bird's foot violet were my favorite. I thought *who sent this? Thank dad. He sent them. He sent them just for me. He knew. He knew how empty I would feel. He knew this would comfort me.*

In August, Rebecca began her college search. She was entering her senior year of high school. In the fall, she would have to apply to various colleges. She needed to select which colleges interested her. My husband, being a fifth-generation Californian, most ardently wanted our daughter to attend a college in California. He insisted that she should visit colleges in California personally since he believed the colleges and the geological beauty of the state would sway our daughter in that direction.

At the same time, in August, William had qualified for the prestigious Zone Swim Meet in upstate New York. My husband wanted to take his son to watch his breaststroke, backstroke and IM. My husband knew that William was still young enough to listen to him in order to perfect his techniques. He hadn't reached that age when his father no longer knew anything. Heather would stay with gramma and I would take Rebecca to California. We would begin in the northern part of the state and would drive the scenic route south, touring eight colleges. At the end of the tour, my husband would bring William to Seattle to visit his sister Helen and her husband, Richard, and Rebecca would fly to meet them there. I would be flying home to be with Heather who was staying with gramma.

Stanford University was at the top of the college list. Everyone in my husband's family had attended Stanford. His great-great grandfather had been in the first graduating class. His dad had attended on a football scholarship and had met his wife there who had been accepted at the age of sixteen. My husband's brother, Scott, had attended. My husband, the rebel, broke the family tradition and attended Stanford's rival, the University of California at Berkeley. I was that glad that he had, as that was where I met him.

Stanford University was about an hour drive south of San Francisco, located on a sprawling circular campus. One circular road took you to the various buildings, athletic fields, and theater. In a large conference room, we sat with other prospective students and their parents and listened to the introductory lecture. We learned of the magnificence of Stanford, of the incredible contributions its alumni had conferred on society and viewed a PowerPoint presentation of its impressive academic departments.

Impressed with the lecture, we leisurely strolled around the Student Life Center and watched the students milling around, talking with one another. After some time, we meandered through the bookstore and continued to people watch. Climbing in the car, we drove the circular road to find the fencing coach. Rebecca wanted to continue her fencing in a very serious way in college. Having had such a poor showing at the World Cup, she vowed she would return and perform well. We found the fencing coach in the gym and introduced ourselves. He was a very relaxed middle-aged man, rather nondescript. I glanced at Rebecca and knew she was having the same reaction. We discussed technique, the enormous time commitment and the various meets for about hour. As we walked to the car, I asked my daughter what she felt about Stanford.

She abruptly and firmly said, "No way. Everyone dresses the same way. It doesn't matter if you are white, black, Asian, chicano. They all wear the same thing, khaki shorts, white polo shirt. They all ride the same type of bicycle. They all have the same type of backpack. They probably all think the same way. No way."

I replied, "Okay, then. Well, that's a definite no."

Usually, Rebecca was diplomatic in her responses, but when she became adamant, her mind was fixed. I knew my husband would be disappointed, but I didn't say this to her. We began the drive south along Route 1, the scenic drive along the spiraling coastline where the drop to the Pacific Ocean is at times hundreds of feet. Rebecca had never seen the spectacular scenery. I had, but only when my husband was driving.

As I approached Route 1 and gazed down the cliffs to the ocean with Rebecca in the passenger seat, I thought *I have never liked mountain driving. I am scared of heights. I am scared of the cliffs with no guardrails and oncoming traffic. Hairpin turns set me over; my stomach churns and my hands sweat. I remember back to the first Greek trip with my parents. My father was angry with me as we were driving in the Peloponnesian Mountains up to Bassae, to Apollo Epikourios's temple that I had very much wanted to see. Otherwise, I would have omitted this from our itinerary with the gutted, winding dirt mountain roads with no guardrails that sickened my stomach. My stomach can take a heaving sea, but not these Greek treacherous roads. But this temple to Apollo had my interest. This temple defied the standard convention of his day. This temple was aligned north to south. Eighty percent of all Greek temples were oriented within the solstitial arc, between the true sunrise and sunset points of the summer and winter solstice. In this way, the cult statue inside always saw the sunrise. Being a morning person myself, I always admired this. This temple was different. There was so much scholarly debate regarding this temple, I was tired of reading it. It was time to see it for myself, but the only way up the mountain for me was in the backseat, lying down, with my sweatshirt covering my face, holding my stomach, while my father drove. He wished I would sit up and look at the spectacular scenery that my mother was witnessing in the passenger seat.*

Having arrived, still dizzy from the ride, I stared at the huge white tent that encapsulated and preserved Apollo's temple. I entered the white tent and walked the length of the temple to the entrance and stepped inside. When I gazed up, I tried to visualize the frieze that should be here, but is imprisoned in the British museum. I moved around slowly in this strange temple with its interior ionic columns towering up to where the frieze of the centaurs and lapiths would have been. I loved the way he put a simple door on the east side so the sunrise could still shine in and warm Apollo. He was the god of music, poetry, medicine and healing. Some say, villagers of nearby Figaleia had prayed to Apollo to purify their village so that the plague of 429 B.C., which devastated the rest of Greece, wouldn't harm their village. Figaleia escaped the plague and in gratitude, they built the temple to him.

I am a chicken shit. I do not like mountain driving.

As I continued driving, a thin fog rolled in from the Pacific Ocean and Rebecca marveled at the cliffs cascading down to the rocky outcropping and to the blue Pacific Ocean. As the hairpin turns became more frequent, the fog increased in thickness. My stomach thanked me for not eating any lunch and I noticed the car had automatically turned on the headlights. I slowed down as I could only see about twenty feet in front of the car. I didn't want to be caught off guard by a hairpin turn or an oncoming car.

I told Rebecca that at least she had a chance to view some of the dramatic scenery. We called this pea soup fog on Cape Cod. We couldn't see anything but the thick dense fog. We continued down the coast slowly and carefully. I increased the heat in the car and turned on the radio to some soft jazz. My daughter curled up and propped her sweatshirt as a pillow and dozed. I thought *of myself in the Peloponnesian Mountains. This is my dad. He knows I can't stand mountain driving. He's bringing in the fog.* Smiling, I rolled down the window and blew a kiss into the air.

We finished the tour by visiting the eighth college in the Los Angles basin. My East-Coast-born daughter was not impressed with the California colleges, but I reminded her she hadn't seen any East Coast colleges yet. I prodded her to keep an open mind as I drove her to the airport. She agreed. She was to fly up north to Seattle to meet William and her father where they would have a nice visit with her aunt and uncle. I took off in the other direction and flew home to pick up Heather from gramma's.

Once home, Heather and I sighed with relief. We had a few days to pick up the pieces of the summer. I was reminded of Bette Davis's famous line, when she walked in and looked around and said, "What a dump!" I didn't think I could have said it better. The house never had a fall cleaning, let alone spring cleaning, during this past year. The windows, the carpets, the light fixtures stared at me with their neglect. I walked out onto to the deck and surveyed the backyard. It wasn't much better. I would start with the yard. Summer would be over soon and then I would be forced to deal with the inside. I loved to garden, to breathe in the evening air and marvel at Mother Nature. Heather wanted desperately to catch up with all her friends whom she hadn't seen during the past week. And of course, this had to be done in the privacy of her room. Friends, Heather's good friends were of the utmost importance to her. I left for the back yard.

Rebecca was scheduled to fly home the day before her father and brother because of her free airline ticket. She was to arrive at JFK in New York City at seven-thirty in the evening. Gramma didn't want me to drive in and pick her up since I would be driving back home at night and well, since granddad had died, we all had become more cautious. She told me that she would pay for a taxi to drive Rebecca home. In the morning, I called Rebecca in Seattle and told her to look for the town's taxi after she retrieved her baggage. She agreed. After dinner that evening, I was outside in the backyard, weeding and cleaning out the flowerbeds, preparing for fall.

Heather came out to the deck and reported, "The taxi service called and they can't find Rebecca."

I slowly put down my gardening tools and walked inside. I walked over to the phone and called Delta Airlines. I asked the woman if the plane had landed from Seattle. She confirmed it had landed on time, keeping with Delta's on-time track history. I asked if Rebecca had been on the plane. She was not allowed to divulge this information. The passenger manifest was confidential, she informed me. I told her my daughter was a minor, that she had been suffering this past spring from mono with a neurological deficit. Sternly, I stated, "Tell me if she was on the plane."

"Hold, please."

I waited and listened to horrible music for what seemed like an eternity.

"Yes, she sat in seat 27F."

I told the woman that my daughter was missing. The taxi driver couldn't find her. Rebecca knew to locate the cab driver outside the baggage claim area. The woman couldn't help me, but she connected me to the Port Authority Police. I reiterated the situation to the police.

I said, "Maybe she went to the bathroom, fainted, hit her head, is lying somewhere unconscious. I don't know. She's missing."

The Port Authority Police immediately evacuated the Delta airline terminal. They brought in rescue dogs to locate her. The police officer called me back within twenty minutes and told me she was not in the terminal. The Port Authority Police told me I could not file a missing person's report until tomorrow. A person was not considered missing until they had been missing for twenty-four hours.

I lowered my voice and spoke very slowly, "That's great. Then I'll know my daughter by her dental plates. She is a minor. Something has happened to her. We have to do something."

The officer at the other end of the phone line paused and finally said, "Okay, take a recent picture of her with your ID to your local police station. We will notify them you're coming. File the report now."

It was now ten in the evening, nearly three hours after the plane landed with Rebecca on board. I ran upstairs and shuffled through my desk and found a picture taken of her as a swim instructor this past June. I looked at the picture. I looked at her wide smile and brown eyes and I thought no. No, this cannot be happening. I grabbed the photograph and raced down the stairs. Heather would wait by the phone to see if anyone called with any information. I jumped in the car and reversed out of the driveway like a bat out of hell.

As I drove to the police station, I thought *the longer a person is missing the less likely they are to be found. I cannot lose one of my children. You can have anything else, but not one of my children. Anything. Absolutely anything. I remember all the horror stories of dead or sexually mutilated missing children, children who are never found: the children's faces I see on the milk cartons. Her wide smile and brown eyes are in front of the dashboard as I drive. I cannot lose her. I cannot lose one of my children.*

Walking into the police station, sweat dripped from my hands. My stomach felt like it was about to convulse. My voice cracked as it tried to form words. My hands trembled when I gave the picture of Rebecca to the sergeant. I looked around for a chair. I needed to hold on to something. He asked the routine questions, how old was Rebecca, what color hair did she have, what was her height and weight. I felt faint. I thought *I can't remember her weight. Is she in her chubby stage? Is she in her thin stage? I don't know. It doesn't matter. What color is her hair? It is not really brown. It has some streaks of red and blonde, if you look closely. Just find her. Find her now. My head is exploding.* I tried to find composure. I said that her weight was one hundred and twelve pounds, but then I realized that was my weight.

My cell phone rang. I couldn't find it. I pulled out my front jean pockets, my sweatshirt pocket and looked in my bag. It was still ringing. It was in my back pocket. I never put my phone in my back pocket. I reached for it and answered it with sweaty hands. It was Heather. She told me that Rebecca had just called the house phone. She was on her way home, but they were lost.

Heather said to her, "Look around you, what do you see?"

She read a local road sign to Heather, not knowing where she was. Heather gave her directions and asked her to write them down. All my children had traveled this road many, many times over the course of the last seven years. It was the road we took to the grocery store every week. But Rebecca didn't know where she was, not by the road sign or by her surroundings.

When I heard this, I believed that she had been drugged. Something was very wrong. I told this to the sergeant. He would send a police officer with me to see if Rebecca actually makes it home. Another officer would be dispatched to Rebecca's current location. I walked briskly to the car and searched for my keys in my bag. I couldn't find them. Tears started to form and I screamed, "Shit!" I climbed into the car and held onto the wheel. I told myself to breathe slowly. I looked down and saw the keys in the ignition. I thought *shake it off, shake it off and start the car. Get a grip. You cannot lose control now. Your daughter may be found. She may not be lost. Start the car. Breathe.*

Driving home, I kept saying, "Be there. Just, please, be there."

I pulled into the driveway and a Jeep with darkened windows was parked in our driveway. I jumped out of my car and ran up to Heather who was sitting on the front porch stoop. She told me she had memorized the license plate, make, and model of the car. The jeep had just driven in.

At that moment, Rebecca opened the Jeep's passenger door and slowly walked up the steps to where we were standing and continued right by us saying she had to get money to pay the man. I told her I had money and I would pay the man and asked her to wait with Heather. Rebecca sat down on the front porch stair and Heather took her hand in hers. I walked over to this young man and inquired how much. I paid him and gave him a fifty-dollar tip. The police officer beckoned and I walked with knees shaking. He asked me if that was my daughter and I responded yes. He told me how very lucky we were. He would drop the missing person report. I thanked him many times and shook his hand.

I returned to my girls and the three of us went inside. Uncharacteristically, I locked the front door. We collapsed in chairs around the kitchen table. I was still trembling inside. I looked across the table and I saw the fragility in Rebecca's face. My eyes turned toward Heather, and as I looked into her blue eyes, I saw her concern and confusion. I breathed deeply several times. I thought *I want answers. What happened? Why did you get into a stranger's car? You've known since you could walk, never to get into a stranger's car. How didn't you see the town's taxi driver outside the baggage claim area? How did this happen? Looking into her brown eyes, it slowly dawned that I might never get answers. She doesn't have answers because she doesn't know. She doesn't know what she's done. The virus is still present in her brain. Thank you. Thank you. I did not lose one of my children. She is alive.*

William and my husband came home the next day, but I was still reeling. Having something awful happen to one of my children kept reverberating in my mind. I thought *learn your lesson. You need to take better care of her. The virus may take many more months to resolve. You need to be more careful. You need to watch her closely.* I devised a plan for her senior year. She would return to boarding school for her senior year, but she would come home every other weekend to rest. On the other weekends, I would drive and we would stay in a quiet hotel, allowing each weekend a respite from the nocturnal noise in the girls' dormitory.

Heather was to begin her freshman year at the high school and William was to enter seventh grade in the middle school. I would resume being chief bottle washer, dog walker, swim team driver, chauffeur and problem solver, but on those swim practice nights, I read Sappho instead of clinical trials. One of my favorites was:

> Beauty endures for as long as people can see it,
> but goodness will always be beautiful.
> *Fragment 50*

> Speak to me, heavenly lyre, and find yourself a voice.
> Plato called her the tenth Muse.

FALL 2001

In the morning, after showering, my husband walked out of the bathroom and into our bedroom with a towel wrapped around his waist. His eyebrows were furrowed and his lips drawn tightly together. I looked at him with raised eyebrows. He walked into the closet to select his clothes for work, returned and placed them on the unmade bed. He glanced at me and told me that his lymph nodes under his right armpit were the size of golf balls. I was not sure I knew we even had lymph nodes underneath our armpits and wondered what did it mean. I asked him if he believed it was due to a viral infection or maybe a bacterial infection. Perhaps, some antibiotics would reduce the swelling.

He slipped his arm into his dress shirt sleeve and looked at me. "And maybe the melanoma has spread," he said, buttoning his shirt.

Stunned, I told him that was not possible. The sentinel node procedure gave him a clean bill of health. He was just borrowing trouble. He asked me to find a good dermatologist in the city. He didn't want to follow up with the dermatologist in the suburbs. He said that he was questioning the wait-and-see approach. I was in disbelief and I reiterated to him that the sentinel node procedure did not detect any metastases.

His eyes narrowed and he said, "I understand. I would like to see a dermatologist at one of the leading medical centers in the city."

I got it very quickly. I saw the fear in his face. I told him that today I would research and find a leading, cutting-edge dermatologist and not to worry. I would call him at work and would make an appointment that fit into his schedule. He pulled on his pants and thanked me. He was late and had to run. I watched him walk out of the bedroom door and heard him descend the stairs and close the front door. I started to make the bed. I thought *oh my god, what if he's right? What does that mean?*

I didn't remember the initial appointment with the dermatologist. I know there must have been one because surgery was scheduled to remove the lymph nodes under his right armpit. I rose at four in the morning the day of the surgery. We had to be in the hospital in the city by five-thirty. The kids were on their own today. They would make their own lunch and walk to school. Another swim team mamma would drive them to swim practice in the evening.

The surgery was just after September 11, 2001. An abundance of flowers lined the sidewalk by the hospital. Above the flowers, taped on the building's wall, were photographs of the dead or missing people. Underneath each photograph was a detailed description of the person. I walked slowly and looked at each photograph and scanned their description. I remembered how each person in each photograph was so incredibly important to the person who wrote their description. The amount of sadness and love poured forth through each word I read. Goose bumps rose on my arms and I slipped my arm through my husband's arm as we entered the revolving door into the hospital. I was glad my dad was not alive. This was beyond what any words have the capacity to describe. I had brought my book to read, *The Best of the Achaeans* by Gregory Nagy. I sat in the waiting room and read about the concepts that defined the hero in Archaic Greek poetry. Nagy insisted that the hero must experience death.

> The hero's death was what gave him glory (kleos) – not only in cult but also in poetry. Achilles entered the Trojan War knowing that he had two choices; either a homecoming (nostos) without glory or die at Troy with glory. Achilles forfeited his homecoming in order to achieve glory. And yet, he is the pivotal character in an epic poem that will never die. In contrast, in the epic poem, the Odyssey, Odysseus was assured of a homecoming, but when Odysseus was certain that he would drown in the stormy sea, he wished he had died at Troy so the Achaeans would carry on his glory. When Odysseus entered

the underworld and saw Achilles, Achilles told him
that he would trade his glory for his homecoming.

Completely engaged with how glory was inherently tied
to death, the surgeon startled me when he approached. I
apologized and stood up. My book dropped to the floor. He
informed me that the surgery went well. My husband's lymph
nodes under his right armpit were successfully extricated. The
initial pathology report indicated the cause of enlargement was
due to the melanoma metastasizing. He assured me, again, that
the removal of the melanoma in the lymph nodes was successful.
I thanked him and shook his hand and asked when my husband
would be out of the recovery room.

I wanted to go home. I wanted our lives back in our routine.
I didn't want to sit in any more hospital waiting rooms. He told
me it wouldn't be long and that a nurse would let me know within
an hour or so. I thought *okay. Normalcy will resume. Breathe. No
more melanoma. No more doctors. No more operations. Good. Life
will be back on track.*

———◆———

At high school, Heather had joined the theatre club. I was
surprised. I never thought she was the acting type. She had never
expressed an interest in it before, but at the same time, I was
pleased she was exploring new ventures. The acting group was
writing their own play to be performed just before Christmas.
She was terribly excited about the performance as well as all
the new people she was meeting. We were looking forward to
attending, my husband, Rebecca, William and me.

The night of the performance, we squished into seats in the
middle of a row midway up from the stage. The auditorium was
packed with parents, siblings, grandparents, aunts, and uncles. It
seemed everyone that we knew and didn't know from our town
was here. The curtain opened. I couldn't follow the sequence of
events and I was not sure if I followed the plot, if there was one.
When the second act began, the curtains slowly opened with

Heather standing on the right side of the stage. She was taller than anyone else with her broad shoulders and was wearing a long bright neon-blue sequined, sexy gown with a silver crown on her head. She towered over the rest of the players who were in one continuous line across the stage. I determined that she must be at least six inches taller than the tallest boy and that was without her crown. She stood out like a lit blue beacon. I had no idea what or whom she represented. All I knew was William, sitting between Rebecca and myself, started to uncontrollably giggle, looking at his sister on stage. I told him to be quiet, but his giggle was infectious. Rebecca began to giggle. William's giggle turned into hysterical laughter. I tried very hard not to laugh. I pulled his sweatshirt hood over his head. People stared at us and told us to be quiet. My husband looked sternly at me. I thought *can I get William out of here? No that would more disruptive. I don't know what to do.* His laughter became more infectious and he had me laughing until tears slid down. My husband and the man beside Rebecca glared at us. Finally, the darkness of his sweatshirt over his head calmed him down.

This was my only memory of the Christmas season of 2001. If you put a gun to my head and asked me what gifts I gave to anyone, you would have to shoot me. I did not remember.

WINTER – SPRING
2001 – 2002

Christmas and New Year's were over in the Northeast and the dead of winter descended with its gray, brittle, short days. The task of taking down the holiday decorations, cleaning the house and settling in until spring occupied my time. One evening, my husband returned home from work, briefcase in hand. I was in the kitchen, cooking chicken with penne.

He came over to the stove and stood next to me. Bending his head toward my ear, he whispered, "We have a problem."

We were all alone and I didn't know why he was whispering. There was no swim practice tonight and the kids were at their different friends' homes. He continued to whisper, "Some of the lymph nodes under my left armpit are like peas, but there are some that are larger than golf balls. They seem to be growing like wildfire."

I looked into his eyes and told him not to worry. They could be surgically removed like the others had been.

"Melanoma can be licked. No worries. I will call the surgeon's office and schedule an appointment tomorrow," I said. He thanked me and opened a bottle of Merlot and poured two glasses.

I thought *why did he whisper this to me? Maybe he thinks if he whispers, it won't be real. But it doesn't matter if it's real. The lymph nodes can be surgically removed. Weird. He's just weird.*

The next morning, after the kids left for school and my husband for work, I called the surgeon's secretary to make an appointment. She inquired as to the reason and I informed her of the recent developments. We settled on an appointment date for the following week.

Later in the afternoon, as I was folding laundry, the phone rang. I went to the kitchen's wall and answered it. I heard the surgeon's voice and I was surprised. He asked me when did my husband first notice the enlargement of the nodes. I told him it was a recent occurrence, not long at all. He was glad that this was a recent development, but we should set a date for surgery on Monday, in three days. He told me that, like before, we should be at the hospital at five-thirty in the morning. I agreed and hung up the phone.

Walking back to the laundry pile, I thought *wow, just like that. I am impressed. No appointment, just surgery. What does this mean? It means that the surgeon wants those lymph nodes removed now. Why the urgency? The other surgery was not urgent. Why now?* I stopped folding the laundry and called my husband to let him know. He wouldn't be able to go to work on Monday. When I finally reached him, I heard the relief in his voice and knew that he would be glad to have this behind him.

The day of surgery, the alarm clock woke us. It was four-thirty in the morning. My husband drove us into the city and we listened to news on the radio, parked in the hospital's parking garage and entered through the revolving doors. We both knew the drill. He went to the room where he would be prepped for surgery and I walked into the vacant waiting room and over to the counter where I poured a cup of the hospital's watered-down version of coffee. I found a comfortable chair, knowing I would be here until late evening. I pulled out the book I was continuing to read, *The Best of the Achaeans.* I began with the chapter "Poetic Visions of Immortality for the Hero."

> Upon having their lifespan cut short by death, heroes receive as consolation the promise of immortality, but this state of immortality after death is located at the extremes of our universe, far removed from the realities of the here-and-now. We in this life have to keep reminding ourselves that the hero who died is still capable of pleasure, that he can still enjoy such real things as convivial feasts in the pleasant company of other youths like him. It is in this sort of spirit that the Banquet Song for Harmodios

is composed, honoring the young man who had achieved the status of being worshiped as a hero by the Athenians for having killed a tyrant:

Harmodios, most philos! Surely you are not at all dead,
but they say that you are on the Isles of the Blessed,
the same place where swift-footed Achilles is,
and they say that the worthy Diomedes,
son of Tydeus, is there too.

The perfect tense of the verb ou.... Tethnekas 'you are not dead' leaves room for the reality of the hero's death: it is not that he did not die, but that he is not dead now.

The surgeon tapped me on the shoulder and I looked up as he sat down next me. I felt that something was not right, but I was not sure what. He leaned close and slowly said that my husband had undergone a CAT scan prior to surgery and he had just reviewed it. He explained to me that this surgery would now be more extensive than the first surgery. My husband would need to remain in the hospital for at least three days, recovering. The surgery would be very aggressive. In addition to removing all the lymph nodes, his back would be opened where the original cite of melanoma was located to determine if there were any metastases there.

He held my hand and continued, "It is worrisome that the cancer has metastasized to this extent."

I told him that I would wait and see my husband in the recovery room. He agreed and left. I didn't move.

I thought *of his word, worrisome. This means that there is something to worry about. There is something to be concerned about. How much should I worry? Worry doesn't do anyone any good. Fix the problem. Take the cancer out. This is melanoma, not glioblastoma. This is not a death sentence. I don't want to worry. Where and how did I miss this? I should have done more research before Christmas. We should have had the sentinel node biopsy immediately, the day after he came home with blood on his shirt. Worrisome. If the surgeon is worried, then what should I be? Worrisome.* My mind would not release the image of the surgeon's lips saying *worrisome*.

I looked at my book. I didn't pick it up. Time stopped. I sat and paced in the waiting room until six-thirty in the evening when the surgeon reentered. I needed to act professional, as if I knew what I was talking about, but I didn't. I hadn't done my research. My mouth was dry. He told me that the surgery went well and that all metastases had been removed. I asked if he knew the stage of the melanoma. I knew that most cancers had four stages: one being the best prognosis, four being the worst. He believed it was stage four, but the biopsy results would give the definitive result. My husband was groggy and wanted only to sleep when I found him in his room. I looked at his face and his eyes fluttered. I walked over to his hospital bed and took his hand in mine. I had no idea if he knew we needed to worry. This was not the time to tell him. I kissed his cheek and told him I should go home for the kids. With his eyes closed, he nodded in agreement.

Leaving the building, it was dark. Walking north on the avenue, the winter wind whipped my wool coat open. I hurried to the parking garage two blocks away and handed the attendant my ticket. I noticed him staring at me. He didn't speak English very well. He gestured for me to zip up my coat. He hugged his arms around his torso and pretended to shiver. I glanced down at my coat. It was completely wide open. I bent down and zipped it up. He smiled. He left to retrieve my car from the bowels of the parking garage. Driving home, I thought *should I tell the kids that the surgeon used the word 'worrisome' to describe their father's condition? No, wait. They don't need to worry. Wait for the biopsy results. Yes, the biopsy results will be in our favor. Then, I won't have to tell them anything but good news. But why did he use that word? I don't want to worry. Why couldn't he have used another word? I don't like that word.*

When I arrived home, the kids were at swim practice. I took off my coat and looked at the zipper and shook my head. I walked into the living room and looked around at the empty room. I looked towards my husband's grandfather's clock on the wall and turned around to see his upright Steinway piano and I wondered about all the men in the family who had owned them at one time. Slowly, I entered the dining room and found an open wine bottle and poured a glass and then walked into the kitchen. Our dog followed me. I looked into his soft, brown eyes as I sat down at the kitchen table. I bent down and petted both his ears with my hands and I whispered to him that the surgeon had used the word *worrisome* today.

The next morning, after dropping Heather and William off at their schools, I drove back to the hospital. We were to meet the surgeon at eleven o'clock. I parked the car in the same parking garage and the same attendant from last night was standing in the white booth. I drove up to the booth and turned off the car, but before I climbed out, I zipped up my coat. I handed him the car keys and smiled. He handed me the ticket and asked me if I would be all day. I thought *god, no*. I told him just an hour or so.

Entering the hospital through the revolving door, I thought *I have my research cut out. I need to investigate everything about metastatic melanoma.* Walking down the long corridor on the fourth floor, I located my husband's room. He was lying in bed with a glazed look in his eyes, being on significant pain medication. I walked over to his bed and asked him how he was feeling. Without expression, he nodded his head. I told him that he should be glad he was in here because outside was bitter, bitter cold.

The surgeon entered punctually and shook both of our hands. He asked how my husband was feeling and he replied that he wanted to go home. The surgeon smiled and responded that because they had to open up his back, the incision was quite large and he preferred to monitor the incision for the next day or so. By Wednesday evening if everything went well, he would be discharged. He continued in a deadpan voice that the biopsy indicated the disease was stage four.

I asked, "What does that mean?" I thought *melanoma is curable. It shouldn't have a stage four. Why does it have a stage four? It's not glioblastoma. Melanoma is not aggressive like brain cancer. Maybe stage four melanoma means something different. When I get home, I will research until no stone is unturned.*

The surgeon stood in front of my husband's bed and told him that his condition was worrisome. I held onto the bed frame tightly with both hands. I listened to him explain that my husband would be referred to another leading medical center which had the best dermatological division for treating only melanoma in the United States. He would be referred to their division head, a guru in metastatic melanoma. The surgeon would make the follow-up appointment for this Friday. It was important to stay ahead of this disease. I looked at my husband, but I couldn't tell what he was thinking. I was not sure how well his brain was working due to the pain medication. I thought *this is a plan. A plan that is going to work. A plan that will allow our lives to resume normally. Our lives will get back on track with the kid's activities, my husband's work, and me, chief taxi driver, cook and bottle washer.*

On Wednesday afternoon, I called the surgeon's office to see if my husband would be discharged in the early evening and the secretary responded affirmatively. His condition was stable, but he would need assistance in cleaning and repacking the wound on a daily basis. I told her that wouldn't be a problem. He would be ready at six in the evening. I thanked her and climbed the stairs to our bedroom.

In the closet, I grabbed a clean pair of sheets and stripped off the sheets that were on the bed and made the bed with clean ones. I found an extra blanket and placed it on my husband's side. I went downstairs to his basement office and scanned the papers scattered everywhere on both desks. Open books lay on the floor. His briefcase was open on his easy chair. I tried to find a book that he would like to read while lying in bed. I gave up. As I left and closed the door, I heard William and Heather enter the front door.

We met in the kitchen and sat around the kitchen table. I told them that their father was coming home tonight and they both wanted to pick him up with me. They both insisted on missing swim practice that evening. I continued that he would receive follow-up care at a leading medical center specializing in melanoma. I saw the relief on their faces. Heather went into the kitchen and started opening all the food cupboards and then opened the refrigerator. Both William and I looked at her inquisitively.

She turned to us and said, "What? I'm going to make daddy something special for dinner tonight. I want to see what we have." She decided on chicken stir-fry as she could prepare it ahead of time and cook it as soon as we came home. She, like her father, was never intimidated by experimenting in the kitchen. She loved creating new dishes. I thanked her. I hadn't gotten that far yet and even if I had, it wouldn't be as delicious as Heather's.

We arrived at the hospital promptly at six in the evening and went directly to my husband's room. He was sitting on his bed, dressed in street clothes, ready to leave. All discharge papers had been signed. He wanted to go home now. At that moment, the surgeon walked in smiling. I prayed that he would not use his favorite word again. He told us that my husband had a ten a.m. appointment on Friday with the division chair for melanoma at the other leading hospital. The surgeon had faxed my husband's test results and hospital notes to him and everything was in order. He wished us good luck and shook my husband's hand.

When my husband rose off the bed, he wobbled for a moment and Heather, who was almost the same height as her father, quickly helped him. She put her arm in his and looked at his back and winced. We walked out together with Heather holding her father's arm. William and I followed. I told them I would get the car and meet them in front of the hospital. In the car, my husband turned slowly toward the back seat to ask the kids how school was going. They both said fine. I thought *they are more concerned for their father than with how they are doing in school. Should I tell them privately that the surgeon used the word worrisome? No, worrying doesn't do anybody any good. I will wait until we see what the new doctor says on Friday. Yes, I will wait. The new doctor may give us good news.*

We hit rush hour traffic and it was stop and go for miles. The highway was littered with potholes from the snow and sleet that had pelted the area. I did my best to avoid each one, but it was impossible in this traffic. Each one I hit, my husband grimaced and held onto the overhead handle above the passenger side window. My stomach growled with hunger, but I was so busy looking for potholes that I paid no attention to it.

At home, our golden retriever galloped to the door to greet us. William immediately ran interference and took the dog outside on the deck. I helped my husband out of his coat and took his left arm and we climbed the stairs one at a time together to our bedroom. Heather began to cook the stir-fry dinner. The smell from the kitchen made us all hungry.

She yelled upstairs, "Dad, where's the dashi?"

He replied, "Tell her it's in the corner cabinet."

She had been learning from him since she was seven every chance she got and he had encouraged her by buying kitchen gadgets that I still didn't know how to use. I helped my husband out of his clothes. They reeked of hospital stench. As I was helping him out of his shirt, I saw the huge bandage encircling his back, going over his right shoulder and around his stomach. I tried not to make an audible gasp. It was massive. I asked him how big was the incision.

He looked directly into my eyes and said, "I don't know. I can't see my back."

I thought *stupid, stupid, stupid question. Sometimes you have way too many questions. You need to listen to yourself before you ask them.* When he was in bed, propped up with many pillows, my daughter brought his dinner on a tray to him. The room still smelled like a hospital and I couldn't eat with the smell in the air. I left them alone and went downstairs to find William.

—————➤•◆•◄—————

On Friday, after a tedious and slow morning of helping my husband dress, we descended the stairs. He carefully positioned his body in the passenger seat as I drove to our appointment, avoiding as many potholes as possible. My husband and I met with the division chair of the melanoma division. He was a young short man with a confident handshake. He had reviewed my husband's medical information from the surgeon and wanted to initiate an aggressive chemotherapy regime.

The chemotherapy would be given through IV once a week either at this hospital or at a local facility by our home. The physician said that he would monitor the progress and requested to meet with us again in one month. That was it. As we waited for the elevator, I thought *neither my husband nor I asked about the prognosis. Ignorance is not bliss. I should have asked, but what would have happened if I did and he doesn't want to know? Maybe this time, ignorance is bliss. We do not know what chemotherapy will really do. We really do not know what this means. I need to start cracking. I need to research in earnest.*

My research:

> Chemotherapy acts by killing cells that divide rapidly: one of the main properties of cancer cells. This means that it also harms cells that divide rapidly under normal circumstances: cells in the bone marrow, digestive tract and hair follicles.

> Side effects: Fatigue can seriously damage quality of life. The patient should reduce the risk of infection by avoiding crowded places and sick people. Nausea and vomiting are very common. They can develop within hours of treatment. Eat crackers during chemotherapy. Patients will typically suffer

from decreased libido and impotence. Alterations in sexual functioning are a normal reaction to chemotherapy.

The bottom line is that, unfortunately, chemotherapy as an overall strategy is not very effective in treating melanoma. Only 15% to 20% of patients respond to chemotherapy. It typically only works for less than a year, and it has little to no effect on survival time – not to mention the side effects.

I thought *this will work. This will work. This is a plan. Normalcy will continue.*

———

Rebecca was home from boarding school the weekend to celebrate her eighteenth birthday. A group of her town friends came over and we ordered pizza. Last summer, I had discussed with my husband that I wished to give each of our children a memorable gift for their eighteenth birthday and graduation from high school. I had saved some of my own money from the years that I had worked before William was born. I wanted to use this money to give each child a trip: a trip anywhere in the world, provided it be out of the United States. It was my hope for them to experience another culture, if only for a few weeks, to understand that other kids grow up without ever tasting peanut butter, without ever going to a mall and these same kids are still happy, really happy. He had totally agreed and thanked me.

After pizza and a small cake her friends gave her small presents. After they left, I cleaned the dishes in the kitchen. Rebecca walked in and thanked me for the little party. I told her I had wanted to do more, but time had slipped away from me. She understood. I told her to open the card on the kitchen table. She opened it and came over to me and threw her arms around my stomach. I had written on card that it was worth one trip anywhere in the world, provided the trip be outside the United States.

She tightened her arms around my waist and whispered in my ear, "I want to return to Greece."

I wheeled around and hugged her back just as tightly. I thought *I can't believe this. I can't believe this. Nostos.* I told her to think of the places she wanted to see and I would organize the trip. We would talk with her father and to see if we could leave as soon as she graduated in June.

My husband underwent chemotherapy during the months of February through April. One evening a week, he drove to a local chemotherapy facility near our house. He sat in a chair and an IV was inserted in his arm. He was given crackers to eat. He brought his reading material and sat for two hours as the drugs slipped slowly into his vein.

I met him there on those nights when I did not play swim team taxi driver. The facility had ugly fluorescent lamps, giving the patients with their IV drips a bluish hue to their skin. The facility smelled just like a hospital. I had the routine of waiting in doctor's offices and hospitals down, but this was completely different. There was no place for visitors to sit. The patients sat in reclining chairs next to their IV stands.

I stood next to him beside his IV stand. I tried to talk about food and what sounded appealing to him since he had lost his appetite and much weight. Teriyaki chicken? Shish-kabob? Pork Loin? Beef Wellington? Steak? Chicken Marsala, his favorite? No, nothing sounded good to him. Merlot or cabernet sauvignon sounded good to him and that was it. I thought *he needs to eat something, something nutritious, but I have no idea what to cook. Maybe I should order dinners from his favorite restaurants, but that will be too expensive. I don't know what to do to make food sound appealing to him. I'll ask Heather. She will know.*

I encouraged him to hang in there. This ordeal was going to rid his body of this ugly cancer.

Secretly, I worried about his fatigue, as he was resolute

in continuing to work and not take any vacation time. Some days, when he knew he had to work late, he scheduled the chemotherapy at the hospital and took an extended lunch. When I had asked him recently if he had told his boss or any of his colleagues, he firmly told me that it was not their business. I didn't understand how he could not tell them, but then I didn't understand how he could not talk to me about his condition. I reasoned that it was his situation and I would take my cue from him. But in the back of my head, I never forgot that the surgeon had used the word *worrisome.*

For the rest of the spring and into the early weeks of the summer, he continued to work after the chemotherapy had ended. He no longer had the look of my husband before all this started. His hair had thinned and his limbs had lost some of their muscle mass. He remained steady in his routine and the rest of us followed suit. We would only know if the chemotherapy was a success if the cancer didn't metastasize.

On the swim practice evenings, I read *The Throne of Labdacus* by Gjertrud Schnackenberg. It was a story of Oedipus and what happened outside the play in the experience of the god who presided over the oracle, Apollo, the god of poetry, music and healing. I memorized the following lines.

> What is: a leaking through of events
> From beyond the bourn of right and wrong.
> What is: a sequence of accidents
> Without a cause.

> And further...

> Who gaze at things tied
> Into a sequence of knots they can't undo.

In Greek belief there existed Unwritten Laws generated on Mt. Olympos. (as the Chorus of Oedipus proclaims in the second stasimos) The Unwritten Laws are the true, deathless, and cosmic laws out of which human laws devolve.

I read this again and again and slowly thought *this describes our family now. "Knots they can't undo".... and I remember the sailing knots I tied as a kid on the pier. No one could untie them. I was an expert at knots.*

———•◦•———

In late May, Rebecca performed her senior piano recital and graduated from the boarding school which she had attended for the past three years. The recital was held in a hall similar to those found in the English countryside. We entered through double wooden doors rising twenty feet high into a foyer with a large marble circular stairwell to the right and a rectangular gilded mirror on the left wall. Passing through the foyer we moved into the reception hall and at the far end stood a grand Steinway piano with its top raised. Beyond, through the large Old Ship Church windows, the pond glistened in the evening sun, surrounded by sprawling lawns. Remembering my father's beautiful basket of summer wildflowers, I had requested a similar arrangement from our local florist. I walked to the grand Steinway and placed the flower basket in front of it.

The audience seated, Rebecca entered from a side door. Striding confidently to the front of the piano, she paused and presented a brief history of her piano career. She had practiced for the past twelve years being taught by various teachers including her grandmother and grandfather. Both her grandmother and grandfather had been instrumental to her growth as a musician. She ended by dedicating her recital to the memory of her grandfather.

This dedication startled me and the small tears that silently meandered along my cheeks surprised me. I thought *of her younger piano recitals when her grandfather had videotaped them and played them back for her so that she could improve. No one is videotaping her final recital, now. This is wrong. I should have remembered to bring the camera. Why didn't my husband think of this? She's worked so hard for this day. I can't believe I didn't think to bring it. Neither of us brought it. My dad would have remembered.*

She took her seat on the piano bench and breathed in slowly, her fingers poised on the keys. She played Rachmaninoff's Second Concerto effortlessly. She ended her recital with his Third. My ears did not detect one missed note or one note off beat. Her grandfather's chest would have been bursting. The audience returned her favor with a standing ovation.

The following day at graduation, we sat under a large tent on the sprawling lawn by the pond. The graduating young women dressed in white dresses walked in a single file down the grassy hill by the pond and took their seats by the podium. I sat next to my husband as he bent over reading the program.

I noticed that his suit, which he had bought a year earlier, now hung on him. His shirt collar was loose around his neck where before it had been taut. His face, while longer and thinner, was spotted with red blotches. I patted his thigh so that he would look up and see the young women as they entered the tent. His thigh muscles that had been firm and strong were now soft. I thought *he looks sick. At least he can see one of his children graduate from high school. How can you think that? There is no indication that the chemotherapy is not working. We are in our normal routines. Focus on your daughter. This is her day. He does not look well. He looks sick. Focus. Focus in front of you.* But I continued to glance at my husband. When the headmistress addressed the audience, at the podium, I turned to pay attention.

Afterwards, at the school luncheon, my husband took pictures of Rebecca with our family and then many more of her with her friends. In the middle of the photography session, I strolled over to him and asked how to use his camera in a simple way. He and my father had always been the photographer of the family, but I wanted a picture of him. I wanted a picture of him with his graduate. I wanted a picture of him and all his three children. He demonstrated the basics and as I was pushing the shutter, my tears fogged the lens.

Rebecca decided to take a year off before attending college.

She chose to work and apply to different colleges for the following year. She was not satisfied with where she had been accepted. I thought *she is concerned for her father. She sees it too. Keep this to yourself.*

SUMMER 2002

June 2002: Epidauros Greece: the site of Asklepios, son of Apollo. Asklepios was the first healer, the first physician of the western world. The sick came to Epidauros to be cured, but before this could happen, they had to adhere to strict rituals; they had to abstain from sex, goat meat and cheese for three days. These sacrificial rituals were essential for the healing process to work. At night, while the patient slept on his couch and dreamed, Asklepios, with his snakes, interpreted the dreams and healed the patient. Snakes were important to Asklepios. Some scholars say that snakes symbolize immortality, transformation and rebirth because they shed their skin and grow it back. Asklepios said his snakes knew the secrets of the earth. In Greek statutes, Asklepios was depicted as a bearded man, holding a rod with a snake wrapped from the bottom left of the rod encircling to the top: the same symbol the American Medical Association uses today except their snake begins at the bottom right of the rod.

Early in the morning, we arrived in this dark green pine forest in the northeast area of the Peloponnesos. As we wandered along the path to the entrance, the wind rustled through the pine trees and we smelled the pine and wildflowers. A stray small lizard darted across the path and into the rocks, which lined the hill. The sun rose slowly beyond the trees where the first hospital stood and warmed our backs. The tourist buses had not yet arrived and we were alone save the archeological excavators to the east.

We paid the entrance fee and climbed the large marble steps to the orchestra. Gazing up to the circular rows in which fifteen thousand people listened to the ancient performances, we were awestruck. Both of us had been here before, but that didn't diminish this feeling as we stood in the middle of the orchestra carved into the hill. We smiled and remembered granddad dropping a coin the middle of the orchestra as the young grandkids scurried to various parts of the theatre to listen. From any vantage point in the audience, the spectator heard the same sound. The acoustics were phenomenal due to the small moat encircling the outer perimeter of the stage. The water in the moat distributed the sound waves equally throughout the surrounding thirty-four limestone rows.

We slowly ascended through the center aisle and took our seats halfway up. I thought *I will I pretend that the year is 425 B.C. and I am watching Sophocles' play Antigone.* But my eyes gazed out beyond the orchestra. The landscape shapes, the curves of the northern hills, the valleys through which the route from the sea passes gave me the best performance. Sitting nestled in the man-made seat in the side of the mountain, I thought *Asklepios was on the mark. The earth, here, is the cure.*

Rebecca broke our silence and quietly said, "The next time I'm really sick, just bring me here."

I smiled and said, "I know."

———————

Back in the port of Piraeus, we boarded the ferry to the Cycladic Island, Naxos. As the ferry departed, we sat on the outside second deck. I scanned the northern horizon for the Parthenon, but smog polluted the air and Athena's temple was indiscernible. In our previous trips, we had visited Crete and Mykonos, but no other island.

We spoke of the archeological sites we wanted to investigate. Rebecca said, "Let us also just relax and enjoy the island." I agreed and reminded her that this was her trip. I was just the cruise director.

When we disembarked, we picked up our rented car and map. Rebecca, the navigator, located our small hotel outside the main port on the map. We drove south along the coast and followed the promontory west. Twilight descended and we were anxious to reach our destination. We drove up a dirt road to a hill overlooking the Aegean on both sides and viewed the white stucco building that was our hotel.

Our room had two Dutch doors. One looked out to the Aegean

on the south and the other offered a view to the northern Aegean. Twin beds were pushed together in the center of the room. A small desk and lamp stood opposite. It was perfect for our needs. The receptionist informed us that there was only one taverna- at the bottom of the hill on the beach- but it closed by nine in the evening. Tired, we didn't want to drive back into town.

We set out meandering down the dirt road. As we wound past the first bend, we greeted the two horses grazing and heard the tinkling of the sheep bells higher up the hill. At the end of the road, a large cove with a wide sandy beach stretched before us. The taverna was nestled in the back of the beach. Other than a few people who were leaving the beach for the day, we were alone. We sat on the beach and leaned backwards into the sand, listening to the sound of the waves lapping near our feet. The muscles in the back of my shoulders, the muscles my husband had determined hammer drills could not pulverize, began to breathe.

As the sun slid over the western mountain, we ventured into the taverna. We were the only guests. A large painted mural adorned the back wall. With greens and blues, it displayed mermaids and dolphins frolicking in the sea. Rebecca with her limited Greek told the woman sitting by the cash register what a beautiful mural it was. The woman smiled and an instant friendship developed. She beckoned us into the back kitchen and filled our plates with a portion from each pot; meatballs, stuffed vine leaves, baked zucchini and stuffed tomatoes. We smiled and thanked her. As we sat down at a table overlooking the beach and cove, she brought a pitcher of red wine and bottled water. She sat with us as while we leisurely ate, conversing mostly in sign language, but communicating.

The following morning, Rebecca wanted to locate the archeological site of Iria. She had read about it and was intrigued. It dated back to 1300 B.C. when Dionysos was worshipped here; later when Christianity reigned, St. George became the deity of the day. The religious use of this particular site had been uninterrupted for over 3,300 years. Map in hand, we set out along bumpy dirt roads and after much reversing, we approached a dirt parking lot with a sign "Iria" and a lone motorcycle.

We climbed out of the car and a large furry black dog growled menacingly at us. Securely chained to his doghouse, we avoided him and his territory. We ambled over to the high chain link fence surrounding the site and peered in. We discerned the delineation of a temple, but not much more. I thought *why in this location? What does the earth hold here that attracted the sacred for so long?* A young man approached and introduced himself. He smiled and shook both of our hands. He was the caretaker of Iria and was happy to show us the site and explain the various buildings. He told us that he had built the museum by himself and was in the process of building an additional room to house artifacts, which were currently in a shed. He had worked here for the past ten years and knew it like the back of his hand. He was from Naxos and had only been off the island once to Athens. He couldn't wait to get back, he said, laughing. Naxos was his home.

As we passed through the gate, he explained that the early votive offerings dating back to 1300 B.C. indicated that the Bacchic mysteries were performed here. These mysteries promised blessedness in the afterlife. Those initiated were called the Bacchoi or the Mystai. They walked in a sacred manner toward their goal of eternal bliss on the Island of the Blessed. A person was initiated through dance and rhythmic music, alcohol and sexual excitement. The state of frenzy was blessedness because it was liberation from the pressures of everyday life. Dionysos was born on Naxos and Naxos had always been known for its wine, so it was a perfect match.

This young gentleman spent the warm afternoon showing us models of the various four buildings built on the same location time and time again. We sat under an olive tree and he served us freshly squeezed lemonade. He explained to Rebecca that the reason the buildings kept tumbling was due to the land shifting. The site was in close proximity to the river whose volume increased dramatically in the spring when the snow on the high mountains melted and then decreased in the arid summer. As he spoke to her, I thought *about initiation. What does it mean to be initiated? A person is initiated through some sort of ritual into a sacred mystery that only the participants understand. Once you're initiated, is it no longer a mystery? Or does the mystery still remain mysterious? Enigmatic? Once you are initiated, there is no turning back. You are there with the other initiates. Do the participants have the same experience when they're initiated? No, they can't. Each person experiences events in their own unique way. But the initiates must form a bond through the fact they experienced the initiating ritual.*

He interrupted my thoughts and asked me if I liked the sacred land here. I surveyed the area, but unlike Epidauros, I didn't feel the sacredness. The sun was beginning its descent and we thanked him for the wonderful afternoon. He smiled and gave us his name and phone number. He eagerly wished that we would meet again one day. We drove back to our hotel to eat our last meal at our favorite taverna and then to pack our bags for the last leg of our journey.

The following day, we boarded the high-speed ferry to Heraklion, Crete and grabbed a taxi to our last hotel near the town of Agios Nikolaos. We treated ourselves to a luxurious hotel overlooking Mirabello Bay, thinking this would soothe our wounds inflicted by the last two years. As we checked in at the large reception desk, a gentleman offered us a fluted glass of champagne.

Not accustomed to this type of luxury, I thanked him and received the fluted goblet. Completing the check in, I scanned the spacious lobby with its deep cushioned armchairs, and placed the glass on one of the many coffee tables. A young woman escorted us to our room down a circular staircase. Our room was situated on the first floor with a balcony overlooking lush gardens with a path down to the beach. We had a sitting room with a couch and easy chairs. By the sliding glass doors, a modern desk and chair faced out to the gardens. Off the sitting room was a massive bedroom with a king-sized bed and a wall mounted television set with speakers encircling the room.

I thought *this has the feel of a luxury American hotel and we are in Greece. The luxury of Greece is in her land, not in an American style hotel. This is only for three nights. This is your daughter's trip, not yours. Try to adjust.*

After breakfast, our rented car was waiting for us. We decided to visit the Heraklion museum. Rebecca had never been there before and it had been years since I had been there. We drove west along the northern coastal route; it was longer than the main road, but the scenery was spectacular with the mountains rising on our left, the sea on our right and the sky bright blue with huge, white cumulus clouds overhead. I advised Rebecca that we should savor the last few days in Greece. We would be returning to our routines all too soon.

The museum, packed with Cretan artifacts, which chronologically spanned five thousand, five hundred years, was overwhelming. I wanted to show Rebecca one of my favorites and I pointed to my necklace. She smiled. I had worn this necklace everyday for the last twenty years.

When my husband and I had been here back in the early 1980's, we had marveled at the Phaistos Disc. At that time, it had not been deciphered. It was a clay disc about six inches in width with hieroglyphics and ideograms running in a spiral from the edge to the center. It was one of a kind, which made it terribly difficult for the code crackers to decode. Some scholars thought it was fake because only one had been discovered. After seeing it in the museum, my husband and I had been strolling the Heraklion streets. He had stopped at a jewelry store window and had walked in. I had followed and watched him buy a necklace. He came over to me and slipped it around my neck. A small gold representation of the Phaistos Disc hung from the gold chain.

He had smiled and said, "This reminds me of you."

We found the disc. It was still in the same location and still a mystery. I thought *he rarely buys me anything. I remember when he slipped this necklace around my neck, how surprised I was. It was beautiful. His hands sweated so much that he could hardly connect the clasp– August in Crete.*

I looked for a display case trying to see if I could see my reflection, so I could see my necklace, but the light was too bright from the sun shining through the high horizontal windows.

We meandered through the first floor and stopped when we came across the unique figurine of the Minoan Snake Goddess. About fourteen inches tall, she held in each uplifted arm two snakes. Her top exposed her naked breasts and a long skirt-like apron draped her torso. I remembered reading that some scholars believed she was evidence that women dominated the Minoan culture. The Minoan Snake Goddess represented the universal mother or earth goddess. I thought *of Asklepios and how snakes knew the cures of the earth. Maybe he learned about snakes from her, the earth goddess.* Rebecca looked at the ceramic figure and said, "One thing's for sure. She's one hot mamma." I agreed. This woman proudly exuded raw sexuality.

We returned to the hotel and descended the stairs to our room for a siesta before our evening meal. I opened the sliding glass doors to the balcony and sat down, breathing the sea air while the view mesmerized me with its tranquility. Rebecca undressed from her street clothes and curled up into the gigantic, soft bed in the bedroom. Something caught my attention and I glanced over to the desk. The red light on the telephone flashed. I picked up the receiver and listened to a message from my husband. He asked me to call him as soon as I received this. I wondered why he called. He never called unless it was something terribly important.

I looked at my watch. It was five in the evening on Crete so it was ten in the morning on the East Coast. I could call him at work. He should be there. I dialed his work number and heard his voice. He sounded like he was in the next room. He asked me how the trip had been, and if we had enjoyed ourselves. I responded affirmatively. He continued that he was scheduled for an MRI and CAT scan today. While this was standard procedure after chemotherapy, he wanted me to be in the loop. The division chair wanted to ascertain that the cancer had not metastasized to his lungs, as that could be a normal course of progression. These tests would determine if the chemotherapy had been effective.

I asked him how he felt and he assured me that he felt fine. I breathed a sigh of relief. I asked him to call me when he received the results and he promised that he would. I hung up the phone and returned to my chair and thought *normalcy. Our lives will continue in their routines when we return. The kids will have their summer and I'll work in the garden. Maybe we should plan our sailing vacation off the Cape in August. Yes, I can sail the boat and my husband can take it easy. Yes, that is what I will do.*

My daughter's stomach grumbled when she rose and implored for an early dinner. She hopped in the shower and I dug out a skirt from my suitcase and slipped it on. We were closing the hotel room door when I heard the phone ring. Startled, I reentered the room and picked up the receiver. It was my mother. I heard the concern in her voice. Immediately, she told me that my husband was scheduled for further tests today. She knew that if the doctor ordered tests, something was wrong. I reassured her that I already knew and that they were routine tests. She was worried and I thought *of the first doctor using the word worrisome.*

With a deliberate and slow voice, I said, "There is nothing to worry about. These are standard, routine tests. Please do not worry."

I knew she was not satisfied. She would call me once she knew the results.

Rebecca's eyes pleaded with me to find dinner. I ended the conversation by telling my mother that we would be home in a few days. I would see her very soon. I hung up and we scampered up the stairs. We drove into Agios Nickolaos and discovered a wonderful restaurant by the lake and ordered chicken with a Greek salad. Returning to the hotel, we walked to the dimly lit piano bar overlooking the bay and sat down by the bay window. Surrounded by dark woods and soft lighting, listening to Cole Porter in the background, we spoke of how the time in Greece had evaporated. We slowly sipped our chardonnay, neither of us wanting our trip to end.

Seven in the morning – the phone rang loudly in my ear. My head was not throbbing, but was definitely not at peace with itself this early in the morning.

I picked up the receiver and heard my mother's trembling voice. She blurted out, "It's cancer. The cancer has gone to his lungs."

I swung my legs out of bed. My mind wasn't thinking straight. I told her I would call her back, after I spoke with my husband. I walked out to the sitting room and slid open the balcony doors and stepped out into the moist morning air and stared at the sea.

I thought *I read somewhere, that once melanoma has metastasized to a major organ, the life expectancy is somewhere between eight and twelve months. Is this the beginning of the end? Why are we here? Why is this happening? We shouldn't be here. We should be at home. My husband is alone right now. What is he feeling? How are we going to proceed? What if he really dies? What is going to happen if he dies? I have never researched the exact definition of a panic attack, but if I had to define it, this would be it.*

I turned around to see Rebecca standing behind me. I stared into her deep brown eyes and thought *the greatest thing that makes you, may also break you. Achilles' heel. I always treat my children as equals, as I would my best friend, at every age. This time is no exception. I do not know any other way. Maybe this is my Achilles' heel. Maybe I should tell her everything is okay. This is a blip on the radar screen. Maybe if I do not say the words, it will not be real. Maybe we can pretend that the phone didn't ring.*

Still staring into her deep brown eyes, I thought *just a moment longer, just a moment longer that our lives will remain the same, in the normal routine.* Slowly, I began to form the words and told her that her father's condition was no longer worrisome. It was serious. It may be life threatening. I told her the cancer had spread to his lungs. I told her that we would call him at three this afternoon. It would be eight in the morning there. We would find out more information then. Her mouth dropped and she looked out beyond the garden. Then she looked at me. We didn't know what to say to each other. It was as if time stopped. We stood there in silence on the balcony together gazing out to the sea.

After some time, my daughter put her arm around my waist and suggested we should dress for the day. We left the hotel and walked down the long hill to the little town of El Lounda Mare. We walked to the water and looked at the fishing boats. We climbed the adjacent hill, which went nowhere. We retraced our steps and sat on a bench and watched the fishermen untangle their yellow nylon fishing nets. We went for a frappe, but neither of us drank it. We ordered toast, but neither of us ate it. We window-shopped. We went into some stores. We didn't buy anything. We kept looking at our watches and felt that three in the afternoon would never arrive. We hardly spoke a word to each other. Neither of us knew what to say.

At three in the afternoon, we found a small alley off a dirt road, away from the locals and traffic. I dialed his number with shaking fingers and felt the knots in my stomach. I heard his voice and asked him how he was. He sounded chipper. I told him that we preferred to come home now.

Surprised, he said, "Hold up, now. No worries. Surgery is scheduled to remove one tiny cancerous growth in my lung. The worst part is recovering. Some of my ribs will have to be broken to access the lung."

I thought *my husband, the ex-football player. What has your body done to you?*

I tried to be upbeat. I would buy better pillows, as he would be lying in bed, unable to move while recovering. He laughed. He had already told his team at work and they were going to loan him a laptop computer so that he could continue to work on the project while in bed. I told him that I would be home in two days. He insisted that we really enjoy the last few days and to take beautiful pictures. He, the photographer, had always loved the light found in Greece.

I said, "Okay" and hung up. I stared at the phone in my hand.

I was completely dazed, confused, distressed. I thought *he is not upset at all. Doesn't he get this? Doesn't he understand that this is a very bad indication of the disease progression? Doesn't he understand? I know that he knows that melanoma micrometastasizes. Once it has moved to a major organ, it is already moving or has moved to another organ. It metastasizes under the radar. Our MRIs and CAT scans do not have the ability to pick up these small growths. We have spoken about this before with various doctors. How can he not get this? This man is the smartest person I have ever known in my life. His IQ is off the charts. He must know. He is just thinking of us. But, I know him. I do know him. He doesn't want to know. And I do not know what I am going to say to him when I see him.*

I reiterated the conversation to Rebecca. We were in irons. The wind had been taken out of our sails. We stood there, looking at one another in disbelief.

The next-to-last day, we drove east along the coast. I spied a dirt road and for some reason, I turned down it. We bumped and rattled past rocks and gutted holes, not past second gear. Rebecca stared at me as if to say, why are you going down this dirt path? I was glad that she didn't ask because I didn't know why I was driving down this road.

Finally, we ended up at a small rocky cove. On each side of the cove grew two spectacular brown mountains and the sea lay beyond. We opened our doors, smelled the salt air and tiptoed over the rocks. There was no sand, only small rocks to form the beach. We had our swimsuits on under our clothes and we stripped off our clothes. Barefoot, we gingerly made our way to the water, arms outstretched, balancing ourselves on the rocks. We swam out past the floating black, stringy seaweed and continued to swim until the cove reached the sea. We stopped and floated on our backs, looking at the rugged, brown hills, the sea beyond and the sky. I thought *only here are the clouds this color white.*

Back in the States, my husband and I waited in the hospital exam room for the surgeon and the oncologist to review the latest tests to inform us when surgery would be scheduled. The oncologist came in by himself and wanted to examine my husband first before any discussion. I left and found the waiting room.

After some time, my husband and the oncologist came in and we moved to a private corner. The oncologist, looking at both of us, said in a deliberate voice that surgery would be delayed for at least a week or so. Not only did the standard pre-surgical tests need to be performed, but further tests as well. The additional tests would determine if the cancer had invaded the groin lymph nodes. This was a common progression of melanoma. If it had, then during the surgery, the metastases in both locations would be removed. The groin lymph node tests would be scheduled at the end of next week. Concerned, I inquired if the tests couldn't be performed sooner. Ten days was along way off considering the nature of this cancer. I was told no. It was the earliest available opening. I sensed my husband's anxiety, but I didn't know what to do for him. I didn't know how to quell my own.

I thought *I get this. My husband is not the only person who is suffering from metastatic melanoma.*

In the evening at home, carrying a delicious vodka tonic with lime, my husband and I walked out to the corner of the backyard, away from the house, where no one could see us from the deck. He looked directly into my eyes. Squinting hard, his voice firm and grave, "I want this cancer out of me, now."

The overwhelming feeling of powerlessness made me dizzy. I thought *there is nothing I can do. No amount of my research is going to alter the course of events. All I can do is to love him in whatever way I can. I will follow his lead in the months to come and do whatever I can to make him comfortable. I do not know what else to do. I do not know what to say.*

I responded, "I know. The surgery will be a success."

I drank my vodka tonic in three swallows. I glanced at his

dark blue polo shirt hanging from his shoulders. My watery eyes scanned the backyard. The evening air was still. It was one of those beautiful, warm July evenings, found only in the Northeast.

Over two weeks had passed since we had met with the surgeon and oncologist. Finally, the pre-surgical results came back. No evidence of cancer was detected in his groin lymph nodes. That evening, when he came home from work, he wanted to celebrate. We grilled shish-kabobs and corn on the cob on the deck and the five of us toasted to good health. The surgery for the cancer in his lung would be next Tuesday. I thought *a glimmer of hope. Maybe, they really will kill the cancer.*

On Monday, I scheduled the children's activities for the next two weeks. I wished to devote my time to care for my husband. I knew how painful broken ribs were. Somersaulting off my bicycle handlebars while speeding downhill one summer afternoon when I was eighteen years old broke four of my ribs and landed me in bed for three weeks barely able to breathe. My daughters were working as swim coaches for the town's swim team and William was swimming for his club's team and the town's. They would be kept busy while my husband recovered at home.

I filled my husband's car up with gasoline, as Rebecca would take my place as the swim team taxi driver. I went overboard buying his favorite food and had stocked the pantry to its limit. In the afternoon, as my children filed in from swim practice, they plopped down around the kitchen table, tuckered out.

I sat down with them and we reviewed the schedule for the next two weeks. At the end, I told them I would appreciate it if they didn't have too many friends over. Their father needed peace and quiet as he recovers. They nodded in agreement. They understood and I knew that they wanted this surgery to be successful.

That evening, I was preparing dinner when my cell phone rang. I dried my hands on my jeans to pick it up. I heard my husband's voice and I knew from the background noise he was in his car on his way home. I asked him if he had cleared his desk at work for the next few weeks.

"There will be no surgery," he articulated slowly.

Breathing in deeply, I held onto the kitchen sink. I gazed to the backyard to my flowerbed around the oak tree and slowly asked, "Why?"

In a monotone voice he replied, "Because there are now nine cancerous growths in both my lungs. They cannot surgically remove all of them. There are too many."

Stunned, I slid down from the kitchen sink to the floor, my knees next to my chest.

Quietly, I asked, "What is the next step?" I thought *it doesn't matter what the next steps are. We are looking death in the face again.*

He said, "I have been referred to a different oncologist who prescribes a different form of chemotherapy. I thought back to my father's glioblastoma. This was the same type of treatment in his last months.

"Perhaps, this will be the solution. How are you feeling?"

He didn't answer. He hung up. My body did not move from the kitchen floor until I heard his car door shut in our driveway, an hour later.

———————

We continued our routines in an almost unknowing way until one late August afternoon when my husband called me from work and asked me to meet him at the oncologist in the afternoon. There was a new protocol that may work and the oncologist wanted to discuss it with us. It was called Interleuken-2 or IL-2. I immediately agreed. Before I left, I had time to do a little research before meeting him in the city.

> Although treatment options are currently very limited for stage four melanoma patients, some people who are treated by IL-2 do survive this most serious stage of the disease. IL-2 is different from chemotherapy. It is given by a fifteen-minute

IV infusion every eight hours for five days. There are two courses that consist of a five-day treatment cycle separated by a nine-day rest period. The side effects, which are serious and sometimes fatal, include; nausea, fatigue, chills, fever, chest pain, mental effects, peeling skin, anemia. It must be conducted in a hospital under direct supervision of a physician specializing in this treatment. Six percent of selected patients had a complete response. Ten percent had a partial response.

After reading this, I thought *eighty-four percent of the selected patients died. Let's bank on the six percent.*

We met the oncologist and it was decided that my husband would undergo the Interleukin treatment during the month of September. We were informed that sometimes a body does not survive the treatment. If my husband's reaction became life threatening, the treatment would be stopped. The oncologist examined my husband before finalizing the decision for Interleukin.

As my husband left for the examining room, I asked the oncologist "What percentage are we looking at?"

"At best, he's looking at a ten percent chance of survival," he responded.

Stunned, I thought *I do not know how. I do not know how we are going to get through this. But, we must get through this. We will get through this. I know we will. We have no choice. One step at a time. Patience. I can do this. I have to do this.*

The day of treatment, we entered a large room with wooden panels, mahogany woodwork, high ceilings and a spacious sitting area with two reclining chairs and a four-poster bed. We were in the older section of the hospital built at the turn of the century. A nurse walked in and informed us that IL-2 patients should have a homelike environment since they would be staying for five days. My husband went into the bathroom and took off his street clothes and put on the hospital gown. I sat down in one of the reclining chairs and played with the remote. The oncologist entered while my husband was still in the bathroom and asked me how he was. I told him just about the same. He continued that I shouldn't have unrealistic expectations as my husband walked out. I stared at this doctor. I thought *unrealistic expectations?!! Isn't it unrealistic to think my husband will die in his early fifties?!! What the hell are you talking about? Unrealistic expectations!*

The oncologist ordered the IV. He would monitor my husband's progress during the day. The first IV drip started and I watched the liquid as it slowly flowed down the transparent plastic tube into my husband's arm. I didn't bring a book today as the scheduling nurse told me that my husband would probably want company. The IL-2 would not make the patient groggy the first day. I watched the nurse take his vital signs. She smiled and said that everything was fine and she left. I gazed at my husband lying in this strange four-poster bed. He looked so small and frail. I smiled and asked him what he wanted to talk about. He said he had been reading a good book about entropy and before I could respond, he continued:

- Increase in negentropy requires an overall increase in entropy.

- The artist lives in a world with lots of confusion, but a high negentropy conversion rate.

- You can talk about an entropy to negentropy conversion ratio.

- On one extreme is the conservative ploy; this establishment ploy emphasizing the retention of established order in the face of wasting (entropy increasing) is subject to the survival of the fittest. Darwin's theory says that improvement (negentropy), which comes with an overall increase in entropy (the attempts that fail) is a function of the number of attempts – a non-linear system.

- This view succeeds by retaining the old order at the expense of suppressing useful innovation.

I thought *he has always been the intellectual, but really, you've got to be kidding me. This is way over my head. I can't follow you. Okay, start taking notes to keep focused.*

I asked, "Please define negentropy."

"In information theory, it is used in reference to a type of ethics based on reducing entropy to the minimum or increasing entropy to the maximum. In this sense, this would be the inverse of the metaphorical association of death with the state of maximum entropy, so that life would be associated with minimum entropy or maximum negentropy principle," he said. "Capisce?"

I rolled my eyes. "Sort of."

I thought *if this is what is getting him through this, at least try to participate. Is this how he is processing what is happening to him? Does this make sense to him? Does this help him? I don't understand. Tonight, review your notes. Maybe you will understand this later.*

After lunch, he was tired and wanted to nap. I was grateful. I wanted to leave. I wanted to go home. He told me to go ahead and he would see me tomorrow.

By the third day of treatment, I was emotionally and physically drained and I was relieved that my mother had driven from the country to our house. I drove her in to the hospital. She would stay with my husband for the day. When we arrived at his room, we saw his body writhing on the bed. He was on fire. His undershirt was soaked through with perspiration. His legs trembled. His eyes were half shut. The nurse assured us that this was a normal side effect and that he was fine.

I thought *he is not fine. He is in pain. He is in agony. This is awful. I cannot watch my husband being tortured. This is what torture is. What is this nurse talking about? Fine. He's not fine.* My mother commanded me to leave. She, with her 90 lb. frame, pushed me forcibly out the door.

"Get out of here," she said. I left with my legs shaking.

The treatment stopped midday on the fourth day. His body did not withstand the treatment. My mind blanked as the oncologist told me the number of white blood cells that had been destroyed. I stared at my husband. I tried not to. His skin had a crusty, bluish hue to it. His hair was matted. He sat on the bed with his feet dangling. The skin hung on the arm that supported him.

I sat down next to him and touched and rubbed his back. It was completely drenched from sweat. I helped him to the bathroom to change. It was time for home and a good shower. He nodded his head slowly. The oncologist instructed us that we should return in nine days to begin the second session of IL-2. I looked incredulously at this man and I thought *how in god's name is he going to survive this?* But I nodded my head. On the way home in the car, he tilted the seat back and slept. Pulling into the driveway, the kids clamored out the front door. As my husband opened the car door, I saw the looks on their faces. They now understood what we were all facing.

———◦◦◦———

Heather insisted on cooking dinner for the next nine days. She wanted to make her father all his favorite meals. She dug out the recipe box and pulled out recipes and began a list. I told her that I was going to help her father take a shower and then we would go to the grocery store to buy the ingredients. When I went upstairs, my husband muttered that he was not in pain. He just wanted to sleep. After showering, my arm around his waist we walked to his side of the bed. He fell into bed and I covered him with a sheet and made sure the ceiling fan was on low. I drew the drapes closed.

By the time I was at the bedroom door, he was already sleeping. I closed the bedroom door quietly and walked downstairs. My children were in the kitchen. The three of them were now working together to plan the next nine days of menus. I understood. They wanted to do something. They wanted to do something to help. I thanked them, but reminded them that school was starting in two weeks. Heather was entering tenth grade and William his last year in middle school, eighth grade. Rebecca told me not to worry. She would help them. They continued to make their list while I sat on the kitchen chair and stroked our gentle golden retriever. I thought *there is only a ten percent chance of survival. Keep this to yourself. Let the kids do what they need to do to get through this. One in ten, the odds are against us now.*

The start of the second round of treatment began and I was dreading the next five days. On the first day, the oncologist informed us that the first round of treatment was indeterminate and that this round would hopefully yield positive results. I thought *sure if he can tolerate it. If he can survive it.* The first day, my husband tolerated the IV solution well. He drifted in and out of consciousness and I stayed most of the day with him. He didn't want to talk, but he wanted me there. When he was sleeping, I wandered around the medical complex and remembered back thirteen years ago, when I had worked here. Not much had changed.

On the second day, William requested to visit his father. I had discouraged all my children from visiting because I never knew what condition he would be in. William was adamant. William wanted to make sure his father could help coach his swim team next month, like he always had. He wanted to be able to tell his swim friends that his dad would be back as assistant coach. He wanted the start of the swim year to be like every other swim year.

It was a beautiful warm day with the sky as blue as it would ever become in the northeast. After we parked the car in the parking garage, we passed by the chain link fence and I hit my head against the protruding padlock. It hurt like hell and William laughed. I held my head and as I looked up, I saw my old boss from thirteen years ago. From across the street, I called his name and he stopped and looked in our direction. He looked the same. He had the same briefcase and same smile. Maybe his hair was a little grayer. He walked over smiling and I introduced William to him.

He firmly shook William's hand and I told him why we were here. My husband had done consulting work for my boss years ago, before the kids were born. I inquired how his department was and he told me that he had some serious personnel issues, but things with him and his wife were good. He had an appointment and had to leave. He was sorry to hear of my husband's situation and said that he would visit my husband tomorrow.

I thought *I am impressed. He has not seen my husband for all these years, but now he wants to visit him. I get it. He, the M.D., understands all too well. He knows the fate of my husband. This is a confirmation of his death sentence.*

My husband didn't make it past the third day of treatment. His blood counts were dangerously low. The oncologist informed me in private that he would be referred to another oncologist who specialized in chemotherapy with a palliative approach. My hands were sweaty and my throat dry. I tried to form the words to say thank you, but they were stuck in my throat.

My Journal:

> September 27, 2002
>
> In order to get through the daily routine, I read poetry – Elytis now – to try to understand what is important. It is in Greece that is still inside of me. It is her inner and outer landscape. I read and write in solitude, while others sleep. Poetic state: It's a third state not subject to daily life's contradictions and distinctions.

FALL 2002

My husband recovered, if you used that term loosely. He no longer felt terribly fatigued and no longer had the symptoms of fever, chills and nausea. The color of his skin had almost returned to a pale pink, but his clothes hung on him. It was as if the IL-2 treatment depleted most of his muscle mass. He wanted to return to work and I tried to discourage him, but he was adamant. He told me that he was the project leader on several important projects and he needed to oversee them. I thought *I understand his logic. If I continue to work, I won't die.*

That evening, his sister Helen called from Seattle and said she and her husband Richard would like to come visit for a few days before he returned full-time to work. I was relieved. Their visit would distract him from thinking of work and they would have a wonderful time. Helen informed that me they had already booked their flight– they were not going to take no for an answer. They would arrive tomorrow at five in the evening. I was stunned, but elated. I thought *of my father's brother coming to visit him from Iowa a month before he died. I know the routine. I know the death process routine.*

The next evening as we drove home from the airport, Helen asked a million questions about her brother's condition. She didn't want me to mince words. She wanted to know all the sordid details. Forty-five minutes later, we pulled into the driveway. I had never articulated so much information about my husband's condition to anyone before.

Before she got out of the car, Helen asked the ten-million dollar question, "How long does he have?"

I slowly turned toward her in the passenger seat and replied, "I don't know."

I thought *I don't know the timeline. I hadn't thought about a timeline. Is there a timeline? What is it? And what happens when the timeline finishes?* I looked up and my husband walked out the front door and greeted Helen and Richard. After much hugging and laughing we entered the house with their luggage. Cocktails were poured and we lounged on the deck in the warm evening air, laughing at Richard's cornball jokes. I had never found them hilarious before, but that night I laughed till my stomach hurt.

They stayed for three days and I hadn't seen my husband as happy for such a long time. He and Helen shared stories about growing up in Newport Beach. She, being seventeen years older, had almost generationally distinct stories. She reminisced of how she met Humphrey Bogart in the Newport Beach Yacht club and had cocktails with him. Stories, delicious food, good wine– it was the tonic we all needed.

Upon returning to Seattle, Helen was diagnosed with a small tumor on her ovary. She had called to inform me and asked me not to tell my husband. She told me that he had enough on his plate and she didn't want him to worry about her. I honored her request, but I was ill at ease. It didn't feel right to withhold this from my husband. If I divulged this to him and she found out, which she would because my husband would call her, she would be upset with me. The following week, she had surgery and emailed me that the tumor was benign. I sighed with relief. Normalcy would resume for her and her husband. This could be put to rest.

It was Saturday late afternoon. My husband had planned dinner in the morning and had been in the kitchen preparing all afternoon. Every appliance was out on the counter with various bowls filled with different concoctions. When I walked in, he explained that he was cooking Mexican shredded beef with enchiladas and tacos. Freshly made guacamole and salsa would begin the evening. Impressed, I scanned the counters and saw a large wine bottle two thirds empty and then I glanced at him. He was almost three sheets to the wind. This had become his weekend habit since recovering from the IL-2 treatment. I wasn't really sure what to do.

I told him it would just be Heather and the two of us for dinner tonight as Rebecca was waitressing at a local inn and

William was at a block party with his friends. At that moment, Heather walked in and was delighted with what she saw. She dug into the guacamole, but my husband tapped her hand. Dinner would be ready in just a little while. She asked how she could help and my husband told her to put the filling into the enchiladas.

I watched them in the kitchen as they worked together as a team. They began to speak about her classes in tenth grade. She told him she was enrolled in Chemistry Honors. While it was difficult memorizing the Periodic Table, she knew how to use the table. She believed she had the class under control.

He abruptly rebuked her. "No, take Chemistry Regular. Chemistry Honors is too difficult. Take Chemistry Regular and you'll be fine. The math you need in Chemistry Honors is beyond you."

She glanced at me with her eyebrows raised. She continued with her second class, History Advanced Placement as I went to the deck door to let the dog in.

He stumbled against the refrigerator and said firmly, "The concepts in that class will be beyond you. There is way too much reading. Don't take that. Enroll in American History."

I thought *of all the kids, she is the reader. Heather eats books. She doesn't get out of bed on the weekends until she can't stand her hunger pains. She'd stay in bed reading all day if somebody brought her food. What is he talking about?*

Heather walked directly over to me and pushed me out onto the deck. Shutting the sliding glass door, she yelled, "How dare he think I'm stupid. He doesn't know my brain. What's wrong with him? Is he serious?"

I tried my best to console her, explaining that he had way too much to drink, that he was not thinking clearly. She yelled at me that she didn't want dinner. She was going out. I watched as she ran down the deck stairs and left through the side yard. When I returned to the kitchen, he had served three plates. I let him know Heather had to run an errand and would eat when she returned. He was not even aware that she had left. I thought *will he remember his conversation with his daughter tomorrow? Will he remember how he put her down?* The dinner was absolutely delicious and I knew the kids would savor it when they were hungry later tonight. We were clearing the table when the phone rang. He was closer to the wall phone than me. I thought *no, don't answer it. Let it ring. You are almost incoherent.* He picked up the receiver.

It was Helen. I heard him say, "What surgery?"

In that split second, I thought *oh, shit, this has come back to bite me. Knowing her, she's had a glass of wine and has forgotten that she asked me not to tell him. Now, he'll be angry that I kept something from him, especially since it's his sister.*

I glanced over to him. He glared at me, holding onto the counter. He hung up. He swayed over to the kitchen sink where I was loading the dishwasher. I swung around and saw his bloodshot eyes. His hands clenched both my upper arms.

"You knew my sister was having surgery and didn't tell me."

He pushed my back against the kitchen sink. "You are my wife and have no right to ever hold anything back from me. You've made yourself attractive, but not for me. I want to know for whom."

The small of my back was killing me and I tried to push him back. My brain was swirling.

I thought *three kids, one dog, one cat, one mother who has a heart condition, one dead father, a husband who is dying and you think I am having an affair? Tell me when do I have the time? What is wrong with you?* I felt the blood rushing to my face. I felt my anger quickly rising.

I tried to pry myself from his grip, but his grasp was firm. I stared into his eyes and begged him to take his hands off me. He slowly released his grip and looked down at me with almost unknowing eyes. I turned back to the kitchen sink and inhaled deeply. I repeated this several times. I wanted to yell at him. I wanted to scream never, ever, do that again, but I suddenly stopped myself short.

I thought *look at this man. Turn around and look at him. Look at the man standing in front of you. He is fifty-one years old. He is dying. On some level, he knows that he is dying. He is angry. He is angry with his daughter with all the possibilities that lie in front of her. He's angry that she will continue to learn. He wants to be able to continue to learn, but he won't be able to. He's angry with me that I will live. He wonders if I'll be with another man. He doesn't want me to be with another man. He wants me to be his wife, but he won't be able to have me as his wife. He knows that he is dying and he's angry. He's angry. Understand that he's angry. Let him be.*

I didn't turn around. I turned on the water as hot as the thermostat would allow, so the steam would mask my tears. I began cleaning furiously. After a short while, I heard him climb upstairs to the bedroom. I finished the dishes and packaged up the enchiladas, tacos and shredded beef and put them in the refrigerator. I walked out on our deck with our dog. I sat down on the stairs and leaned my back against the railing. I gazed to the night stars to try to find the North Star.

> Demosthenes discovered among the Athenians of the fourth century, before Christ, that the more liberated the individual was, the more difficult it became for him to accept the tyrannical fact of death.

His anger in the days that followed was unpredictable. Some days, when he came home from work, he took his dinner and descended to his office, closing the door. Some days, he stayed with me and spoke of inconsequential things. I couldn't find a pattern in his behavior. I simply followed his lead.

Rebecca assumed the duty of the swim team taxi driver as I stayed home with my husband almost every night. One evening, after he went to his office, I waited for an hour and then went to see if he wanted any dinner. When I tried to open the door, it didn't open all the way. I squeezed into his office and peered behind the door. A large, new bass amplifier stood in the corner.

I asked him, "What is this?"

"It's a new bass amplifier. I am going to learn bass. I bought it last week."

Stunned, I inquired, "When were you going to let me in on this? Was it expensive?" Since I had stopped working when William was born, money had always been tight.

"It was just five hundred dollars," he smiled. I shuddered. "Not to worry. There will be plenty of money." I looked at him inquisitively. "I'm going to beat the stock market."

He beckoned me to his desk. I leaned over his shoulder and saw on the computer monitor every type of chart known to mankind indicating all the variables associated with a given stock. I was concerned, but I showed him that I was impressed at how he programmed these charts. I questioned the amount of money he was investing, but he didn't answer. He clicked on more screens displaying detailed analysis of puts and calls. My insides were reeling. I thought *he is going to lose all the money he has.* I nodded and suggested it was time for dinner. We climbed the stairs together. I thought *I don't know what to do. How do you say to an intelligent man, no one has ever beaten the stock market? What in god's name are you thinking? My dad could have talked with him about the stock market, how no one has beaten it. I don't have a clue how to begin that conversation. I need to think of what to do.*

<hr/>

It was Friday night in November when we ate at our favorite Italian restaurant in town. It was a cozy warm restaurant whose food warmed our insides as the fall was turning into winter. We just needed to get out. We just needed a break from our routines. When we returned home, the kids scattered to their various activities and my husband poured us a nightcap. We sat by the kitchen table. He looked tired and I asked him if he couldn't take some time off, especially since Thanksgiving and Christmas were upon us.

He didn't answer me. Rather he looked slowly at his drink. I knew that something was on his mind. Quietly, he said, "Today at work, we had our staff meeting in which projects were assigned and project leaders were appointed." I nodded. "The next step was for the project leaders to select their team. Well, today, I was selected to head up a project that is complicated with various facets. When it came to selecting my team, two of the guys I selected refused to work with me."

Shocked, I demanded, "Why, was the project too difficult for them?"

Slowly and deliberately, he answered, "Because, they said I may not be around to finish the project and they didn't want the responsibility to finish the project if I weren't around."

I was incredulous. I couldn't believe anyone would behave this way. I asked him who they were. I wanted to write a letter. Yes, I would write a letter to the chairman of the department. This was out of the bell curve. These men were mean-spirited. Leaning back in his chair, he took a sip of his nightcap. He placed his glass down carefully on the table and leaned forward towards me. Looking directly into my eyes, he said, "No, I am just reminding them of their own mortality."

I thought *I will never forget this. No slack, even if you are the person dying.*

WINTER 2002 – 2003

My Journal:

Christmas 2002

A beautiful air-dried prime rib, aged with home
grown herbs, roasted in the newly acquired
Calphalon roasting pan and after carefully
carving while guests seated in anticipation,
my husband's energy depleted, his sense of
awareness numbed by disease and not from
drink, the roast juices sliding off the platter
onto the carpet. With intervention and everyone
served, he is too weakened to eat his pièce
de résistance. We toast to the company we
keep and later, after brandy, he sleeps and the
children and gramma follow. Rebecca says I
sleep too much. It is a sign of depression. I
reassure her it's merely a sign of replenishment
as I memorize Cavafy's "Growing In Spirit" in
the early, early morn.

He who hopes to grow in spirit
will have to transcend obedience and respect.
He will hold on to some laws
but he will mostly violate
both law and custom, and go beyond
the established, inadequate norm.
Sensual pleasures will have much to teach him.
He will not be afraid of the destructive act:
half the house will have to come down.
This way he will grow virtuously into wisdom.

After New Year's, we were beginning a new routine. My old
boss, the one who visited my husband during his IL-2 treatment,

had asked me to consult with his department. He and I had emailed each other after he had visited my husband. After the kids got off to school, I would drive into the city and work for five to six hours a day and then return home to resume being "mom."

The evening before I was to begin this new routine, I was watching TV, trying not to think about returning to work when my husband appeared. He sat down next to me on the couch. We were by ourselves. I knew something was wrong. He looked so tired and so pale.

"I have a problem," he whispered. I reached for the remote and decreased the volume. With a deadpan face, he said quietly, "I can't write my name."

Stunned, I agreed, this was a problem. I thought *NO, this is not a problem. This is a catastrophe! I remember reading that melanoma can metastasize to the brain or liver after invading the lungs.* I put my arm through his arm and said I would call the oncologist in the morning as soon I arrived at work. I asked him how he was feeling. He smiled and said that he was tired. I climbed the stairs to our bedroom with him and pleaded with him not to go to work in the morning. I helped him into bed and tucked him in. I slid in on the other side, but sleep was hopeless. I tossed and turned and eventually went downstairs and tried to sleep on the couch with our golden retriever beside me.

In the morning, when I rose from the couch and went upstairs, my husband was already dressed, ready to go to work. The only problem was that he was wearing the same clothes he wore yesterday. I asked him if he considered it a good idea to go to work. He told me that he had to go in. He was at a critical juncture with one of his projects. My mouth opened and I stared at him. I thought *I don't know what to say. How can I prevent this man from going to work? How do I tell him I don't think you're going to make progress with your critical juncture if you can't write your name? How do you say this and not embarrass him, not make him feel worse? I don't know. How do you? He's dying and I can't talk to him about it. Honor his wishes. If we don't talk about it, maybe he won't die. I remember my mother saying, "If I hadn't gone to the kitchen to eat a cookie, maybe he wouldn't have died."*

In disbelief and terror, I watched him go downstairs and out the front door. I stood in the middle of our bedroom and in that rare moment, I simply didn't know what to do. I couldn't move.

At work, I immediately found my boss and informed him of my husband's condition. I needed to speak with his oncologist immediately. My heart raced as I picked up my cell phone to speak with the oncologist. After listening to my description of my husband's symptoms, he replied that a neurologist should evaluate him. He would arrange for the appointment. I inquired which neurologist he recommended and when he answered, I gasped. This was the same neurologist my dad had seen before we transferred him to another medical center.

At eight that evening, my husband and I waited for the neurologist. It was difficult to sit in the same waiting room, looking at the same dismal wallpaper as I had done sixteen months earlier with my father. I couldn't believe this was happening. I didn't know why this was happening. My husband sat next to me as if in a trance. I thought *sixteen months before tonight, I sat in the exact same chair, except with my father. Now, I am sitting next to my husband. Pray this will be the last time I ever sit here.* We were the only people in this huge waiting room. Finally, the neurologist called us in. As she was examining my husband, it was quite evident that something drastically was the matter. She instructed him to extend his right arm perpendicular to his side and then to bring his hand to his face and with his index finger touch his nose. She asked him to repeat the same procedure with his left arm. Both times, his index finger consistently touched his cheek, about three inches from his nose. She declared that he had suffered a stroke and recommended us to proceed to our local hospital for further diagnostic tests. She would call the local hospital and order a CAT scan to confirm her diagnosis.

As we walked down to the parking garage in the frigid night air, he said, "You think, on top of all of this, I had a stroke." I thought *no, it is not a stroke. The melanoma is invading your brain. This is why you can't write your name.*

In the car, I asked whom should I contact at his work to let them know he wouldn't be in tomorrow. He couldn't remember his boss's name. I asked him a name of his closest coworker. He stared out the window. I thought *I will look up the administrator of his department.*

Once admitted to the local hospital and in the exam room, the physician asked my husband to perform the same test as the neurologist had. The fluorescent lights were bright and almost surreal. Again, he was unable to touch his nose with either index finger. The physician looked at me with an astonished look and inquired, "Is he usually this uncoordinated?"

I thought *what an idiot. Did you read the diagnosis on the admitting form? It's metastatic melanoma. It is invading his brain. Do something instead of looking at me thinking he's uncoordinated. I can't believe you.*

The physician ordered a CAT scan of his brain and my husband was admitted for the night. Hospital procedure dictated that I could not accompany him to the CAT scan. The nurse would call us with the results of the scan later in the evening.

As I drove home, I realized I had to tell the kids the situation. I gathered them around the kitchen table and quietly explained that their father was undergoing further tests at our local hospital and the results would inform us if the cancer had metastasized to his brain. I saw the horror in their eyes and I felt the horror in my heart. Looking at their stunned faces, I gently told them we would know more later. There wasn't anything we could do except get some rest. My body was physically exhausted. My head and heart were emotionally drained. I collapsed on the black leather couch in the den and fell into a restless sleep. Rebecca nudged me an hour or so later and handed me the phone. I heard the radiologist voice. He told me the CAT scan indicated that the melanoma had invaded both hemispheres of my husband's brain.

——•◦•——

Melanoma micro-metastasizes. The actual cancer tumors are quite small, but hematomas grow around the tumors. Blood clots form and continue to grow. If you can reduce the hematomas, you give more space for the brain cells to function. The next afternoon, at the local hospital, a small Chinese radiologist was wheeling my husband to radiation. I grabbed the handles of the wheelchair and told her "No." He was not going to be treated here. She adamantly said she had her orders. Sternly, I said I had authorization over his health care. Radiation on blood clots was pointless. I took control of the wheelchair and wheeled my husband back to his room and helped him into bed. I looked directly into his eyes in hopes that he would focus and understand. I told him he was going to be transferred to the leading medical center where he had been receiving treatment. I told him I would return shortly. As I left, I informed the nurse at the nursing station that he would be transferred later today.

I didn't know how I was going to get him transferred, I just knew that he must be transferred. He couldn't stay at a hospital where they radiate blood clots. I drove home and raced upstairs to my desk in our bedroom. I opened my file cabinet and found my father's folder with his medical information. I didn't know why I had not thrown this out yet, but I hadn't. I leafed through the papers and found the telephone number of my dad's neurosurgeon, who performed his craniotomy at the same medical center. I called. He was not in, but his associate was. I spoke with him and relayed all the information that I could remember. He told me that before he could comment, he would need to review the CAT scans of last night. He would be in his office until six pm today. I told him I would drive them in now. I would not wait until tomorrow. I returned to the local hospital and located the medical records department on the fourth floor. I waited in line and kept looking at my watch. It was four-thirty. I prayed I would not hit traffic and wished this line would move faster. Finally, at the counter I completed the request form detailing the patient's name, date of birth, medical record number and the record being requested. I hastily handed it back to her. She read the request form slowly and replied she couldn't release the scan to me. My husband, the patient, must sign for them. It was the federal law. I looked at her incredulously and told her that was not possible. The patient was unable to write his name. His brain was being squished by blood clots formed by cancerous melanoma. She didn't care. She couldn't release them. She needed his signature. Having worked in a medical center for ten years, I knew the ropes, so as to speak, of medical records and I knew my husband's medical record number. It was on his hospital wristband. I slipped behind the counter as the woman began to assist the next person in line. The door where the actual medical records were kept was to the right of her. She didn't see me as I scooted past the counter. I entered the records room and located his CAT scan rather quickly and dashed out.

The woman saw me and yelled, "Lady, you can't take that."

I walked very briskly out of the waiting room area, bolted down four staircases and dashed out to my car. I drove into the city with my heart beating in my ears. I double-parked outside the neurology building, praying the parking ticket god was with me, and took the elevator to the twelfth floor. I located the neurologist's secretary and gave her the CAT scan. She was a pleasant woman who assured me that the neurosurgeon would review it as soon as he was finished with his patient. He would call me. I thanked her and left to face the rush hour traffic out of the city. About an hour and half later, my cell phone rang as I drove into the parking lot of the local hospital. It was the neurologist. He said, calmly, "I think I can help your husband. May I see him tomorrow at ten in the morning?"

I thought *yes. Yes. Someone can help. Someone can help me. Someone can help my husband.* I hung up and pulled into a parking space and put my head on the steering wheel. I felt my adrenaline begin to subside.

Heather met me in the hospital's main lobby. She had roasted chicken and made mashed potatoes with a mixed medley of vegetables for her father's dinner. We took the elevator to his floor and I let her know about the neurosurgeon. She was relieved. As we walked into his room, we both saw his face light up as he looked at Heather's dinner. She smiled and placed it on the pushcart in front of him in bed. As he devoured the chicken, I told him that I would pick him up in the morning and that he had a morning appointment with one of the best neurosurgeons. I didn't ask him if he understood what I had said because I was not sure he did. When my husband finished his dinner, the plate was covered with gravy. I took it from the pushcart and walked over to the wastebasket and dropped it in. I cleaned off the silverware and put it my bag. I had never liked that plate and I was not going to clean it. Heather stared at me.

The next morning, at ten in the morning, my husband and I walked up the street, which was a virtual wind tunnel, blasting ice-cold air. We sat in the neurosurgeon's office. He explained that radiation would be ineffective in my husband's case, but that a craniotomy would remove much of the melanoma with their surrounding hematomas. The surgery would not stop the growth of melanoma, but would give the patient quality of life. The oncologist would be responsible for continuing the course of chemotherapy afterwards and for submitting the disability papers. He continued that my husband should not work and that I should inform his department that a return to work date could not be established at this time. I was relieved. Someone with authority had advised him that he could not work. I was not sure how much of this conversation my husband understood, but we both agreed to the craniotomy and my husband agreed that he would not work until the oncologist approved. The neurosurgeon explained this in a quiet, compassionate way. He didn't have the huge mahogany desk like my father's neurologist. He had a small office filled with pictures of his wife and children. He was a tall man, with a genuine smile. The surgery was scheduled for the next day. Waiting for the elevator, I thought *I can't believe I am in the same building with my husband as I was with my father. I can't believe my husband is going to have the same operation as my father did, sixteen months later. This is more than a coincidence. This is unnerving.* I reminded my husband to put on his gloves before we went out into the frigid air.

The next day, the craniotomy was a success. My husband recovered nicely. I sat by his side and fed him ice chips as I had done for my father. The following day, my children came to visit him. When we arrived, we checked in at the nurse's station. The nurse said, "I didn't know your husband was a physician."

"He's not," I replied.

"He told me that he was an anesthesiologist and then removed both his IVs. He was going to check himself out," she continued.

I thought *oh my god. Is this what we have in store for us? He is supposed to recover some of his cognitive abilities. Are we going to have an altered person living with us?*

William giggled and I tapped the back of his head. We entered my husband's room and saw him lying in bed, looking serene and comfortable. His head was shaved and he was wearing a huge, white bandage as a skullcap. His face was not swollen as my father's had been. He looked good, considering what he had been through. I didn't ask him about being an anesthesiologist. The nurse came in and informed us that he would be discharged in two days. This would give me enough time to continue to work while stocking the pantry with his favorite foods.

Two days later, after work, I walked over to the neurology hospital and found him in his room, dressed in fresh street clothes. The oncologist who was overseeing the continuation of his chemotherapy was discussing further treatment. I greeted them and sat down on the bed next to my husband.

The oncologist continued, "You know, you never know when it's your end. I could walk across the street to the next building and get hit by a truck. We're all going to die someday."

They began to talk philosophically about life and death. They spoke of Socrates and why he chose the hemlock. I looked at my husband's reaction. He was nodding his head. My brain was shutting this out. I thought *is this really helpful? Yes, Socrates was right with his last request. It was on the mark. Sacrifice to Asklepios a cock. A sacrifice for his birth. Some say Socrates did so because he was metaphorically giving birth to his own death. Dying is like childbirth and death is like being reborn. Okay, enough.* I left the room to find some water.

Once home, everyone felt the release of tension. The stress was out of the air. We settled in. My husband had a sense of calmness about him. He would not be working. He could do whatever he liked during the day. Heather and William would be in school and Rebecca would work in the evenings and would be able to be home with her father during the day. I began working almost full-time as the department was undergoing a radical change and needed my assistance.

One of the drugs prescribed for my husband was a steroid. Steroids reduced the swelling of the nasty blood clots surrounding the cancer tumors. Steroids also make the patient hungry – hungry all the time. By February, he began to read cookbooks and research recipes online. He started this process in the morning and by early afternoon, had made a list of ingredients that he needed for dinner. The ingredients were specific, by brand. It couldn't be just any hot sauce for the chicken wings. It had to be Frank's® RedHot Sauce. Sometimes Rebecca searched several stores to find these exact ingredients. She was a trooper and didn't complain. One day, she went to four stores, but couldn't find the right type of mushrooms for Veal Scallopini with Mushroom and Marsala. My husband was adamant about having the right mushroom, so out she went to the fifth store. After several hours of looking for mushrooms, she discovered them in a Korean store almost an hour away from home. By late evening, after swim practice, we had a gourmet meal served to us. Sometimes, we sat in the dining room to eat. Sometimes we ate at the kitchen table. It didn't matter where. The conversation, the delicious dinner the five of us eating together satiated us emotionally and physically.

At about the same time, Heather was having a terrible time in her Advanced Placement History class as well as having a generally terrible time with her peers at the high school. Everyone knew that her father was dying and everyone approached her in the hall or at lunch to express how sorry they were. She couldn't stand this. She didn't consider ninety percent of these kids to be good friends and she believed this kind of conversation should be reserved for only good friends. She felt as though she was wearing a scarlet letter. She was becoming unglued. We spoke about the situation and I agreed to meet her Advanced Placement History teacher to see if I could help somehow. I was not sure how I would be able to help, but she made the appointment.

The teacher had a stellar reputation in the high school as being not only extremely intelligent, well-read, and socially conscious, with a heart of gold, but also a champion of an Ethiopian village. All the parents of the smart students had forewarned me she was an exceptional teacher. We met in the cafeteria, sitting around a small circular plastic table. She introduced herself and explained how difficult and challenging this course was. I nodded. She handed me a paper. It was Heather's essay on Patrick Henry and the issues he tackled. I read it and I thought *not bad. It is not perhaps the top of the line, but it is definitely coherent and well thought out. What is this teacher's issue?* She then handed me another paper. She told me this paper was A+. It was written with insight, understanding and a clear command of the issues. I read the paper. In the first paragraph, I did not find a verb. I had no idea what the student was trying to communicate. The second paragraph left me in a sweat due to its incoherence. I skimmed the rest. I handed the paper back. The teacher smugly smiled and said, "Now, do you understand?"

I thought *I get this. I get this in so many ways.*

"How, specifically, would you want Heather to improve?" I asked.

She explained in detail how the second paper was compiled with factual data and insightful interpretation, but didn't answer my question. The conversation continued, but I wasn't listening anymore.

The teacher elaborated, "It doesn't matter what else is happening in your daughter's life, this is an advanced placement class."

I thought *I get it. No slack; not even if you're the child of a dying father.*

I glanced at Heather and saw the sadness in her blue eyes. I thanked the teacher, but did not discuss any further next steps as we left. We walked down the long corridor to the main entrance amidst the students' stares and I imagined that this was what she had to endure daily. Once we climbed in the car, I started the engine to warm the car. The air was brittle with its winter chill. We spoke seriously. She wanted to be homeschooled. This was setting her over. I completely understood after this conversation with her teacher, the stench of the lockers, the fluorescent lights in the hallway, the students' stares. I got it. I would make an appointment with the principal and her advisor. I told her that she would not have to go back and she didn't. She was homeschooled for the rest of her sophomore year.

Late February, Helen called from Seattle. Their brother, Scott, a year older than she and eighteen years older than my husband, had suffered a sudden heart attack and was in critical condition in an ICU in a San Francisco hospital. It was unclear if he would live. My husband insisted that we fly out to see them. I made arrangements at work to be out for a few days and figured out the kids' schedules. I helped my husband pack, thinking we would be there for just two days. We arrived at the airport, and waiting to board the plane, I looked at my husband and saw a changed person. He had gained probably between fifteen to twenty pounds since his craniotomy six weeks ago. His face was puffy, his eyes had sunk back inwards and he was developing large red blotches. He was wearing a cap since his hair hadn't grown completely back and his stomach now extended way over his belt. We were listening to the airline representative announce the people whose seat numbers began with a specific row to board. All of a sudden, my husband grabbed my arm and said, "We need to board now."

I quickly turned and said, "No, our seats are before those seats. Those numbered seats are behind ours."

In that one instant, I knew that he was aware of his mistake and shaken by it. He couldn't fathom the concept of before or after. I told him that the announcement was muddled and not to worry.

Helen and Richard had discovered a wonderful hotel in San Francisco: inexpensive, but close to everything. We drove immediately over to the hospital to visit Scott. We checked in at the main desk of the hospital and took the elevator to the ICU unit to meet his wife. She was shaken. She said that Scott had been having chest pains for the past few days, but he had believed it was just he flu. He hadn't gone to the doctor, but then when the pain become excruciating, he dialed 911. She had been at work when the hospital called her. We offered our sympathy. I didn't really know this woman, but I felt her anxiety. The three of them went into the ICU unit. I waited in the ICU lobby.

They didn't remain very long as the patient was in critical condition, but Scott assured them that he was ready to see Jesus. When we left the hospital, we ate lunch in a local restaurant and they all returned to the hotel for a siesta. Perfect. I planned to walk to Chinatown.

Having worked in San Francisco for two years after graduating Berkeley, I knew the town like the back of my hand. Chinatown was about two miles away and it was a warm, sunny afternoon. Walking down the hill, I thought *this is a beautiful, sunny afternoon in San Francisco. I remember back to when my husband and I lived across the bay, in Berkeley, right after we met. That was the best time we had together. We roller skated in the Golden Gate Park, ate brunch at the Cliff house, listened to jazz in the Castro District. We were free. We had no kids, no mortgage, no worries. Living hand to mouth, we camped in the mountains of the Sierra Nevada. I laughed out loud: upon waking up in our two-man tent up in the mountains of the Sierras, I had seen a huge paw print. My husband immediately found his book on the Sierra Wilderness and identified the paw print to be a puma. Then he frowned. He said, "Pumas live at the three thousand foot level and we are way below that."*

I asked, "Do you want me to make a sign which reads, 'Puma – climb higher. You're not supposed to live down here.'?"

We laughed. He replied, "I will play my mandolin to scare the puma off."

I loved how he played the mandolin and the twang of his bluegrass voice. What happened to those times? Try to remember the last time he and I did something fun together, just the two of us. It was before the kids were born. Stop this. Think of something positive. Stay positive. You live in a different time and space now.

I strolled up and down the little streets of Chinatown and bought three rope necklaces for my kids. They had the Chinese emblem of life hanging from their chain.

That night, after a wonderful dinner of seafood, we retired early, as everyone was exhausted from their respective trips and the time change. In the morning, my husband and I woke to a loud knock on the door and then another one and another one. I bolted out of bed, feeling the way my head felt in Crete when my mother called. I opened the door. It was Helen. Scott was dead. He had died early in the morning. Helen wanted to wait until eight am to tell us. He had suffered another massive heart attack. I thought *I wonder if he is seeing Jesus. I wonder what it would be like to see Jesus. It must be calm. He always exuded an aura of peacefulness, of tranquility.* I glanced at my husband to see his reaction, but he was expressionless. I was not sure what he was thinking or feeling. Helen told us that she and Richard would stay for the service and my husband agreed it was the right thing to do.

Later, we were informed of the schedule of events. A memorial service would be held in the church they both attended in two days with a reception following. Helen and Richard needed to buy clothes for the service. Not knowing how much money my husband had lost trying to beat the stock market, I decided that we were not going to buy clothes. I called Rebecca and told her of the news. I asked her to ship the black dress I had bought for work and my husband's suit that he wore at her graduation. She agreed and she would notify gramma of the turn of events. The next day, we drove around San Francisco in search for appropriate funeral attire.

Scott and his wife were ardent born again Christians. To say they took their religion passionately and seriously was an understatement, and they wanted everyone to share in their beliefs. They believed that there was only one true god.

The day of the service, we drove into a massive parking lot and I gazed up at the church. I had never been this physically close to this type of church. It was of modern architecture bellowing up to the sky with its triangular tower. I had only seen churches like this from the perspective of driving on Southern California freeways as they towered on the hills. I was used to the chapels built by the fishermen and villagers of Cape Cod, built in the 1600s with their original stained glass windows and hard wooden pews with their one belfry. This metallic structure soared to the sky, I guessed to be closer to Jesus.

As we passed through the main door, we entered a lobby. I was unaccustomed to a spacious lobby in a church. There was a crowd of people waiting to enter the church proper and we took our place in the queue. I was amazed by the sheer number of people. I didn't think I even knew this amount of people. As we walked into the church proper, I felt as though I was entering a high school auditorium. There was a stage equipped with microphones and a podium, but I saw no altar, no religious icons, and no crosses depicting the sacrifice of Jesus. There was no pulpit. The chairs were the kind whose seats flipped up when you were not sitting in them. I couldn't seem to feel any god in this massive room.

The Greek temples were homes for their gods and goddesses. Inside their temples, in the naos, there stood a cult statue of the god or goddess, set up on a pedestal. A table of offerings, incense stands and sometimes an ever-burning lamp would stand before the cult statue. I didn't feel as if this place was a home to anyone. This was an auditorium where someone stands at the podium and speaks to an audience.

The immediate family sat in the front rows, while the rest of the huge church was completely packed by friends. The deceased had three sons and one daughter. During the service, each son spoke. The oldest son climbed the stairs to the stage first. He spoke of how each member of his family had found the richness of Jesus each in their own way, each in their own time. His belief in Jesus gave him solace and an acceptance that his father was now with the almighty father. The second son rose and instead of standing behind the podium, took the microphone and paced the staged. He had found Jesus in a county fair ground where an evangelistic preacher was proselytizing the power of Jesus: that his belief in the power of Jesus gave him his power in life. Another son said he discovered his connection while watching a minister on TV. They all said their father was with Jesus now and that their father was at peace, in an eternal resting peace. I sat and listened. I thought *what is my husband thinking? What is he feeling? His brother is at peace. What is my husband feeling?* His face was expressionless. His hands were folded in his lap. I placed my hand on his knee and kept it there for the rest of the performance.

At the reception, all of my husband's extended family were genuinely happy to see him. It had been years since he had seen some of Scott's children. Being eighteen years younger than his brother, my husband was closer in years to Scott's sons and had been considered their big brother, even though he was technically their uncle. One son, recently married, was traveling to Morocco with his wife to spread the word of Jesus there. As they talked to him with much enthusiasm, I wondered how the Muslims were going to enjoy knowing the power of Jesus. Standing next to the table with the food, my husband was happy enjoying all his relatives. I sensed that everyone knew my husband was sick and dying, but no one spoke of it.

I took a break from the reception and walked out to the parking lot. My husband's niece, his sister's daughter, joined me. I was close with her and she was close to my husband. It was a spectacular beautiful afternoon with clear, blue skies, white puffy clouds, and a warm breeze. We sat on the parking square and talked. "How long?" she asked.

I replied that I didn't know. She told me she wanted to drive my husband back to the hotel after the reception. She wanted some alone time with him. He was her favorite uncle and she was his favorite niece. He had coined the phrase, "I hate nieces to pieces" when they were toddlers. She had rented a red, snazzy convertible and it was a perfect afternoon for a ride in it. We agreed to drive the longer scenic route back to the hotel in order to enjoy the afternoon sun.

The next day, before leaving for the airport, my husband, Helen and I strolled to Fisherman's Wharf to eat fresh seafood on the pier. Once again, the warm afternoon was beautiful sitting next to the bay. We sat outside in the sun and leisurely ate our lunch in a quiet, secluded café by the waterfront. I gazed out to the sailboats on the bay and I thought *of the times my husband and I had sailed on this bay. It had been our Sunday ritual. I glanced over to him and his sister and thought this might be the last time these two will have a chance to be together. I should leave to give them time to themselves.* After a while, I excused myself to buy some Ghirardelli chocolate, telling them that I would meet them back at the hotel. Sipping their wine speaking about their family genealogy, I left and an empty feeling flowed throughout my body.

SPRING 2003

My work had become very demanding, as the dean who supervised the department was restructuring the department and the personnel. They needed to hire an administrator. My old boss recommended me. I knew that I had to work somewhere full-time, as we needed the income. I had compiled my resume and had sent it to various medical centers, receiving favorable responses. But I had worked here before and, in my ignorance, believed this would be an easy job since I was familiar with the responsibilities. I told my boss that I needed a decision on whether the dean wished to hire me or not as I needed to secure permanent employment soon. He made an appointment with the dean for later that afternoon. We walked to his building and rode the elevator to the tenth floor and met with him in his conference room. I glanced out to the river and saw a red-tailed hawk flying breathtakingly over the river. She glided gracefully through the air, over the water. The dean beckoned for us to have a seat around the conference table. The three of us discussed the functions of the position and finally arrived at the salary, which was the deciding factor for me. The dean mentioned a figure that was seven thousand more than the other offers I had received. I decided to take it. I shook his hand firmly and thanked him. I reiterated the salary figure as we shook and he nodded in agreement. He would have Human Resources review the personnel paperwork and would inform me when the offer was official. We left and I felt relieved that my family would have sufficient income.

In April, my husband's niece and her boyfriend from San Francisco were scheduled to visit my husband. My husband was having trouble remembering things and having difficulty dressing these days and his niece very much wanted to see him. His dinners had become sporadic. Sometimes he still cooked like the gourmet chef he once had been, but then there were evenings we pushed our food around on our plates, pretending to eat it. We never said anything. My children and I only praised his efforts. My niece wanted to come the first week of April, but I told her to come sooner than later. When I said this, I thought *I don't know why, but just come now if you want to see your uncle.* The anxiety knot in my stomach twisted and I couldn't release this feeling, no matter how I tried.

During the next week, my husband started having trouble navigating the stairs. When he climbed downstairs to his office in the basement, he stayed there for hours. Once he came up, he did not go down again. It seemed like he had the physical ability to climb up and down one flight each day. One night, as he was trying to climb the stairs to our bedroom, he reached the third step, but he couldn't go further. With his right hand clenched on the banister, he was unable to lift his right foot to the next stair. I was at the bottom of the stairs watching his difficulty. I climbed up to him and put my arm around his waist to help him. He turned abruptly and told me sternly that he didn't want my help. He wanted to sleep on the couch tonight. I took his hand in mine and we descended. Once he was lying down comfortably, I scampered upstairs to fetch blankets and a pillow. Reaching up to the closet for the blanket, I thought *how much does he remember? Does he know that he can't climb stairs? Is this similar to what happened to my dad? His oncologist had told him he would fade into la-la land and that's exactly what he did. Is my husband entering la-la land? I will call the oncologist tomorrow and tell him of this recent development.* When I returned to my husband, he was fast asleep. I covered him with the blanket and squeezed the pillow under his head.

The next morning, my husband was sleeping peacefully when I left for work. I asked Rebecca to keep an eye on him. Not being able to climb upstairs the night before left me quite concerned. Late morning, I was sitting at my desk when my private phone line rang. I answered it and heard the anxiety in Rebecca's voice.

"Mom, he can't sit up. When I get him to sit up, he slides back down on his side. He just urinated all over himself."

I thought *why am I at work? I should be there. This is awful for my daughter to experience this. I should be home with him. This is not right. I think way too much about money and the future. I should have been thinking about him.* I told her I would call hospice and come home as soon as I could. She told me she had already called gramma and that she was on her way in.

I hung up and called the local hospital's hospice division. I was told that the earliest hospice could come would be sometime next week. "No," I said, "We need help now." I explained the situation.

They were very sorry, but couldn't have anyone out before next week. I hung up. I called the oncologist and implored him to intervene. He stopped me short and said he would call. He told me to take a deep breath. I elaborated that his niece and her significant other were on their way from California to see him. He then offered to increase the level of steroids to the maximum. In this way, he could maybe give my husband another week of quality life so he could maybe participate in his niece's visit. My hand was sweating, holding the receiver. He continued, that when it came closer, he would admit my husband to the hospital.

I interrupted, "On what grounds?"

"We can say that we're ruling out an infection," he replied.

Calmly, I responded, "Cancer is not an infection. It is a virus. He will stay home with us." I hung up.

I thought *we've come this far. An infection. I don't think so. He needs to be at home with us, his family, not in an antiseptic hospital room.* I looked out my office window and saw the dark, icy, polluted river with ice chunks floating down. The sky was gray with wisps of clouds. I thought *I have never thought before of defining hell. But at this moment, this is the perfect description.*

The phone startled me. It was the oncologist. He had arranged for a hospice representative to be at our house within two hours. I thanked him very much and felt a twinge of guilt that I had corrected him on the definition of cancer. He was trying to be helpful. It was three-thirty in the afternoon and

I could beat the rush hour traffic. I called my boss. He would relay the information to the dean. On the way home, tears slid down my cheeks and then more tears. My vision was blurry and I thought *stop this, stop now. How awful for my daughter to deal with her father in this way. Did I hear the oncologist say one week, one week of quality life? What exactly does this mean? I have one week of quality life with the man whom I slept with the first night I met, with whom I gave birth to three children, and have not been away from for twenty-three years? One week? One week of quality life left? My mother's words after my father died. "If I hadn't gone into the kitchen to get a cookie, he might not have died." One quality week? This is all? This is it? Then what? Tears and driving. I'm good at this.*

When I arrived home, I hurried over to my husband who was lying on the black leather couch. She was right. He couldn't sit up. If I raised him to a sitting position, he would just slide back over and collapse into the couch. The doorbell rang. It was a nice middle-aged woman with two large briefcases. She identified herself as the hospice representative and I thanked her for rearranging her schedule. We sat at the kitchen table. She proceeded to inform me what they would and wouldn't do. First, she had ordered a hospital bed and a wheelchair. It would be a matter of days before he wouldn't be able to walk, she said. She gave me a prescription for a box. The box would contain morphine for pain and medication to help with the fluid retention in his lungs. A hospice representative would come twice a day to see how things were going. As we talked, in walked my husband's niece and her boyfriend. I had believed that they were coming tomorrow. No, she told me. It was always today. I thought *I usually don't get things like this confused. Take a mental note. Start writing things down.*

The hospice rep continued, "I want you to know that what you are experiencing now is beyond stress." I thought *thank god. Somebody gets this.*

I was glad to see my husband's niece, but I felt things were chaotic. The hospice woman finished and instructed me to get the box as soon as possible. I promised her I would. Once she left and the greetings established I left to get the box and the new prescription for the maximum steroids. When I returned, Heather and my husband's niece were cooking up a storm. Every pot and pan was out, every burner going, oven, microwave, and blender. I thought *leave the dishes. I'll do them. It's what I do best. I clean up messes.*

I went over to my husband and gently pulled his head up. I coaxed him to open his mouth and I placed the steroid pill on the back of his tongue and urged him to sip some water. After swallowing the pill, I leaned him back down and sat on the side of the couch with him. I watched him as he drifted into la-la land. I waited to see if this pill was really going to work. I waited for few minutes and then, the flash of coherency. It was not going to work in minutes. I realized I needed to watch myself more.

The weekend was upon us and the steroids were kicking in. While my husband would never walk again, he could sit up in a wheelchair. My niece's boyfriend wanted to go into the city to the Harley Davidson Motorcycle Store on Madison Avenue. He wanted to buy a T-shirt. This was high on his priority for his trip to the East Coast. I thought *I have one quality week left with my husband. Why do I want to spend it at some motorcycle store? I can't ride motorcycles. The one time I did, I lost control of it.*

But my husband wanted to go so I agreed.

After acquiring the wheelchair and wrestling it into the car, we headed into the city. It was just my husband, our niece, her boyfriend and me. Having parked the car in a city garage, I helped my husband into the wheelchair and begun pushing. He was heavy and one of the wheels kept jamming. This was arduous. When we arrived at the Harley Davidson store, the door was too narrow for the wheelchair to pass through. I beckoned them to go in and I would wait on the sidewalk with my husband. It was not cold, but it was a damp, raw day in New York City, the kind that leaves your bones chilled. I was tired, my arms were sore from pushing the wheelchair and I was coming down with a cold. I wanted to go home and climb into bed. I asked my husband if he was doing okay, but he had a faraway look in his eye. He didn't answer me.

After awhile, they returned and the boyfriend said to my husband, "Look what I got for you! A Harley Davidson T-shirt!" I thought *this guy is crazy! What is wrong with you? My husband has less than one week of quality life and you think he wants a Harley Davidson T-shirt.*

My husband took the T-shirt, held it up, looked at the Harley Davidson insignia and said, "I've always wanted a Harley Davidson T-shirt. Thank you."

———※◦※———

That evening, I encouraged everyone else to try a new seafood restaurant nearby for dinner. I preferred to stay home with my husband, as I was worried about his fatigue. Everyone agreed, except William. He insisted on staying with us. I very much wanted him to go as I was not sure what I would cook him for dinner, but Heather said she would bring something home for him. After they left, William and I stood by the hospital bed as my husband dozed. The New York City trip had depleted his mental and physical energy and I worried that we wouldn't have our six more days of quality life.

William spoke and said, "Dad never told us who should receive his prized possessions."

———※◦※———

Let me digress for just a moment. In all the years I had known my husband, he never asked anything of consequence of me. Yes, he would ask for my opinion or to help him with a household task, something along those lines, but he never asked me anything important. Basically because I tried to do what was important without being asked and this seemed to work for us, until I was pregnant with our son. We knew we were having a son and were trying to figure out a name for him. I would suggest several and then he would suggest several, but nothing ever seemed to suit. One night going to bed, when I was almost nine months pregnant, he came over to my side to tuck me in. He whispered in my ear, "I would like to name our son." I looked at him inquisitively. He wanted his son's first name to be after himself with his middle name being my maiden surname. He had never before asked me anything of this magnitude and I agreed. He wanted his son to carry on his family traditions as he had done. He insisted that he was but a steward of a genealogical family tradition. This tradition entailed preserving some very special antiques that had been passed down from generation to generation. I knew that my husband wanted William to have these, because my son was male and carried his father's name. But, I also knew that it was inherently unfair to our two daughters. We were not living in the fifth century before Christ and this was not Greece and even if we were, I would argue for an equal distribution. I honored his request without pause. These were his prized possessions. These were not mine.

I turned toward William and said, "Let's ask him. Let's ask him who he wants to receive his family heirlooms." William nodded.

I gently touched my husband's arm and his eyes opened. I asked, "Your son and I are here and have a question for you."

He turned toward his son and smiled. I asked specifically if his son should inherit the grandfather's clock. My husband nodded in agreement. I asked if his son should inherit the oak roll top desk. He nodded. I asked if his son should inherit his grandmother's Steinway piano. Again, he nodded.

William grew impatient and said, "He doesn't know what he's agreeing to. He's just nodding his head."

I took a slow, deep breath in. "Okay," I said, "Let's see."

I held on to my husband's arm and he looked directly toward me. I asked, "Dad, do you like girls in bikinis?" He nodded affirmatively.

"Dad, do you like guys in speedos?" He shook his head no.

I laughed. I looked at William. He was satisfied. I smiled, too, thinking we only agreed upon a few of the antiques. William left to play guitar upstairs in his room and I took a seat by the hospital bed and gazed out the bay window past the deck to the backyard. My vision blurred as the tears formed. It was quiet in the house. I heard the churn of the furnace cranking up in the basement. Outside, it was becoming dusk and grey. Twilight was upon us. This was the last day of March and I wondered when spring would return with her warmth. I heard the sheets rustle and turned around to see my husband pulling himself up, his arms using the hospital bed's guardrails, trying to sit up. Propping himself up with one arm, he reached out with his other arm and extended his hand. He touched the side of my nose where the tears were silently falling and slid his index finger down my cheek, ever so gently. Unable to keep the position, he collapsed back into the bed and closed his eyes. I sat quietly looking at him. As the evening became night, I didn't move. I didn't turn on a light. I didn't move from that position until I heard the front door open with everyone returning from dinner.

—••—

The next day, I drove my niece and her boyfriend to the airport as they were headed back to California and then I went straight to work. We were feeding my husband steady doses of morphine now as hospice recommended. He rested comfortably. Rebecca, who was home with him during the day, promised she would call if anything changed. The department in which I worked was in such turmoil that I felt obligated to be there to help alleviate the staff's anxiety. When I arrived, I called the oncologist to let him know the morphine dose and he agreed that it was appropriate. He again suggested my husband be admitted to the hospital, but I remained resolutely opposed. I could not think of a worse death than to be alone in a sterile, cold hospital room. He explained that he was going to devise another combination of chemotherapies, which might help, and he would get back to me. I thanked him and turned my attention towards work.

It was Friday morning and I was at work when Rebecca called. "He's going to die soon," she said. While her voice was calm, I knew that she did not want to be alone with her father when he died. I called my boss to tell him that I would have to leave early. I called hospice to meet me when I arrived home. Once home, my husband was somewhat lucid. The hospice representative approached my husband as he lay in the hospital bed floating in and out of consciousness.

She touched his arm and asked, "What are you feeling, now that the time is close at hand?"

In a garbled voice, he tried to articulate that he was waiting for new drugs. I was surprised that he had understood this information that I had explained to him earlier.

She continued, "Are you afraid? There is nothing to worry about. Are you feeling at peace with yourself?"

In a slow and deliberate voice I asked her to come over to the kitchen table. There was paperwork I didn't understand. I was outraged. If my husband wanted to talk about his death, then he, and only he should begin this conversation. I thought *if you are going to die, be allowed to die in the way you want to.* I tried to be diplomatic with her, as I escorted her to the door. Closing the door, I thought *what if he wants to have this conversation? What if he just needed someone to begin with an opening paragraph? Should I have allowed her to start this conversation? I am not sure. Should I initiate this conversation? I don't know what I should do.*

But once the front door was closed, Rebecca signaled me to the dining room. We looked at each other incredulously We had invited a group of people weeks ago for a party, tomorrow night, to celebrate my husband's fifty-second birthday. I had completely forgotten about this. The invite had gone out a month ago when my husband was still cooking and cognizant. I couldn't believe I had done this. Now, he could barely move.

He hadn't eaten anything for two days. It was just a matter of time. I told my daughter we would have the party, but we would call everyone and let them know of the particulars. It would be up to the guests to decide if they wanted to attend.

⋙ ◦ ⋘

The next morning, I woke up early and rose from bed. It had been lovely sleeping in a bed these past few days. Since January when he underwent the craniotomy, I had been sleeping on the black leather couch in the den, leaving the king-sized bed for my husband. Now roles were reversed. I walked downstairs and as I was rounding the banister, I smelled something putrid, so foul. I pulled my sweater over my nose. I walked into the kitchen, thinking maybe William made a late night snack and left the remains somewhere. No. I then opened the sliding glass doors to allow our golden retriever out for his morning ritual and looked around. Maybe, the dog had an accident. I looked to where the dog usually slept, but didn't see anything unusual. I then walked over into the den and my feet stopped dead in their tracks.

There was a white, fluffy discharge foaming out of my husband's mouth, cascading down his neck onto his shirt and chest. I literally gagged. This was the putrid smell and as I stared, the white, fluffy foam just kept flowing out of his mouth. I had no idea what it was. After moments of simply staring at this phenomenon, I realized I had to clean this stuff up before the kids climbed out of bed. I sucked in a deep breath and then the adrenalin hit. I opened all the windows in the den and went over to the kitchen and opened the windows above the sink. The freezing air blasted in. Taking paper towels and a plastic bag, I returned to my husband's side and started to scoop this foam-like substance from his chest and mouth. The stench sickened my stomach. I used almost a full roll of paper towels and in the middle of cleaning I thought *I should have worn gloves to do this. Shut this thought out. This stuff is part of a human being. This is not taboo, even if it does reek.* I did the best job I could and I thought *is the oncologist right? Should I have allowed him to be admitted to a hospital so a nurse could do this? Maybe she would have done a better job. She is a professional. I'm just me.* And then, the mental slam hit. *How dare you second guess yourself? This man is your husband. A nurse wouldn't do the job as well as you. She wouldn't care. She would look at him as another patient, another body. This man is your husband. I will take care of him. I will take good care of him.* I looked at the plastic bag. It reeked. I didn't know where to dump it. The trash cans were in the garage. I thought *if I put the bag in there, it will just stink up the garage. I will take the trash cans out of the garage and drag them to the side yard and dispose of the plastic bag there. The trash collectors should be tipped generously this week.* His stinking undershirt needed to be removed. I ran upstairs to get a washcloth, soap and a clean undershirt. My blood was on fire. It pulsated through every vein in my body as I scampered downstairs silently. It was Saturday and my kids were sleeping late. Bowl with warm, soapy water in hand, I carried them over to the hospital bed. I cranked the bed up so that my husband's body was in an almost sitting up position. I tried to take his undershirt off, but his body was dead weight. I couldn't pull his arm out of the shirtsleeve. I went to the kitchen to find scissors and returned. I cut his undershirt up the middle. This shirt was not going to be saved. Once off, I stared at my husband's chest. This was no longer my husband. This was no longer my husband's chest. This was no longer my husband, the ex-swimmer, the ex-football player. This chest and stomach were fluid. They had no definition. The skin was pale and hung. I thought *stay focused. Clean him up before the kids get up. Get this plastic bag and shirt out of here. Stop looking at his chest.* I took the washcloth and wiped his skin down once more. The foam had stopped flowing. He was absolutely without any consciousness.

I took a step back. I thought *is he dead?* I took his wrist and applied my index finger to his vein. I felt a strong pulse. I cranked up the bed to a higher position so I could easily slip on his clean undershirt. Over the head it went smoothly. I lifted his left arm up and inserted it into the shirtsleeve. His arm was heavy to hold. I did the same with the other. I climbed on top of the bed and pulled his sitting body towards me so that I could pull the shirt down in the back. I had never had an almost dead body lean on me. Goose bumps rose on my arms. But it was done and he hadn't moaned. I hadn't caused him pain. I sighed with relief. I swung my legs off the bed and cranked the bed down and prayed that no more foam would ooze forth. I tucked the covers over him so that he wouldn't feel the chilly air. Out in the garage, I pulled the trash can into the side yard and stuffed the plastic bag full of the paper towels and his undershirt in it and secured the lid tightly. I saw a large rock under the Rose of Sharon hedge. I picked it and placed it on the trash can lid. Neither the dog nor the wind would be able to topple this thing over.

Coming back in the house, it was freezing inside, but there was only a remnant of the stench left. I thought *we should fumigate the house, but how?* I looked at the coffee machine and decided no. The adrenalin was not going to need a jump-start this morning. I went upstairs and as I climbed the stairs, I pulled my sweater off over my head and began to unbutton my shirt. I left my clothes in a pile outside the bathroom door and turned on the shower to the hottest water I could stand and climbed in. I was numb. I didn't feel the hotness of the water. I scrubbed every inch of my body with soap. After sometime, my body began to feel the warmth and I stood there, letting the warm water flow over my body. I thought *how much longer? What other surprises?* I stared at the rubber duck decal Heather had glued on the shower tile for her father and me when she was ten years old.

I slowly turned off the water, but my blood did not stop pulsating. I wrapped the towel around me and walked into our closet. I opened my drawer and dug around for the softest, most comfortable clothes I owned. I found my jeans with the holes in the knees and back pocket and a faded sweatshirt that still had the soft fuzz on the inside. I searched for my warmest socks. And as I was dressing, I breathed in slowly and deeply. My body would not stop trembling. I felt as though my body was about to explode. I walked over to the desk in the bedroom and turned on the computer. I checked my email. I saw one from an old friend whom I hadn't seen for years, but who knew the situation. I clicked on her email and read.

> How awful. I wish that I could reach across this continent and just give you a huge hug… let some of the pressure and sadness escape from you into me, and give your mind and soul a rest from what sounds like a tremendously hard and emotional time.
>
> I will be praying for your husband. I hope that he is comfortable and his sense of humor is what he carries with him in these last few days. I would love to come meet you in Newport Beach, if you would like some friendly company. Catalina island is one of the most beautiful places in the world, and with his love of the ocean, it seems like a beautiful place for his soul to soar once his body is too tired to hold on to it. In many ways, his body is fading, but he has made his impression on you, and taught you, and loved you. Like the lessons we learn in life, and like our memories, those things don't have limits. They don't fade. They are part of who we are; all and that he gave you will always be a part of who you are. He will be gone and you will miss him terribly. But, I think you will find that you feel his presence in the many years to come, as you did when he was with you over the past years. You will talk to him and he will be there. Anyone who has touched your heart while they were alive will continue to be with you always.
>
> I wish him peace. And, no matter how many years go by, I love and respect you and will always be there for you.
>
> You never need to ask. Just call. Carry my number always with you. I'll be there.
>
> Your Friend

I read it again through tears and thought *this is the silver lining. This is love. Years have gone by, but she speaks to my heart, like I had seen her yesterday, cutting through time and distance. With such warmth, she reassures me, in her understated way, life will continue. It will be okay. I will be okay. Even if he is dead, I can still talk with him. I will still be able to feel him. These things don't have limits. I won't lose him.* I breathed deeply and slowly. I felt my muscles relax. I wrapped my arms around my torso and sat in my wooden chair by the desk with this email staring at me. I heard the kid's bathroom door shut and glanced at my watch. I had been sitting in front of the computer for more than an hour. Quickly, I logged off the computer and ran downstairs to make sure no more foam was flowing forth. The kids were up.

Downstairs, I quickly closed all the windows in the kitchen and the den and sprayed the air with Lysol to make sure the air was clean. I thought *what if the white fluffy foam has some sort of bacteria in it? What if it's contagious? What if the air is infected? Spray more Lysol. You can't let your kids get infected. Stop it. Death is not contagious. Get a grip.*

⟫•◦•⟪

April 5th, 2003. This was the day of his party. He was now officially fifty-two years old. My mother drove in and brought a happy birthday banner and hung it on the standing bookshelves behind the hospital bed. The kids were all up and we had designated tasks for each of us in order to prepare for the party.

We had no idea who would really come, if anybody. I thought *someone dying in your home can have a strange effect on people, especially if the party is for the person dying.*

I couldn't believe that we were pulling this off, but we were. The party began and the doorbell didn't stop ringing. More than forty people attended. I could only think of two couples who had stayed away. I couldn't remember when there had been so much warmth, so much love in this house. People were laughing and having a wonderful time. The food was warm and delicious. I mingled with guests and enjoyed the variety of the company.

⟫•◦•⟪

I set my alarm clock for five the following morning. I wanted to make sure that no more foam was rising from his throat. I rose from bed and walked down the stairs, slowly, preparing myself. There was no foam, thank god. I made coffee and sat at the kitchen table with my coffee mug, but I didn't drink it. I stared at my husband. I stared at his body. I thought *how much longer is this going to take? How long? He's not in pain. Does he know, now, that he's dying?*

Much later, I heard rumblings from the second floor. The kids were up. I went upstairs and told them to get dressed. We were all going to the grocery store. I was not sure why we are all going to the grocery store. We just were. We were all going to get out of this house together and go to the grocery store. They looked at me oddly and went to dress. They were not sure why we were all going to the grocery store, either, but they all knew I was adamant that we were going to the grocery store. It was Sunday and the grocery store was very busy. All the mammas who didn't go to church were here buying their weekly supply of groceries. This was the church for mammas who didn't go to church. I figured that was why we were here, too. This was our church today. We were in the aisle with the canned vegetables. My three children were in front of my shopping cart: Rebecca, age nineteen, Heather, fifteen, and William, thirteen. I stopped cold and thought *is this what our family will look like from now on? Is this how it's going to feel from now on? It will just be the four of us? I can't imagine this. I can't imagine this at all.*

When we got home, there had been no movement from the den. We put the groceries away together. Somehow, we wanted to be together doing something, anything. I told them we were going out for an early dinner. We were not going to cook tonight. Heather exclaimed that I was nuts. We just bought two hundred dollars worth of groceries.

I told her, "Never mind. We are going out for dinner."

Being early on a Sunday evening, I took them to a local restaurant in town. I didn't think in advance about seeing anyone we knew. God knew we all didn't want to see anyone we knew, not now. I knew I would not be able to open my mouth if we did. Being a Sunday early evening, there were only a few elderly couples eating as we entered the restaurant. I glanced at them and thought *this will not be me in thirty years. Maybe, I will be dead in thirty years. Who knows? Who knew we would be facing this now?* We sat in a booth in a quiet section of the restaurant. Rebecca sat beside me and my two other children sat opposite us. I ordered a salad, but I couldn't eat it.

I looked at William and Heather facing me and I looked over to Rebecca. I thought *is this how it's going to be? Is this how our family will look from now on? What about my husband? He needs to be here. He needs to tell the kids to eat new things. He needs to describe the various ingredients and how they combine together to create the whole. He needs to be here asking them intriguing questions about music, astronomy, Einstein, philosophy, about their lives. I can't do this solo. I'm not as learned as he is. I don't have his dry wit. He always fills in my gaps. He always sees what the rest of us miss. He needs to be here. I can't imagine our family looking like this.* After a glass of wine, I felt the tears form. I told them to stop. I pierced my fingernails into my leg to feel something different. I thought *don't form. Wait. You will have your chance, not now. Not now. I am looking at three very special people whose lives are about to tailspin. Do not cry? Don't!* Instead, I looked at my children with a depth of love I had never known before.

Back home, Heather's boyfriend came over and they went to her room. My husband would have frowned on this behavior, but I couldn't. I simply did not have the strength. William was trying to study for school in his room. I looked into the den and saw there had not been any movement. His chest moved slowly up and down. I climbed upstairs and went into our bedroom to prepare my dress clothes for Monday morning. Rebecca sat with her father for a while.

It was about ten in the evening. I was preparing for bed when Rebecca came in and said, "Mamma, it's time."

I knew what she meant. He had died. I didn't hear anything

else she said because my heart was pumping the blood too loudly. My ears heard only the throbbing blood. I walked downstairs with her and held his limp wrist in my hand. I tried to find a pulse. There was none. I tried the other wrist. None. I repeated this four times. No pulse. I still couldn't hear. I looked at his face and thought *this can't be the last time I see his face. This face is part of my life. This face is part of who I am.* I didn't feel anything except the blood racing through my body.

I turned around to see my daughter standing behind me. She had a glazed look on her face, like the deer caught in your headlights. I hugged her with every ounce of strength I had. We didn't cry. We just stood there holding each other. I thought *this must be the definition of shock.*

She climbed upstairs to find her brother and sister. I went to the phone to call hospice so that a nurse would come and declare him dead for the record. I then called the funeral director to retrieve the body. I hung up the phone in the kitchen and looked over to the den.

My three children had circled around their father, lying in the hospital bed, our treasured books lining the bookcases behind him. Each one of my children was touching a part of him: our ritual of death. I could only imagine the pain in each of their hearts. I could not think of what was in mine. The amount of sadness from their bodies flowed into mine. I didn't know what to do for them. The ache in my body started in my stomach and permeated to my extremities until all I felt was this ache. I walked slowly over to them and quietly asked them to say their last goodbye. I asked them to go upstairs when the hospice nurse and the funeral home workers arrived. I still had vivid memories of the two funeral home workers struggling to remove my father in a black body bag. I did not want my children to have this as their last memory of their father. This memory would not leave me alone some nights.

They went to their rooms. My body went into overdrive. I didn't know how it was functioning. I didn't recognize my voice. I didn't know who was talking inside of me. The hospice nurse asked me where the rest of the morphine was. She must discard it. I opened the refrigerator and took out the box. She flushed all the liquid down the toilet. I thought *did she think I might use the morphine on myself?* She completed the paperwork. Time of death ten minutes after ten in the evening on April 6th, 2003. She offered the standard condolences and left.

I waited for the funeral home workers. I was dreading, but preparing myself for the last view of my husband. I didn't know how my body would behave. The doorbell rang. They were two short Mexicans who barely spoke English. They nodded at me and I led them to the den. They carried a stretcher covered in a dark beautiful flowered velvet material. I didn't see any body bag. My husband would be carried out in comfort. They gingerly removed him from the hospital bed and placed him on this stretcher. They secured his body with two straps and then put a blanket over his body, but not his head. The door to the garage was in the den and they signaled that they would like to take him out through the garage. I nodded.

As they reached the door, I put my hand on the stretcher. I looked at his face one more time. I thought *take a photograph with your mind of his face and freeze it until you die. I want to see his eyes, but they are closed. I want a picture of him with his eyes open. I want to wake him up and tell him to open his eyes. I want to see his hazel eyes full of life. I took the picture with my mind of his face with his eyes closed.* I put two fingers to my lips and kissed them and then gently pressed the same two fingers on his mouth. They lifted the stretcher down the stairs into the garage and I remotely opened the outside garage door for them. I watched these two men roll the stretcher out into the black night air onto the driveway and slide him into the hearse, which they had thoughtfully backed into the driveway. I stood there, arms wrapped around my torso, while the garage door rattled shut. I closed the door to the garage slowly and turned around and stared at the empty hospital bed.

My feet walked my body over to the phone on the kitchen wall and I called my boss's work number. I heard his voice mail and I left the message that my husband had died at ten minutes after ten on Sunday, April 6th and that I would be coming to work a little late tomorrow. I had to meet with the funeral director in the morning. I hung up the receiver. I couldn't believe that I was going to work, but I was worried about money and keeping our house. The house smelled of death. The ancient Greeks would have sprayed their house with seawater, smeared it with earth and then swept it out. A sacrifice would have been made on their hearth and then their house would have been purified. I didn't know how to remove this stench. I didn't know how to purify our home. I slowly climbed the stairs with my right arm pulling my body up each stair. My children were sitting on my daughter's bed and I sat down with them. We all knew this was coming. We had to have known. But now that it had happened, we just looked into each other's eyes in disbelief. We couldn't talk. We sat there in silence on the bed.

No one slept well that night. We were all on automatic pilot. The next morning, Rebecca and I met the funeral director. He insisted on all the pertinent details. He had to obtain the oncologist's signature stating the cause of death on the death certificate.

He questioned, "How many certified copies of the death certificate will you need? How many bank and brokerage accounts did your husband have? Will his employer need one? His lawyer will need one for the file. Did he have life insurance? You must immediately file the death certificate with Social Security. You know that, right? Let me know as soon as possible how many certified copies you will need."

I didn't have any answers. I didn't know. All I knew is that I needed his body cremated. I needed to take him to California, where he was born, to be buried. That's all I knew. I couldn't think beyond this. I didn't know.

After the meeting, I left for work. I needed to snap out of my fog. I needed to become organized. I had to remove the death smell from the house. I had to deal with the hospital bed and all the hospital supplies. I had to make the plane reservations. I had to call his sister. I had to call my mother. I stayed at work and made the phone calls and scheduled the funeral. We would leave Thursday for California and the service would be Saturday. His sister would take care of the hotel and notify my husband's extended family on the West Coast. I would find a minister through hospice.

When I returned home, hospice had already removed the hospital bed. I wasn't sure if my kids went to school that day. I wasn't sure if I called their schools to inform them that their father had died last night. I saw all the food on the kitchen table and on the kitchen counters. The living room was flooded with flower arrangements, spilling into the dining room. Word had spread like wildfire. I still smelled death through the fragrances of the flowers. I was in the kitchen when the doorbell rang. It was a woman I had known for several years. Her son and William swam together on various swim teams over the last six years. She walked right in, eyes sad and gave me the hugest embrace. I felt her strong hands on my back and smelled her perfume. She lived in the wealthy section of town. She stood in front of me, cutting to the chase. She was the first person to greet us. She was not afraid of death. She knew we didn't need flowers, food or sympathy cards. We needed the touch. We needed to know that we were still alive. We needed human comfort and here she was. We sat down by the kitchen table and she held my hand. I told her I was only having a family service in California.

In a firm tone, looking directly into my eyes, she said, "You can't do that. People in this town need to be able to grieve and say goodbye to him. He coached too many children on the soccer, softball and swim teams for all those years. The children need to come and say goodbye to their coach. Their parents and his friends need say goodbye. You need to have a service in town for them."

She told me to call the funeral director and to schedule it

for the weekend after we returned from California. The notice would be included in his obituary in the newspapers, she said. People will read it there. I said I would. She told me she and her family wouldn't be there. They were going to their winter house somewhere in Florida. I thanked her for coming. She hugged me goodbye and walked out into the evening.

Rebecca came into the kitchen and said that a local newspaper reporter was on the phone. The reporter wanted to write an article on the life of my husband. She wanted to discuss this with me. I didn't remember the phone ringing. I took the receiver in my hand. The reporter asked me what made him special. I thought *what makes anyone special? He was a human being. The tears. No, they can't start.* I replied that he had grown up in a beach town in Southern California. He hadn't attended first grade. His parents and he had sailed from Mystic, Connecticut down to the Panama Canal, through the canal and up the coast, back to Southern California. It had taken them a year. She inquired, "How would you describe him?"

My mind flashed back to the man I had fallen in love with and I replied, "He was really just a beach bum."

And then I thought *shit – you shouldn't say this. But that's who I fell in love with.* This dialogue continued in my head while she continued to ask questions and someone else was answering them. I thought *of my husband teaching the kids when they could barely walk how to body surf, how to skip rocks, how to tie knots. I couldn't think of who he became. I didn't really know that person. I knew the man I fell in love with, the funky, long-haired bluegrass musician who designed solar panels in Southern California. The man who introduced me to the Sierra Nevada Mountains, with the smell of pine, Douglas fir and the red dirt and the old abandoned gold mine. The man who supported my interest in the ancient Greeks and took me to the motherland for the first time. Eight weeks we camped throughout her land.* I didn't remember hanging up the phone and I didn't remember answering the reporter's questions. I remembered remembering the wonderful man I fell in love with. I hadn't thought of him for years.

————◆◆◆————

The following Tuesday and Wednesday were just hazy blurs. I went to work, but I didn't work. On Wednesday, I prepared to pack for our trip the next day. Another woman whose kid swam on the swim team rang the doorbell. She brought a large plant as a condolence gift. It was one of those plants you see at Easter time with a distinctive smell. She placed it on the kitchen table as my kids and I sat down. All of a sudden, she slammed her hand down on the table and said, "This is awful. This will be very hard for you."

It was like an explosion and I snapped out of my outer body feeling. I felt I was living again. I agreed with her. She went on to say that she had read it takes the average widow many, many years after her spouse's death to regain her former level of life's satisfactions. I looked at her with raised eyebrows. I thought *is that what they call someone like me? Widow? Where did that word come from? It should be obliterated from the English language. It's just wrong. And what…. And what about life's satisfactions? What are they? I've been living with the process of death for the past three years. Life's satisfactions? What are life's satisfactions?* She left to get food from her car and returned with more food than we could possibly eat in a week. She and her husband ran a restaurant in town. I went to bed that night and thought *of what this woman had said. How many years are many, many years? Is it two years? Is it four years? Is it six years? I can only think of next week. I can't think in terms of years. And life's satisfactions? Exactly what is a life satisfaction? Our trip to California is important. This is what is important. This is a life satisfaction.*

————◆◆◆————

On the plane to California, I suggested to my children that they might wish to say something at their father's graveside funeral. There would be no church service. My husband had held the bigger picture of all religious views. His service would be outside on a sloping green hill next to his mother and father's grave surrounded by shade trees. William and Rebecca said they would like to say something, but Heather in her resolute way declined. I understood.

The next day, I met with the hospice minister while my children went with their cousins, aunts and uncles to Newport Beach. I stayed behind and waited. It was a damp, raw spring day in Southern California filled with the smell of the Eucalyptus trees. I went out on the hotel's balcony and rehearsed my eulogy and the tears did not stop sliding down my face. I could talk through my tears. My voice didn't waver, but the tears would not stop flowing.

I thought *no. You are going to stand in front of the congregation without crying. You are going to honor his life with your eulogy and you are not going to cry. Think of something serious. Almost losing Rebecca. That's serious. Think of this. Think of only this. Don't cry.*

The tears abated and I read the eulogy without crying. Coherency then flashed through my brain. I needed to call my boss back in New York to ascertain that Human Resources approved me for the full-time position. Without their approval, I would have to find another job as soon as we returned. I called him and felt him smiling on the phone. He couldn't believe that I was calling him at a time like this. But I needed to know. This would make a huge difference to three kids lives, not to mention, mine. He replied yes and I felt my shoulders slump into relaxation. *We would have money. Thank god.* I hadn't yet figured out how much money my husband had lost in his attempt to beat the stock market, but somehow I knew the result would be dismal.

When my kids returned from the beach, William walked in with dripping shorts. I looked at him inquiringly. He had been swimming. He had to swim in the Pacific Ocean on Newport Beach, the same beach where his father had grown up. His skin was marbled and almost blue. I walked over to him and encircled his small boy frame with my arms and tousled his hair.

"Get in a warm shower," I said.

All of us stayed in the same room, while my mother stayed in her own room down the hall. During our Greek trips, my children always had their own room and the adults had their separate room, but today, we wanted to be together. I thought *does this mean that they are adults, sharing a room with me?*

It was an afternoon graveside service on a Saturday. The sun's rays were warm coming over the hill. The green grass was moist from the inground sprinklers spraying the earth the previous night. White chairs were placed in rows in front of the small empty brown hole in the ground. A small square awning held up by four posts shielded the audience from the afternoon sun. The time was three-fifteen. People sat and with no chair vacant, others stood on the sides and in the back. There was no podium. There was no microphone. There was no altar.

The minister stood in front of the chairs, by the brown hole in the ground, next to which was the container of my husband's ashes. He began talking and silence fell. He said words and more words. They didn't make sense to me. I didn't understand the religious significance. After a while he looked at me. I knew that was my cue to stand and walk to the front near the brown hole and give my eulogy. From the back, I stood up and with each slow step, my high heels sank into the moist earth. It was hard to pull the long heel out of the ground and take the next step. Then it hit me.

I thought *I should not be going first. The Greek libation bearers should be going before me. They should pour the libation into the brown hole for the earth to drink, the libation destined for the dead and for the gods who dwell in the earth. Lucian wrote, "The souls are nourished by libations." They make us realize the power of the dead. What is spilled into the earth cannot be brought back. It is irretrievable. It is the purest and highest form of renunciation.* Each time I dug my heel out of the earth and stepped toward the front, I visualized my Greek libation bearers pouring the wine into the brown hole in front of me. I thought *this ritual dictates that a prayer must accompany their libation. My prayer to my husband. "Fly in peace. Find love."*

My voice strong and calm, I began.

> *I've probably said this to many of you over the last few months, but I'll say it again for the record. Over the course of the last two and a half years, I've lived my life by finding the silver lining in every situation. And such was the case with my husband's illness. I came to know a man whom I had thought I had known and loved for the past twenty-three years in a new and absolutely wonderful way. Since January as my husband's disease began to progress in a rapid and serious way, his sense of humor, his wit, his ability to comfort us increased in direct proportion to his disease. He never once lost his optimism for life, his interest in our daily activities, his determined will to serve us the most exotic and healthy dinners, his faith in our abilities. He was our rock to whom we'd return to daily.*
>
> *And in keeping with these qualities, he wanted a wonderful birthday celebration to commemorate his fifty-second birthday on April 5th from four to six pm at our home. As the day approached and he declined, retreating to a hospital bed in our den, we called the guests to let them know of the particulars. We would still have the party, but it was up to them – a personal choice – to attend or not. Approximately forty people filled our house; those with intestinal fortitude and compassion addressed themselves to my husband. As I scanned our living room and dining room and felt the energy, I realized I had never been surrounded by such quality of character. Each person there from all walks of life had been a significant player in his life and what a high level of intellect, wit, laughter and love filled our home. To say it was sustaining is an understatement. It was his birthday gift to us. I was grateful for the party and to him. He knew it was the right thing to do. And afterwards, and*

only afterwards, it was time.

And again the silver lining – even though I had been with him all those years, I never realized what a significant and important role he played in so many different people's lives. I guess it doesn't surprise me because he was the most tolerant, patient and intelligent man I have ever known. He had friends who were orthodox Jews who could not travel until after sunset to the party. He had Hindu friends who brought balloons. Doctors, dads, softball coaches, swim team coaches. He was a good and true friend to all of them.

Going through airport security to bring his cremains to California where he will rest with his father, mother and brother, overlooking the island of Catalina, the security officer stopped my bag for inspection. He looked inside at the plastic container containing the cremains and said, "You have crystals in there." I said, "I know. It is my husband."

I couldn't see the audience. I couldn't see their reaction. I could only see Rebecca. She was rising and walking to the front. I walked two steps and then bent over. I slipped off my shoes and walked barefoot over to the side of the gathering. I watched Rebecca take her place at the front and I admired how beautiful she was. I glanced over to Heather who was sitting next to her grandmother and the sadness in her face was almost unbearable to me.

She began.

Since my father's death, I've learned that he had a lot of different relationships with a lot of people. And I've also realized that those relationships changed. As I look back at our relationship, I can see that no matter how it changed, or we changed, there was something there that never left. If I were away at school, or he was busy with work, that something never changed. It didn't have a schedule.

My dad gave me the gift of wanting to know why. He taught me to analyze things, not to settle and memorize a theorem, but to do the proof and find out why and how it worked. I have early memories of coming home from elementary school with math problems. We would sit after dinner and scrawl equations on paper napkins. He taught me how to ask the right questions. He showed me what it is to desire knowledge.

In seventh grade, I sat next to him on a ferry in the Aegean Sea. "Dad," I asked, "Why is the sky blue?" Instead of typical responses, "It just is." or "It's reflected off the water.", I was told that blue is the shortest color wave in the spectrum. The reds, oranges, and greens are longer and absorbed in the atmosphere. But blue is the shortest. It travels through the atmosphere faster. And that's why the water is blue.

My dad taught me to analyze things. When he died, he left me with a lot of unanswered questions. How am I supposed to analyze his death? It wasn't until I stood on Newport Beach this morning that I understood. I saw someone run into the water. And I thought, that's it. Running into water; the transition from running to swimming, from land to ocean. He won't stop moving and neither will I.

And then, this thin, thirteen-year-old blonde-haired boy rose. I thought of him dripping wet coming into the hotel room and I wished I had seen him swimming in the Pacific yesterday. I remember the many times my husband and I swam off of the same beach. He gracefully diving through the oncoming waves, only to surface smiling, turning around after the wave passed. I watched William walk up and felt my heart about to break.

Standing with one foot on the pile of dirt beside the hole and inches away from his father's ashes, his voice crackled.

> *If my dad hadn't passed Sunday, I would currently be competing at the YWCA Nationals Swim Meet in Charlotte, North Carolina. Only the elite swimmers on the East Coast compete there. I was seeded first in the 200 IM and ranked in the top 8 of my other events. I owe much of my swimming success to my dad.*
>
> *I remember when I was in the eight and under program, he was my coach. He would videotape me at meets and play it back so I could improve. While he cared about my times, he cared more for the correct way to swim the stroke. He never cared what place I came in.*
>
> *He would take us to free swims on Sunday afternoons and would work with all of us for a while and then we'd play in the water. He could hurl me like a basketball high out of the water and I would cannonball back in. Ever since, he followed my swimming – even two weeks ago at the NJ Junior Olympics, he wanted to know how I swam.*
>
> *Another interest we both shared was music. Not just listening to it, but playing it. I started taking bass guitar lessons last April from him. He would always tell me some tricks of the trade. When he would come home from work, he would come up to my room and tune my bass. Then at Christmas, I got a guitar: dad's specialty. He taught me a lot in a very short time.*
>
> *But not only instrumentally, we liked the same artists. One night we must have talked for at least two hours about Jimi Hendrix and what music would be like if he were still around. We would talk about dad's gig days with his bluegrass band;*

> *about his glaring mandolin solos and about how met my mom.*
>
> *I will truly miss you, dad, and not just for replacing my guitar strings, but about who you were.*

As he finished speaking, William crumpled his notes and stuffed them in his pants pocket and as he did, he looked down to his feet at the brown hole in the ground. I held my breath. I looked at his young face and thought *how is it possible to comfort this anguish. It is so deep.* The minister began to speak and William moved slowly back to his seat next to his sister. More words and the service ended. People milled around in groups, talking with one another. I looked up the hill to a large shade tree and noticed two Mexican workers with their wheelbarrow and shovels.

They were waiting for us to leave so that they could fill the hole with their dirt. I started to climb the hill to tell them to wait. As I began, the minister touched my elbow and advised me that the administrator needed to see me in the office. More paperwork needed to be discussed. The bill was ready. I looked at him in disbelief. I asked if it were possible to have a few moments. No, the office would be closing at four-thirty. It was Saturday. Leaving the people milling, I walked down the hill to the large building at the entrance to the cemetery.

As I entered, organ music sifted through various small speakers in the ceiling. Fake flowers adorned the marble table in the entrance hall. My heels sank into a thick burgundy carpet. A short chubby woman with thick black glasses greeted me and introduced herself as the administrator. She led me into a large conference room, wallpapered with dark purple flowers. There was a wooden rectangular conference table with eight cushioned chairs on each side of the table. The chairs had wheels on them so you could roll them on the thick carpet. She asked me to have a seat. She needed to retrieve my husband's paperwork. And, oh, she needed to know what I wanted engraved on his grave marker. I needed to choose that as well. I sat down dazed. *He still had paperwork. Maybe he was not dead.* But then, the words '*grave markers*' reverberated in my brain.

I thought *I haven't thought about this. His grave marker, so years from now, people passing by will know the name of the person who is to be remembered here. But his soul is what's important and it won't be here and then swoosh,* my mind is flooded by our conversation on the beach near Itea twenty years earlier. We were sitting in the sand, drinking cheap wine overlooking the bay of Corinth. Our pup tent pitched a few feet behind us. We lay back in the sand and gazed up to the night sky. He began to describe and name the various constellations. My eyes followed his raised index finger as he traced them in the air for me. He turned on his side to face me, propping his head up with one arm. His other hand caressed my stomach. He said he thought Plato was right about souls in the Phaedrus and I asked what he meant. He continued, *"Just as every man has his own face, ideas have their own specific shape. These ideas are outside space and time. It is the soul of man that is capable of the knowledge of being, of ideas. It carries in it a knowledge that is not of this life: knowledge is recollection or anamnesis. In this way, the knowing soul rises above existence as stretched between birth and death. Death affects only the body. The soul is immortal. The gods call on it to ascend. This ascent is a passionate undertaking which seizes the whole man, an act of love, Eros rising up to madness, mania. It is the beautiful that points the way. It touches the soul and excites it to a loving approach. From physical beauty cognition leads to the beauty of the soul, from there to the beauty of knowledge, the pure being, imperishable and divine, the idea of the beautiful."* He lay back down on the sand and snuggled next to me. Looking up to the stars, he said, *"At least that's what I remember."* I smiled and tried to connect the dots in what he had just described and envisioned beyond the night sky, way beyond heaven, a peaceful place filled with these ideas and souls. It seemed about right to me, too.

"Have you decided?" the chubby woman asked as she reappeared with three green envelopes.

I looked at her. "With the grave marker?" she asked.

I nodded. "I want a rectangular stone with his full name on the first line, his date of birth and date of death on the second line. And on the third line in script, I want the words 'Lover of Knowledge'."

I rose from the table and told her to send me the bill. I was leaving. I needed to be at the reception. I needed to honor my husband with his family. She started to say something, but I didn't listen. I walked out. I wanted to find my children. I wanted to go to the reception. I wanted my husband to be alive.

The reception was held in a kind of courtyard in the hotel where all the relatives and we were staying. Helen ordered the dinner and organized it. Scott's grown kids gathered by themselves at a remote table. Someone whispered to me that they were going to take their dad's ashes out to the Pacific Ocean on a boat and let the Pacific swallow them. They weren't going to invite Helen, yet she was here with us. I didn't understand. Here was a woman who had lost both her brothers in less than two months time and they were excluding her from saying goodbye? I thought *maybe this is a born-again-Christian thing. Maybe only Scott's immediate family should participate. Maybe this is their ritual. This is beyond me. I don't understand.*

The flight home and our return was a haze. When we arrived Sunday evening, I walked upstairs and into our closet to determine what I was going to wear to work the next day. I stopped, frozen in my tracks. I looked to his side of the closet where his suits were hanging and then to his dress shirts and I thought *someone needs to deal with his clothes. Someone needs to go through all his clothes and figure out what to do with them. He isn't here. Who is going to do this? Oh, no. Not now. Sometime.*

I looked over to his dresser in the closet and opened his top drawer. He had left his worn brown leather wallet in the corner. He had never bought a new wallet in the twenty-three years I had known him. I didn't know why, but he never did. His folding wallet was barely held together by the stitching in its seams.

I lay in bed that night with my eyes wide open staring at the ceiling. I then propped the pillows behind my head and scooted up and switched on the nightstand lamp. I looked from one side of the room to another, from the portrait pictures my father had taken of each of his grandchildren, nicely framed, to a picture of my husband and me on our wedding day. I didn't sleep. I turned off the alarm clock at four-thirty the next morning. It was time to shower and take the dog for his four-mile walk before driving into the city to work.

———————

The following day, Monday, I arrived by seven-thirty in the morning and walked into my office. There was a note on my desk from my boss, written in his distinctive script. He needed to see me immediately. I took the elevator to the fourth floor where his office was located. I knew he would be in early. He saw his hospital patients at six in the morning. When I walked into the foyer, he was sitting behind his huge desk in his office. He beckoned me to sit down.

He asked me how I was. I replied, "Fine. What's the situation?"

He said, "We have a problem."

I thought *problem? You think we have a problem? I just buried my husband. He was fifty-two years old. That was a problem. Anything else is not a problem.*

He informed me that the dean wanted to reduce my salary by ten thousand dollars. My mouth dropped open. My throat scraped out the words, "He shook my hand. We had an agreement."

I thought *back to last month when I was in the dean's conference room watching the red-tailed hawk. He walked over to the side of the conference table where I was standing. He extended his arm. We shook hands. I reiterated the salary figure. He shook my hand again. My insides are screaming. Screw you. Great timing. You hit below the belt. I don't know how you sleep at night. You shake someone's hand in agreement, then renege. This is how a dean at a leading medical center professionally behaves? I had two other job offers, but no, took this because of your meaningless handshake.*

I asked my boss on what grounds. He said that the dean thought it was too much. My boss was retiring in a month. There was little he could do. I asked him if there were anything else. There wasn't. I walked out of his office, waited for the elevator. Riding down in the elevator, I thought *of my mother when I was small, warning me to be wary of short men. She said that they were usually mean and not to be trusted. They had inferiority complexes due to their lack of height. I scoffed at her remark. While she was an extremely intelligent person, sometimes she saw things differently than the rest of us. Maybe I should pay more attention to her from now on. I'm five feet, four inches and I look down to meet this man's eyes when we're standing.*

One day during the week, I was sitting at the desk in my office when my phone rang. It was Rebecca. She and her sister and brother were sitting around the dining room table. They had all the photograph albums on the table and were leafing through each one, page by page. They were creating a memorial booklet for their father to be distributed at his funeral in town this coming Saturday. They found a picture of him at the helm of our chartered sailboat with his son standing between him and the wheel. They were both holding the wheel, looking at the compass. It was taken on the last vacation we took as a family: the one when I left for the day to take my dad to the neurologist to listen to his death sentence. They wanted to use that picture on the front cover. I knew the picture. Rebecca had taken it. I remembered Homer's metaphor and asked her to use it as the caption.

> As in the generation of leaves, so is that of humanity.
> The wind scatters the leaves on the ground, but the
> live timber burgeons with leaves again in the season
> of spring returning.

I hung up the phone and thought *I should be there, not here. This is not right. I want to help create his memorial book. He was my husband. I want to be with my kids. This is not right.*

On Saturday, in the morning, after walking the dog, I climbed the stairs to our bedroom and walked into the closet. I had started not to look at his side of the closet. If I didn't see it, I won't think I will have to deal with it. I selected my black dress and took it into the bathroom and started the shower. Standing in the shower, I heard the knock on the door. It was Heather.

Gramma was here. Gramma and I were going to the funeral home ahead of everyone else to meet with this new minister. I hadn't known before how easy it was to rent a minister. I had believed that you had to have a relationship with one, established by going to church every Sunday and listening to his sermons. That was how I grew up. And every Sunday, as a kid, I had listened to the minister and thought he was talking directly to me, thinking that he knew the nasty comment I had said on the playground. I had believed that the minister standing in front of the congregation every Sunday had been talking directly to me. Then, after the service, he would stand outside and greet every person leaving the church. I had hated this. I had always thought when he looked directly into my eyes, he had been saying, "Did you understand? You won't do that again, will you?"

But today, I rented a minister. As I was putting on my makeup, William peered into the bathroom door. I looked at him and knew something serious was on his mind.

He said, "Mom, a lot of my friends are going to be there today." I nodded. "I don't want to read my eulogy."

This was not the time to ask why. This was the time to accept this. I gave him a hug and asked if he wanted me to read it.

"Yes, will you?" he asked. I told him it wasn't a problem. I saw his shoulders relax and urged him to get ready. I knew that he knew what to wear. We were all wearing the same outfits we did last Saturday.

My mother and I were sitting on a couch in the funeral home that we literally sank into, making us uncomfortable. I preferred to be sitting with a straight back talking to our rented minister.

He asked how I wanted the service to be conducted. I thought *shit, I don't know. I got through the one with his ashes. I'm having this service because I was told to. I don't know. Isn't this where you're supposed to come in?* I said that I wanted it simple, that I would give the same eulogy as I had a week ago, that I would read William's and that Rebecca would recite hers. He told me he would give a few opening and closing remarks and I thanked him.

He walked us into the room where the service was to be held. It was a very large room with folding chairs in fifteen rows from the back to the front area where we were to speak. My mother said there were chairs for one hundred and five people. My mother always counted things. Math made the world safe for her. A pedestal holding a beautiful vase with overflowing flowers adorned the front of the room. It was from my friend who insisted that we have the funeral. It anchored the room. Three in the afternoon, people began to arrive. I stood by the side of the room and watched. I had no idea who was going to come or who was not going to come or how many people.

I watched as the people kept entering the room after signing the guest book. I saw my cousin from Virginia enter. I had no idea that she would be here. I didn't remember talking to her. I had no idea she knew this was taking place. Softball coaches, swimming coaches, they all came. Kids started to enter and then William's buddies. They must have taken up two rows. My brother came. Heather sat with her grandmother once again as the minister began the service. I looked to the audience. People were standing in the next room, as there wasn't enough space in this room. Many people from my husband's office came. I didn't even know who they were.

I went into my automatic pilot mode and kept focused on the flower arrangement. After the service, I continued to stand by the flower arrangement and then it happened. Everyone began forming a line facing me so that I could personally greet them. I thought *oh, no. I'm tired. My feet hurt. I just want to go home and climb into bed and pull the covers over my head. I have to greet these people and listen to how sorry they are, and what a great*

*guy my husband was, even if they didn't want to work with him
because he was dying.*

I stood there, frozen and then I extended my right arm and
began. I looked around for my mother. I had stood with her at my
father's funeral service. I didn't see her anywhere. I looked around
for Rebecca, but no sight of her either. From the corner of my eye,
I saw William. His buddies surrounded him. I was impressed
with how many there were and how they were all genuine, good
buddies. I couldn't ask him. Thanking each guest for coming and
hugging and shaking hands, some people with tears sliding down
their cheeks, my insides began to feel hollow. I thought *what is
this? What is this emptiness? My heart put the word in my brain.
Loneliness. I have always been able to be alone and not lonely. But
now standing among all these people, this is lonely.*

The reception following at our home was filled with people.
It reminded me of his birthday party, just two weeks before,
except today was a warm spring late afternoon. The forsythia by
the deck was bursting into a sea of yellow. People congregated
on the deck, in the kitchen, dining room and living room. I
was surprised at the sheer number of people. I didn't remember
ordering the caterer or what was served. During the reception,
I was standing in the hallway by the front door. I took off my
high heels and put them on the stairs. My feet ached. One of my
husband's colleagues approached me. He and my husband had
known each other for the last fifteen years. Even though he no
longer worked with my husband, they had remained in constant
contact. He had lost his wife about one year ago to breast cancer.

Now, this tall man was in front of me. He thanked me for the
reception. He was not surprised at how many people attended
my husband's service. My husband had been a good man, he
told me, but he had to leave. He had a date at seven for dinner.
I looked at him inquisitively. He went on to say that he had
started dating several woman two months after his wife died
and that I should do the same thing. Jolted, I thought *about the
concept of dating. Is this one of life's satisfactions? Is that what
the woman meant? I can't think about dating. I can't think about*

the rest of my life. He smiled and walked out the front door. I emitted a large sigh of relief. People started to find me to say goodbye and after about five people left, I scampered upstairs while no one was looking. I just couldn't shake another person's hand. I couldn't listen to another person speak of my husband. I couldn't listen to any more stories. I walked into my bedroom and went into the closet and shut the door. William found me hours later, asleep on the floor in the closet. I had taken off my dress, hung it where it belonged, put on my jeans, sweatshirt and comfy socks. I had taken a few of his softest sweaters from his drawer, made a pillow and gone to sleep.

———◆◆◆———

When I arrived home from work the following Monday, I walked into the house. William was sitting at the kitchen table scrutinizing a chart spread out on the table. I inquired what it was and he told me that it came in the mail today. His dad's brother's wife had purchased and dedicated a star for his father and had given it to him. He continued that the star, whose name now and forever would be his father's name, was permanently registered in the International Star Registry's vault in Switzerland and recorded in an astronomical compendium. His father's star was located near the constellation of Perseus with the astronomical coordinates of Right Ascension two hours, forty-five minutes, twenty-one point thirty-seven seconds and the declination of fifty-five degrees, forty-one minutes, thirty-three point ninety-four seconds. I told him to hold on. I didn't have a clue as to what he was talking about.

He read from the accompanying pamphlet that Right Ascension was equivalent to longitude, but was measured in hours, minutes and seconds of time. Each hour of RA was fifteen degrees of arc and twenty-four hours were equivalent to three hundred and sixty degrees. Declination or D was the angular distance north or south of the celestial equator, the extension of the earth's equator into the sky. D was equal to the latitude. He asked me if we could buy a telescope since the magnitude or brightness of his father's star was invisible to the naked eye. It was further than sixty light years away. Now, my interest was piqued and I went over to the table and sat down next to him. I had no idea the distance of a light year. He handed me the pamphlet and I read:

> A light year is about 10 trillion kilometers. These distances seem huge, but they are small in comparison to the scale of our galaxy and the universe itself. The majority of the bright stars and faint stars in the galactic disk, which astronomers have catalogued are really local neighbors of our sun. Your special star is located in our own galaxy, the Milky Way and probably within a few hundred light years.

I knew that our universe was enormous, but thinking in the terms that I had just read, I was awestruck by its vastness. William told me that he would begin to investigate different types of telescopes. He wanted to see his father as a star in heaven. And I thought *of our conversation in Itea: Beyond the stars, beyond heaven, that's where ideas live, that's where souls live. That's where my husband is.*

—————◆————

SUMMER 2003

Each year, as my husband aged and the children grew, he became more and more conservative and traditional. When I first met him, he had long hair that he pulled back in a ponytail, and he wore faded blue jeans and a flannel shirt. He drove a ten-year-old VW van, which he had converted into a camper after he had rebuilt the engine three times. He had been finishing his first undergraduate degree in his own sweet time. He savored and memorized each word he learned. We had moved in together into an old brown-shingled cottage, just weeks after we first met at the bar where his band was playing. We spoke endlessly into the night about any topic. He would take my handwritten outlines before my exams and quiz me. He learned what I knew about Alexander the Great and how his empire was to be divided. We both agreed that you couldn't trust what historians said about deathbed wishes, not even Alexander's. He had been a member of the musicians' union and was proud to carry the card in his wallet. His mandolin and fiddle were his constant companions.

But as each year passed, he slowly became dogged in his conviction that life should be lived in an ethical and conservative manner. No one in our family was allowed to swear. If he said it once, he must have said it a million times, that the only expletive his mother ever, ever had said in her entire life was "Hellfire, damnation." Each time he said this, the children rolled their eyes. Suffice it say, we were to use the King's English with correct grammar. Slang was not tolerated. No member of the opposite sex was allowed in any of the childrens' bedrooms. Curfews were abided. At dinner, everyone had their napkins in their laps, elbows were off the table, left hand in your lap, and of course, the conversation was either of current events or another intellectual topic with each member of the family expected to intelligently participate.

After he died, and after the funeral services, my children and I began swearing, slowly but surely. It started out with just a few "god damnits," but escalated quite rapidly. It felt good. William's favorite slogan was "fuck this shit." Heather didn't speak a sentence without at least one or two "mother fuckers" in it. I used the whole spectrum of swear words. Rebecca didn't participate with the same voracity as the rest of us, but every so often a few choice expletives would flow from her mouth. Sometimes we would forget and swear in front of our neighbor's young children and then apologize profusely. It was during this time period that my children and I developed our family's mantra: Shit happens. When William dropped a glass on the floor and it broke, Shit happens. When Heather got a C on her History Advanced Placement Exam, Shit happens. When I got stuck in rush-hour traffic on Friday night and didn't get home until past seven in the evening, Shit happens.

<hr />

During the month of May, I walked into Heather's room to check on her. She was continuing to be home schooled as a sophomore. She couldn't cope with returning to the high school and I couldn't cope either, so tutors came to our house. When I walked in, she was sitting on the floor with papers all around her. She was creating a project for her health class.

She looked up at me and said, "Don't be upset. I have this under control. I am going to graduate from high school next year as a junior. I've talked to my advisor. I can accumulate all the credits I need by next year to graduate. I want to go to the college where you went in Southern California. I've got this, mom. I am going to do this."

She was my Taurus daughter. When she became determined, when her mind was set, we had all learned in our family to either accept her verdict or if you argued, be prepared to duck. I thought *she is going to California in a year, a year from now. She will be but seventeen years old. That's young to move three thousand miles away. A year, that's far away. Maybe it will be all right then. A year, that's in the future.*

Stunned, I said, "Okay, if that's what you really want."

I left the room thinking next year. I couldn't wrap my brain around the concept, next year.

I hated my routine. I hated working. I hated being away from my kids. My boss had retired and everyone in the department was angry. The dean had hired consultants to tell him how to run the department and the consultants dictated new job descriptions for which many staff members would not qualify. They would be let go. The Human Resource term was "released." The dean instructed me that it was my responsibility to handle the releases. Everything was to change and everyone was upset. The dean said that it was merely a "reorganization" as if that helped the staff understand why many of them would become unemployed. A new director was coming on board in June and when he came, it was as if a hurricane swept in. He was a tall, affable young man, enthusiastic about medicine, and was genuinely concerned for patients. I was happy he had arrived. I had been running the department for two months solo. It had been two months of upheaval. I wanted a normal job.

My routine as it existed was to wake up at four-thirty in the morning, shower, dress in jeans, walk the dog his four miles, come home, change into professional attire, leave by six am, drive through early morning rush hour traffic to work, arrive by seven-thirty, leave by four-thirty, drive through early evening rush hour traffic to get home, walk the dog, and begin cooking dinner by six in the evening. It was during this time period that I began drinking vodka tonics as I prepared dinner, during dinner and after dinner.

I learned the trick that if you have enough vodka in your system, no one can ask you to do anything or if they do, you can't do it. I was so tired of arriving at work, listening to more than twenty voicemails, only to return each one, turn my computer on to see the screen flooded with angry emails from patients who didn't like what the dean and his consultants were doing, having to email each patient back after resolving their conflicts, listening to the legitimate complaints of the retained staff, training new staff, not having time to eat lunch, not having time to use the bathroom, coming home, looking at the clock, realizing that if I were to get eight hours of sleep, I needed to be in bed in less than two hours.

Yes, this was when I discovered what vodka tonics could do for you. It was during this period of time when I sat in commuter rush-hour traffic for hours and listened to one specific radio station, which played only hard rock. All the songs said something poignant to me and I realized my husband was the disc jockey. I didn't know how. All I knew was that I was certain he was selecting which song played. This was when I became an expert at driving with blurred vision. Each song my husband played contained a message for me.

One morning in late September, on the way to work, I had to stop at the county courthouse to file my husband's will with the surrogate court. This meant that I would be late to work. This was almost a sin. When I walked into the courthouse, I passed through a security screening just like the ones at the airport. I thought *of going through security with my husband's ashes to board the plane to California, when I had been stopped. The security guard who opened up my bag and pointed to the glass container said that there were crystals in there. I told them they were my husband. He smiled and closed my bag and allowed me to skirt around the x-ray machine. I never thought ashes would be classified as crystals, but I was glad. There was a comfort knowing they weren't just ashes. And now, passing through this security system, all I have is his Last Will and Testament. This is it. He is dead.*

The lady who examined the will in order to give me the letters testamentary so I could access his bank accounts, inquired as to the cause of death, because he was awfully young to die. I told her. She patted my hand and said not to worry. I would find another husband very soon.

Startled, I withdrew my hand quickly. I did not want to find another husband very soon. I did not want to find a husband at all. I wanted her to give me what I needed and get to work so I wouldn't be fired so we wouldn't have to sell the house. I had ascertained that most of our savings had been lost from his cancer infected stock market scheme. I thought *What? Why would she think I wanted to find another husband? Why?* She gave me the letters and I dashed out. In the car, pulling out of the parking lot, I called the receptionist at work. It was nine-thirty in the morning. I asked if any catastrophe had occurred. It seemed like they were a daily occurrence in this department.

———◆———

My girls were working again as coaches for the swim team and William was swimming only for the town's team. He wanted a break from club swimming. I didn't argue with him, even though I knew this would set him back. He was an extremely talented swimmer. He had the gift. My husband had been very proud of his technique and his speed, but I knew I couldn't play that card. When I looked into his eyes, I only saw gray emptiness. It was all I could do to work forty-five to fifty hours a week, buy the groceries, do the laundry, clean the house, do the yard work. I couldn't argue. I was too tired.

Coming home one evening I brought in the mail and noticed an envelope from hospice and wondered about its contents. I walked through the front hall and sat down at the kitchen table and opened it. It was a letter addressed to all four of us. They suggested that each of us individually and then as a family seek their grief counseling. What we had all experienced was way outside the bell curve. At dinner that night, I broached the topic with the kids and I was amazed. I had always been leery of psychiatry, psychology, and social workers. Those whom I knew in those professions had a rather difficult time managing their own personal life and I had known more than a handful.

My two daughters were the first to react. They thought it a good idea and they would call tomorrow. I almost fell off of my chair. I had been so blindsided by work that I didn't understand how much they were hurting. I thought *maybe this is a good idea.*

Maybe it will help. I guess they really need help. William declined. His buddies were his therapy. They made him feel normal. They made him forget. Plus, he had his first girlfriend, a smart girl and the desire of all the boys.

The next evening at dinner, I sat down and looked at my daughters and knew something was different. Rebecca said that she had been to see her therapist today and the word "her" swirled through my head. After one session, it was "her" therapist. She continued that while she had been accepted to a college in the city, she was having second thoughts. Her therapist, a young black woman, was going to help sort this out with her. I raised my eyebrows and thought *this is the first I'm hearing about this. Usually, I'm pretty good at knowing what's going on with my kids.* Heather announced that she would be seeing the same therapist tomorrow. I thought *I am no longer being the mother I want to be. The mother in me is missing in action. I feel like a workaholic and then an alcoholic when I get home.*

The next evening, after dinner, I was washing the dishes when I heard doors slamming violently upstairs. I went to the base of the stairs and listened. I heard Heather slam a door with her strong arms, yelling at the top of her lungs at Rebecca. I waited at the bottom of the stairs for a moment, hoping this would stop. More nasty comments were hurled back and forth in the upstairs hall. A door opened, someone yelled, the door was slammed. I began to climb the stairs slowly. I was trying to determine what they were arguing about.

Heather was standing in the doorway of her room, tears streaming down her cheeks, and then came the flood of information. Rebecca had decided she wanted to attend the same college Heather had already decided upon. That was why she was graduating next year. The state of California was not big enough for both of them. This was completely unfair to her. Rebecca opened her door and said she could attend whatever college she wanted. They continued to shout at one another. I didn't know how to bring reason into this argument.

Rebecca's therapist had encouraged her to do this. She

thought that a small college in a relatively small town would yield a tranquil environment, while attending a large university in one of the largest cities in the world would be overwhelming. Her therapist told her to inform her sister immediately. She did so while they were coaching on deck watching the little children swim in the lane lines. When I heard this, I knew things were out of control.

To tell anyone something of this magnitude while having twenty-five little lives dependent on your eyes was over the top. Many of these little swimmers could barely swim. The coaches were responsible for their safety, to make sure they didn't drown. To have this conversation in a place and at a time where Heather was incapable of responding was not fair.

I asked, "This is what your therapist encouraged you to do?"

"Yes, and I did so!" screamed Rebecca.

I replied, "I can't believe you told your sister in a place and time that she was unable to react. And besides, you had chosen your college. What made you change your mind?"

She yelled, "That was before Dad died!"

Heather burst into tears and slammed her door and yelled, "Leave me alone."

Rebecca slammed her door right afterwards and I stood there in the hallway looking at both closed doors and thought *we have a problem and I'm part of it. All their old sibling rivalry is surfacing. Combine that with the fierceness of their anger they feel towards losing their father and you have this. This is out of control.*

I went into my room, walked into the closet and started throwing his suits, his dress shirts, his ties into a pile on the bedroom floor. I tore open his dresser drawers and threw his sweaters, polo shirts, shorts, socks, and underwear into the pile. I stopped myself when I opened the top drawer and saw his wallet. I paused and looked at the pile. I stared at this pile in the middle of the bedroom floor. I stepped over it and went to my desk and sat down.

My Journal:

August 19, 2003

I am tired of being the glue. I'm tired of being
the strong one and that's where my anger comes
in. William says that I'm always angry now. I
am angry that he left his shoes at the bottom the
stairs. I'm angry that he left his coke can by the
couch. He's right. I am operating with a short
fuse and it's becoming shorter. We're all angry.
Each time we look at each other, we remind each
other of who's not here, and then we're angry.
Both my daughters want to be as far away as
possible. Then they won't have to look at us and
be reminded of who is not here. They're in so
much pain that if they flee, they think the pain
will be less. I don't know how to ease their pain.
I don't know how to ease my own.

No one was the same after this fight. We were civil to one
another, but it was as if we had all become ghosts. Nobody
really wanted to be around each other. My girls barely spoke
to one another. I began to work more hours, many of them on
the weekend to prepare for the fall when our facility would
become extremely busy. The rest of the summer, I was a robot.
My automatic pilot steered me in my routine and each day, when
I went to sleep, I tried to forget the day. Late in the summer, I
helped Rebecca pack for college. She was going to attend the
university college in the city after all. I was not sure how she
circled back to her original decision. I took the morning off from
work to drive her and all her stuff into the city. We waited in line
with the other freshman to receive her dorm room key. It took
forever and all I could think of was that I should be at work.
After hauling her stuff into the elevator and into her dorm room,
I left, looking at my watch. It was already past noon.

FALL 2003

William started his freshman year, and Heather returned to taking classes at the high school. Both walked two miles to school and back each day. Unlike the other mammas, I couldn't drive them. I was at work. William did not want to swim at all this year and I suggested that he and his sister swim for just the high school team. I still hadn't sold my husband's car. I had almost paid off the mortgage on the house. I had the lawyer convert the deed to my name. The lawyer had inquired if I wanted to change my name back to my maiden name. I thought *I have not considered this an option. No. My children's name will remain the same and mine will too. Why do I want to sever the last connection I have with him? Why did the lawyer ask me this? Do other people change their name back? Maybe I don't think like normal people.*

September 9, 2003. Today would have been our twenty-first wedding anniversary. The alarm hadn't yet rung when I switched it off. Slowly I pulled the covers off and walked into the bathroom and turned on the light. I went into the bathroom, turned on the shower and wondered what we would have done today. I had no idea. I climbed into the shower and began to make a mental list of the tasks to accomplish at work.

———◆◆———

One late September morning, I was driving to work in the Sienna, about to merge on to the ramp to the bridge. It was six-twenty am when I picked up my cell phone. I looked at the number and saw the time. I knew the prefix of the number was from my mother's county, but I didn't recognize the remainder of the phone number. I answered it. It was the county's hospital. The woman asked me to identify myself. She informed me that my mother had suffered an aortic aneurysm and was being medivacked to the city hospital where she had previously undergone her pig valve surgery. I told the woman that I would meet my mother there. I pulled the car over to the shoulder of the road and switched on my flashing lights. I called the new director. I knew he would be on his way to work as well. When he answered and heard my news, he told me to go directly to the hospital. He understood, but to let him know the outcome. I assured him I would.

I called Rebecca at college and my brother at work. I told them to meet me at the hospital. When we arrived, the three of us watched the paramedics race the stretcher with my mother on it through the hall to ICU. Her surgeon from her previous surgery had been paged and he was there. He reviewed the CAT scan. He said she needed immediate surgery. The dilation of her aorta was more than five and half centimeters. I had no idea what this meant, but I trusted this surgeon. She would be taken into surgery immediately. He would cancel his previously scheduled surgeries. He warned us that this could be life threatening. Her condition was gravely serious. I thanked him and told him I would wait.

I looked at my daughter and my brother. I told them I would call them when surgery was over. My brother needed to open his shop and my daughter needed to attend her college classes. They agreed and left. I looked around dazed, stunned. I didn't have a book. I didn't have anything to read. I walked outside to the street. It was a warm autumn morning. I glanced at my watch. It was eight-twenty. I walked up the hill to a local coffee shop and bought myself a large cup of coffee, hazelnut, milk and sugar and sat down by the street window. I watched the pedestrians scurrying to work, leading normal lives and I thought *I wonder if I can get into one of their bodies, like the body snatchers did.* I sat, sipping my coffee and thought *my children came in three. Is death going to come in three? Am I facing my third death? I cannot allow this to set me over. I need to earn a living. Three lives are dependent on me, just me. Get a grip. I need to retain a sense of composure.*

I know. I'll go to the grocery store when no one is there. Yes, Friday night. Friday night will be good. Everyone usually has plans on a Friday night. I won't see anyone I know. Good plan. I remember this past summer when I was food shopping, I would be in an aisle and glance up and see someone I knew, a parent from the swim team or an acquaintance from town. Our eyes would meet and then when I pushed my cart toward them and looked up, they had scooted down another aisle. I understood these phenomena. I made people uncomfortable.

Now that my husband was actually dead and the funeral a few months behind us, people didn't know what to say to me. They didn't want to be reminded. Just by being me, just by having a husband who died at the age of fifty-two, reminded them up front that shit does happen. I was getting tired of this. The ancient Greeks thought that death polluted the deceased's house and those who had a family member die were contaminated, especially if you touched the corpse. These contaminated people were prevented from contact with the gods until the appropriate purification had been performed. But I can do this, even if I am contaminated. I won't let anyone know that my mother perhaps is facing death. I will pretend to my colleagues at work, to my neighbors, to my friends that I am normal. That just because my mother may be dying, no one needs to know, just like no one needs to know that my husband is my disc jockey every time I am alone in the car. I'm going to gut the house. I've saved some money. I'm going to gut the house. I'll start with my husband's office. Yes, it's time to gut the house.

I waited all morning until the early afternoon. Dozing in a cushy chair in the waiting room, the surgeon found me.

"The operation was touch and go," he said. "But your mother survived it. She will be in the Intensive Care Unit with a feeding tube for several days, if not a week."

He continued that this was a wait-and-see situation. I asked if I could see her and he led me through the massive swinging doors into the unit. We walked past patients who looked like cadavers, lying listlessly in their beds with every sort of tube coming out of every orifice in their body. I put my hand over my nose. The air smelled of death. My mother was lying in the last bed, the furthest away from the door and the furthest away from the nursing station. She looked like the rest of the patients. She had a huge tube inserted down her throat, an oxygen mask over her nose and various and sundry tubes inserted into her arms. Somehow I was not upset when I saw her. I walked over to her, picked up her limp hand and stroked it. The surgeon left and I stood there smelling the air of death, stroking her hand.

> *My Journal:*
>
> September 28, 2003
>
> I will try to write about what I spoke with our dog today while on our evening walk.
>
> The process of dying is such an overwhelming, time-consuming task in that you have to deal with the day-to-day events, getting more morphine, calling the various doctors, making sure the patient is comfortable. Yes, you know at a very basic level that the person is dying, but you are too busy dealing with the daily process of death, that you forget about what death really is and what it really means on a soul level. And now, five months after my husband died and two years after my father died, I feel a steady current of strength drain from my inside, from my inner soul, a slow, but steady erosion. Death is like a drug. It anesthetizes you, makes you numb to your everyday surroundings. It pulls you into a space unknown to those who live their normal daily lives. And once you're in that space, you're alone – awakened to your real senses.

My mother stayed in the ICU for two months. After several weeks, she slowly gained consciousness, but she wasn't herself. One day, while lying in the ICU bed, she instructed me to go to the hall closet and get her a box of kleenex and report back to her how many boxes she had left. She tried to lift her hand to point where the linen closet was. She must have at least six boxes in the closet. I quietly told her that she was not at her home. She was in the hospital, but she didn't understand. She wanted her inventory of kleenex boxes.

I visited her every other workday and then on Saturdays I stayed with her for the afternoon. On Sundays, I drove to her house in the country and dealt with her mail, paid her bills, arranged for someone to mow the lawn and rake the leaves.

———•◦•———

The first renovations on the house began with my husband's office. William, Heather and I moved his antique oak roll top desk and the oak engineering bookcase from his basement office to my bedroom. We hauled his easy chair and his two metallic desks to the street for bulk pickup. I took out all the relevant files from his desk, including the ones that documented his stock market scheme. I found his journals and took those too. I thought *not now, but sometime, I will read these. I don't know when, but I do know, not now. Sometime.* We packaged his computers and briefcase and saved them. Someday we may want to access the information to see what he was thinking in the last months of his life.

William wanted to turn my husband's office into his bedroom. It was larger than his small room on the second floor and being in the basement, he would have more privacy. He and his buddies picked out the paint at the hardware store. They chose a pale green color. We bought a futon couch at IKEA that could be made into a bed, so a buddy or two could sleep over. While we were there, he asked for a bunk bed so that more buddies could spend the night. I agreed, if he would assemble it. I had been privileged when it came to tools. This had always been my dad's or my husband's domain, not mine. We bought a thick green carpet to be laid over the thick padding on the concrete floor.

It was at this time that I became quite serious about the renovations. I had always hated the cheap carpet we installed upstairs when we first moved in. In fact, I hated the carpet in the living room and dining room. I hated the large white tiles that spread from the kitchen into the den. I wanted to refinish the hardwood floors, which were hidden underneath. The contractors began upstairs in my room. All my furniture was moved into my older daughter's room, who was away at college. When I came home from work one evening, the workmen had completed sanding and sealing the hardwood floor in my room and the upstairs hallway. The only problem was that they had also finished the stairs and a huge yellow tape was tied across the entrance to the stairs with a dangling sign reading "Don't walk on for twelve hours."

The contractors hadn't told me they were going to do this. I was standing in the hall with William.

I asked, "How am I supposed to get my clothes in my closet for work tomorrow if we can't walk up the stairs and into my room?"

He asked me what I wanted to wear. Anticipating the various meetings I had tomorrow, I told him my dark pin-stripe suit with the blue blouse. He told me he would get them. He would climb onto the garage roof and climb in through the window by my closet and jump from the window into the closet and fetch them. It was raining and I warned him that the roof was too slippery. He was out the back door before I could finish speaking. Up the roof he scampered like a squirrel, pried open the window and only made one small imprint on the drying hardwood floor. He successfully picked out exactly what I needed and slid back down the roof. I thought *I don't know what I would do without him. I am not sure I could have done that. Yes, you could have. You would have. But, nice, I didn't have to.*

That evening, we sat down to dinner marveling at how natural the floors appeared when the phone rang. I went to the kitchen wall and picked up the receiver. A man identified himself as William's freshman advisor. He apprised me of how William conducted himself at school. He walked with his sweatshirt hood over his head, always looking down. It was evident that he was going through the motions, but wasn't engaged in his classes, particularly in his math class. The advisor said that students weren't allowed to switch classes this late in the fall, but William was in an algebra class with some very undesirable kids. He was going to transfer him to a more challenging math class. He was maneuvering this under the radar and he asked me not to mention our conversation with any other parent. He told me that he was going to take William under his wing and that we should stay in communication throughout the year. He was concerned for him. I thanked him and promised to stay in touch. I hung up and walked over to finish dinner. I asked William about this man and he smiled. He said he liked him very much and I thought *thank god for guardian angels.*

On Halloween, I bought the usual amount of candy and told the kids to open the door to the trick-or-treaters. I had an evening meeting and wouldn't be home until late. William said that he and his buddies were going to be hanging out and wouldn't be home either. Heather was going to be with her boyfriend. I looked at all the candy and put it in a pail and left it on the front porch. When I came home late that evening, I noticed all the toilet paper strung over the telephone wires and sidewalks. Lots of toilet paper carpeted the sidewalk. I smiled and thought *this is one way the kids release their energy.*

Over the weekend, I was folding laundry from the dryer when the phone rang. A lady whose daughter was in my William's class was on the other end. I knew the daughter. We called her "Ms. Perfect." She never got a grade less than an A– since kindergarten, always wore pristine clothes and in ninth grade had the same haircut as when she entered kindergarten. Her mother was on the phone, speaking very sternly to me. I didn't know the mother. She informed me that my son had been seen throwing an egg onto her living room window. Unmistakably, it was he. She continued that he should be punished. This could have caused massive damage. If the egg had gone onto the house, her entire house would have had to be repainted. When she continued that William should do fifty hours of community work to make amends, I grew impatient. I told her I would handle this and that I had to go. I hung up the phone and thought *this woman needs to find something else to do. It was one egg on one window. It was Halloween.* I found my son and told him Ms. Perfect's mother had just called, quite irate. He started to giggle when I told him about the fifty hours of community work. I thought *I am going to have to raise my son through all four years of high school. I am going to have to do this solo. How am I going to combine my husband's authority over his son with my soft style? How can I do this? I don't know how I'm going to do it. This wasn't the deal.*

———◆◆◆———

WINTER 2003 – 2004

We couldn't celebrate Christmas here, at home. We just couldn't. We needed to get out of here. We needed to go somewhere warm if only for a few days. I called Helen to see if they would join us. The four of us could not go by ourselves. If we did, we would have just sat around looking at each other, reminding ourselves of who was missing. They were game and Richard suggested Jamaica. He had been a professional buyer at a major aeronautics firm and was a sleuth at finding deals. He would be in charge. My mother would remain hospitalized until the New Year at which time I was to find her a nursing home specializing in rehabilitation. I told my children about the plans and everyone was happy. We would flee our home, even though the hardwood floors throughout the house made it feel more warm and natural. We would enjoy the new floors when we returned.

We were going to Jamaica. We stopped in Miami for the night on the way down and took a cab to South Beach. None of us had ever been to South Beach. We walked along the strip by the beach that had many outdoor restaurants with the large heating poles and selected one that was playing jazz. It reminded me of my dad playing his jazz. When we sat down to order, the waitress inquired if we would like to begin with drinks. I requested a vodka tonic. Rebecca requested a glass of white wine. I stared at her. She was nineteen years old and the drinking age was twenty-one. The waitress asked her for ID to prove she was twenty-one. I tried to keep my mouth closed when she took out of her wallet an ID stating her birthday was in 1981. The waitress was satisfied and handed the ID back to my daughter.

After the waitress left, I asked her to explain. Heather was intrigued. Rebecca informed us that fake IDs were quite easy to obtain in a certain section of the city and that she and her friends had taken the subway down a few weeks ago and paid twenty dollars to buy them. I warned her to be careful. She assured me she would be, but I was not convinced. She continued that she had a new boyfriend whom she had met at a crystal shop in a funky section of the city. She really, really liked him. She showed us pictures of him dressed in biking gear, standing next to a speed demon bike. He lived about an hour outside the city and she was spending weekends at his house on a huge beach. She said she felt safe with him. She felt protected. She said that she was falling in love with him and I thought *of the concept of safe. It wasn't a familiar concept.*

When we arrived in Jamaica, we met Helen and Richard at the airport and took the bus to our resort. The lobby was spacious and overlooked the sea. It reminded me of an old Victorian mansion with high-back chairs which you melted into. Richard had negotiated a package deal that included meals and drinks so there was an endless amount of rum punches and food for everyone. We checked in and were escorted to our bungalow along a path with ferns dipping down to your head. Our bungalow was large, equipped with a kitchen, living room and bedroom. All the girls would bunk in the bedroom and William would sleep on the pullout couch in the living room. We explored our new surroundings and settled in. We met back in the lobby to enjoy the cocktail hour followed by dinner in the dining room below. Richard had quite the sense of humor and he and my son took to exchanging dirty jokes on their side of the table. I hadn't seen him laugh like this for years.

Activities were bountiful. William and Rebecca scheduled scuba lessons, while Heather met a holiday boyfriend. I warded off a cold. I felt my chest tightening. Helen offered to treat me to a Swedish massage that she arranged for next day. The morning of the massage, I rose only to feel fatigued, like an iron vest was wrapped around my chest. I met my sister-in-law at the spa. This woman had been a silent but strong support for me ever since my husband's cancer metastasized.

When we entered the spa proper, the receptionist instructed us which room to enter. As I walked into my designated room, several candles illuminated the space and very soft, calming music played. I undressed and slid under the sheets. A black woman came in and introduced herself. I had never had a massage before and was unsure what to expect. She quietly told me to think of something peaceful. I knew that was going to be a challenge. I thought *something peaceful. Swimming off the rocky beach on Crete with the two brown mountains rising from the cove. Floating on my back, staring at the white cumulus clouds and the light blue sky. Suspended. Time stopped. Floating. Stay focused. Stay focused on this. But that was after the phone call. That was after the phone call when I knew life would be changed. I didn't know how we were going to get through it. I still don't know how we're going to get through this. Stay focused on floating. How are we going to get through? This is just the beginning.*

The woman initially massaged my legs and by the time she was massaging my shoulders, my brain stopped focusing on my peaceful image. While my physical body was relaxing, my insides were becoming tense. My chest was tight, my ears were popping, and my throat felt as if it were swelling shut. The flu gripped my body. After the massage, I relaxed with Helen on a wooden bench in our terry cloth robes, drinking water. I couldn't help myself. I didn't want to cry, but the tears just came. She didn't say a word. She didn't have to. We just sat together while I continued to cry.

Back in my bungalow, I succumbed to one of the worst viruses known to mankind. The others enjoyed their holiday by scuba diving and taking excursions throughout the island. I retreated with my book of poetry, kleenex, and herbal tea. In the evening, I joined the others for cocktails and dinner, but didn't venture out during the day.

> *My Journal:*
>
> 22nd December 2003
>
> Jamaica
>
> I feel compelled to write. I need to take
> measures to heal myself – all by myself. I want
> to spend more time with my children and

gramma. They'll be gone so soon. We need to
learn how to heal as a family. I need to nourish
my soul, my body, my heart. This is what I must
do, for myself, by myself. And memorize Rilke.

Ignorant Before the Heavens of My Life

Ignorant before the heavens of my life,
I stand and gaze in wonder. Oh the vastness
of the stars. They're rising and descent. How still.
As if I didn't exist. Do I have any
share in this? Have I somehow dispensed with
their pure effect? Does my blood's ebb and flow
change with their changes? Let me put aside
every desire, every relationship
except this one, so that my heart grows used to
its farthest spaces. Better that it live
fully aware, in the terror of its stars, than
as if protected, soothed by what is near.

———◆———

When we returned from Jamaica, we went back into our
automatic routine mode. Heather was tolerating her classes,
William was going though the motions of being a freshman at
the high school and I drove to work listening to the songs my
husband played for me on our special radio station. One night at
dinner, William asked me if he could go to therapy. He couldn't
get out of his funk and I didn't know how to help. I had no
idea what it was like to be a thirteen-year-old boy and have your
father die on you. I was still leery of therapy, having witnessed
what it did for my daughters, but I told him, "Sure. Why not
give it a shot?" If he didn't like it, he could always stop it. I told
him I would research and try to find a very good one that our
insurance company would cover.

The following day at work, I took some time to research on
the internet therapists who specialized in an adolescent's grief

for a deceased parent. I found several and made calls to feel them out. I had my questions in order. I wasn't about to turn this fragile boy over to just anyone. I finally selected one and made the appointment. His office wasn't far from our house. William could walk there without a problem. Satisfied with my progress, I put on my coat and walked out into the frigid city air to buy a cup of coffee, hazelnut, milk and sugar.

Waiting in the small diner, I glanced at the steamed windows and I thought *of the steam from our kitchen faucet when I turned it on as hard as it would go so it would mask my tears the night my husband blew up at his daughter and me. Did he really think I was having an affair? I don't know. I don't know what he was thinking. I don't know what he was feeling. He didn't want to share them with me or anyone. He experienced death by himself. I know he experienced it fully. He was that type of person. He wouldn't have let an experience like this go by without fully embracing it. It was a once in a lifetime experience. I wonder what he felt. I wonder what he thought. Maybe you should investigate therapy yourself. Maybe. My mother's right. We are living in a house of cards. If I cave, the house comes down. Maybe you should take a chance with it. Maybe.* When I got back to my small office, I shut the door, hung up my coat and started my research. After much perusing, I settled on one male psychologist who saw patients in the evening. I called and made an appointment.

The next week, William had his initial appointment with his therapist in the evening. I drove him to the medical office. A short, middle-aged, balding man introduced himself to us. He seemed pleasant enough, but now I listened acutely to my mother's warning about short men. I kept this to myself as William was led into the therapy room. Exactly after one hour, my son appeared. I couldn't tell if he believed this was going to help or not. He wanted to leave. As we drove home, I inquired how it went. I didn't want to know details. I wanted to know if he wished to continue. He told me the jury was out. He would let me know.

Several weeks later and after two visits with my therapist, I was on a business trip, stranded in the airport. Sitting, waiting for the delayed plane home, the winds gusted to unsafe speeds for airplanes to take off and land. There was nothing to do but wait. I sat in the uncomfortable lounge seat. I looked through my bag and found a professional insurance journal describing statistical analysis documenting premium rates. The idea of reading that on my personal time was an abhorrent thought. I took out a piece of paper from my notebook and wrote:

> Free Association Time: And the gods are not appeased as the winds create havoc with air travel... Is it a curse that fate makes me stand still for a moment?

> Do I continue past two visits with my therapist or is it a type of mental masturbation that robs me of time? If I have learned anything, it is that while time may or may not be linear and may or may not be forever, your time with time is temporal. It must be cherished, savored, spent ever so wisely. I told my therapist, all I wanted was some time for me. I had no time for me. Between working, taking care of my kids, the house, the finances, the estate legal work, my mother, her bills, her house, I had no time just for me.

> My therapist's question to me, "And if you had the time alone, do you think you would crumble?" No.... Perhaps – and so what if I did? Would it replace the tears spent sliding down the car seat on the different highways? Would it absolve all grief, the emptiness? They say memories are sustaining. I say they can deteriorate. They can squash life. They annihilate. They rob the lungs of oxygen. They make you remember. If you didn't remember, you wouldn't feel the hollowness, the empty space where you swirl around alone.

The airline representative announced that the plane was ready to board. It was ten-thirty at night. I would be home by one in the morning. I would have about three hours of sleep. I stuffed my writing into my wallet. I wanted to keep it somewhere safe.

My New Year's resolution was to reinstitute traditions we used to have when my husband was alive. I curbed back on my swearing. I needed to be some kind of role model for my two children who lived at home. I couldn't do anything for Rebecca. She was with her boyfriend now, madly in love. I told my two children that every Sunday for one hour we were going to have a sit-down Sunday dinner in the dining room. I would learn to cook and the dinners would be healthy and delicious. It was impossible to have weekday dinners together on a consistent basis. Everyone's schedule was too chaotic, but we could make time on Sunday just for an hour, just to be in each other's company. We would have intellectual conversations. We would look at each other and not be reminded of who used to sit at the head of the table. We would look at each other. We could do this, the three of us.

We began our tradition. On the third Sunday that we had been eating a nutritionally healthy dinner together, sitting in the dining room, I had roasted a chicken. If my husband were alive, he would have carved it at the table and served everyone from the platter. Instead, I carved the chicken in the kitchen and put the slices of meat, mashed potatoes and green beans on each plate and brought the plates into the dining room. We sat down together. I began the conversation by asking Heather how her classes were going. She replied that her health class was quite informative. I inquired as to what were they learning. She informed us they were studying reproductive health. My thirteen-year-old son gazed at her inquisitively. She continued that while they learned about the basic technical facts of the sperm fertilizing the egg, she had taken it upon herself to research outside of class. She wanted to know why people desired sex.

I glanced at William. He leaned closer over his plate. She continued that it was because of the orgasm. An orgasm was a thrilling, sensual, physical sensation. I was not sure where she was going with this and I was not sure if I should curtail her. I knew my husband would have been on the floor at this point, but this was factual. It was part of life.

She leaned forward and looked into her brother's eyes and said, "Sorry, the female orgasm is much more intense than the male orgasm. The female clitoris has far more nerve endings than the head of the male penis."

At this point, I said beneath my breath, "Holy shit." I was glad my husband was dead. He would die if he heard this. I looked at William. His eyes were popping out of his head. I reached over and touched her arm and thanked her for the information and told her this topic of conversation was not really appropriate at the dinner table.

She smugly said, "Well, you asked me!"

We continued in silence for a while. I changed the topic of conversation to my impending trip to California in two weeks for a college reunion. Rebecca would come home for the weekend. I would only be gone for three days. This was my last time to be away before our new director came on board for my department. The director from last summer had accepted another position. The new director was a woman and she would be starting in the spring. The dean requested that I work closely with her so she would be able to learn all the facets of the department. He didn't want me to take any time off until she was well oriented. We cleared the table together and as William and I were doing the dishes together in the kitchen, I thought *I am not quite sure what to say about the information his sister imparted to him at the dinner table. Where are you when I need you? I am going to have to raise my son solo. I wonder about all those things William will miss in the coming years because he has only a mother. I cannot possibly give him what his father could. A father's contribution to his son's life is unique to a father. A mother cannot replace a father's gifts. But somehow I must try. Somehow,*

I must try. But, I don't know how to compensate for this. I don't know what I can do.

———◦◦◦———

The next morning, I woke up and began my routine. But when I turned on the shower, I noticed a white lined piece of paper on the shelf beside the shower, the shelf my dad had installed. I picked up the piece of paper and read. I turned off the shower and sat down on the toilet and read each word slowly.

Mom,

> *It's your birthday today. Whenever you will read this, if you ever find this, just take a second to absorb this. You have been through what more than most people go through. But it only makes you stronger. And as you know, you are the strongest person I know. There are still tougher battles ahead and they will only make you stronger. There is always a battle ahead. And if you ever need to sit one out, just call me up and I'll take care of it. You are the single most important human being in my life. I know I can be an ass and be selfish and only hang out with friends, but I will always love you. You are my guide in life, mom. You show me where to and not to go. Anything I do to hurt you, just know I will always love you, even after we die. You mean everything to me, mom. If one night you wanna hang out just ask me to stay in and I will. And if we ever get into a big argument and we hurt each other, I hope you just come back and read this. Because this letter is true and genuine, just like my love to you.*
>
> *I will always love you.*
>
> *William*

I read his letter, reread it, and read it again. Each time my chest became a little warmer. The sense of hollowness succumbed to the glowing feeling of warmth. I put my hand right to my chest to see if I could fee the warmth. No, it was on the inside. My thirteen-year-old son's words made a physical reaction. I thought *I am the luckiest person in the world. I am the luckiest mother to have this son and his birthday present.* I turned on the shower water and climbed in.

Two weeks later, I headed to Southern California for my college reunion. I wasn't sure why I was going. I had never been to a college reunion before, but I knew I wanted to see an old friend. The trip ended up being a whirlwind and afterwards, on the long plane ride home, I wrote the following in my journal.

My Journal:

24th February 2004

California

I didn't realize that I was to end up on Newport Beach in February 2004. I went to my college reunion to see my old college partner. He and I went back thirty years. He and I were keepers of each other souls back then, reading each other's journals, knowing one another's next thought, playing in the dusty San Bernardino Mountains where the dirt was clean. I didn't really want to see the college. I maybe wanted to see the professor with whom I had an affair a long time ago. He was a warm and gentle lover who was structured in his sex, not adventuresome, but warm like his cashmere sweaters. I saw my partner and we talked and smoked Native American Indian cigarettes he brought from Albuquerque. We sat on the concrete wall outside the new Student Union. He couldn't believe my husband had died. He remembered him from visiting us when we lived in our old farmhouse. He remembered him from the only New Year's Eve we celebrated in the city with his wife. He couldn't believe that he had died. I didn't know what I believed. I could recite the events. I could tell him that my husband had a mole on his back: that the first dermatologist wanted to take a wait-and-see approach. I could tell my college partner all the steps I took to make sure it didn't metastasize. I could tell him the sequence of tests and doctor visits. I couldn't tell him about the white sputum rupturing from his mouth in the early morning before his death day. And I didn't tell anyone that my husband had pulled himself up as I sat beside him two days before he died and that he stroked my cheek with his index finger. That was mine. But I didn't realize that I went to Southern California to be on Newport Beach in February 2004. I remember only talking to my college partner, sitting on the concrete wall, talking about my husband. The next morning, there were reunion functions. I didn't know where my partner or the professor was. I went to some financial management seminar led by an alumnus who was their golden boy of success, but I didn't learn anything that my dad hadn't already taught me. When it was over, I couldn't find my partner or the professor. I left. I started driving and realized I was going to Newport Beach. I remember the warm wind and the smell of the salt driving down Route 55 towards the beach. I entered the beach by the pier and walked towards the waves and as I was walking, slowly, steadily, looking toward the horizon and the waves – a mind freezing, gut-wrenching force encapsulated my whole being: Anguish. I could breathe. You can breathe. I steadied myself, arms encircling my torso. Gasping air, heaving, tears streamlining. Anguish is soul

pain. My husband and I had been on this beach
so many times. He grew up here. This was his
playground in elementary school, touch football,
quarterback during middle and high school.
We smoked pot in the wedge when we would
drive down from Berkeley to visit his dad. He
taught me the constellations from this beach,
how to dead reckon, how shells have ambient
sound, how to listen to their vibrations. He
taught the kids how to body surf here. This was
his. I thought I'm being shown snippets from
his life; a scrawny blonde haired boy skipping
rocks at the edge – he had the art. It was in the
wrist. A young couple, madly in love, further
up in the sand. PDA. A family with three kids
entering the beach. I remember crying from
the navel when the gut goes into spasms. I
remember thinking I always want to remember
this. No other experience comes close to the
depth this feeling penetrates. Soul pain. I
remember my boot heels sinking into the wet
sand. I remember collecting shells and being
angry with myself that I couldn't remember the
names of the shells. My husband's grandfather
had catalogued shells. Some shells were even
named after him. He had found them first. And
I couldn't remember the garden variety of shells
on Newport Beach in February 2004. I don't
remember how long I stayed on the beach and
I don't remember how I got to the hotel on the
Back Bay in the early twilight. After I checked
in, I walked across the street to the Back Bay
of Newport Harbor where boats are organized
like cars in a parking garage in New York City:
one boat parked atop another in a rack. There
was a beautiful sloop nestled against the pier
and on its mainsail cover, the logo of National

Geographic. A man was at the stern, grilling his
dinner. Eye contact. He beckoned by gesture,
but I wasn't ready. I think I remember trying to
smile. I wanted to, but I don't remember if I did.
I walked away thinking "men." And afterwards
walking down the road, entering some club,
listening to a raunchy country band, alone, not
lonely, just alone among the Saturday night
country crowd and I thought of the man grilling
his dinner on the stern of his graceful sloop.

———————

When I returned home, my kids sensed there was something
different about me. I was tired, but I was calm. I wasn't on
automatic pilot. I felt my internal compass regaining magnetic
north. I threw my bags into the living room, admiring the
hardwood floors and suggested that we change up our routine. I
recommended that we go out for dinner tonight. Rebecca would
stay Sunday evening and we would drive into the city together in
the morning. We agreed on a Japanese restaurant in a neighboring
town, one that we'd never been to before. I thought *we are going
to do this. We are going to forge new memories together, the four of
us. We can do this.*

At dinner that night, I broached the subject of continuing
the renovations. Heather asked me what I had in mind. I told
them I wanted to tear down the deck that ran only along part of
the back of the house. I wanted to build a larger deck that would
run the entire length of the house. In the dining room, instead
of ugly windows, I wanted French doors to open onto the deck.
The sliding glass doors entering the deck from the den would
remain. I wanted a hot tub. I wanted to soothe my body from
working so hard. I hated wearing high heels, but I refused to
wear sneakers with silk dresses. The pain in my calves woke me
up at night and I would painfully stretch them until the tension
subsided. Yes, a hot tub. I wanted to put in new windows in

the entire house. Our old windows were not energy efficient. I wanted to paint the living room and dining room in natural earth tones. We needed a new roof on the house.

The three of them looked at me in shock. I confessed that I had been saving money. I had painstakingly saved every month for over a year now. We had been on a strict budget and had scrupulously adhered to it. I wanted to do this. I wanted to throw out the couches in the living room. They were ugly, and besides, the cat had scratched them to pieces. I told them the end result would be beautiful. The house would be peaceful and tranquil. I told them I would start my research on contractors. Heather was enthusiastic and said she would help pick out the paint colors and paint. She would come with me to look at different couches. Rebecca said our house would be in an upheaval and she was glad she wasn't going to be around. We hardly saw her. When she wasn't in classes, she was with her boyfriend every moment. They had become inseparable.

———◆◆◆———

SPRING – SUMMER
2004

The new director joined our department in May. My job was to escort her to Human Resources in order to ensure that her paperwork was in order and then to the licensing department where her medical license would be verified. I was to acquaint her with her new professional environment. The medical licensing department was located in the administrative building, behind two large doors. Upon reaching the department, before I opened the door, I stopped short. I looked at the name on the door. It was a doctor with whom my husband had worked closely for several years developing a computerized patient tracking system. My husband had always spoken very highly of him and I remembered receiving a card addressed to my husband from him after he died. I had never met the man. We entered through the doors and the secretary informed us that he would be with us shortly. Sure enough, he came out and inspected the director's paperwork. Everything was in order and she would have permission to practice medicine in this complex. He shook her hand and went back to his office.

I asked the director if she would have a seat. I would be back in two minutes. She sat down, and I returned to the doctor's office and softly knocked on the door. He opened it. I introduced myself. I told him I was the wife of the man who had worked with him several years before on the patient tracking system. I wanted him to know how highly my husband had regarded him. His body quickly leaned on the wall as if someone had gently pushed him. He looked at me directly and said how much that meant to him and that he was extremely sorry about his death. I thanked him. I didn't want to make him feel uncomfortable, so I quickly left. When I returned to the waiting room, I could tell the director was upset with having to wait. As we left through the massive doors, I shook my head.

Every Saturday afternoon during the spring of 2004, Heather was my constant companion. We would go clothes shopping. Not having worked professionally for more than thirteen years, my wardrobe was in dire straits. One morning when I had first started working, I had walked into her bedroom to kiss her goodbye. She looked at me and said, "Wait."

She'd found her glasses on her nightstand and slipped them on, scrutinizing me. I asked, "What's the matter?"

She looked horrified and said, "Fashion Emergency!!!"

She'd told me not to worry, that she would help, but she would not allow me to go to work dressed in that outfit. She told me exactly what to change into and I'd gone back to my bedroom and followed her instructions. She was the artist. And in keeping with her pledge, she accompanied me almost every Saturday in search of sleek, fashionable attire to wear to work. She would sit on the floor in various dressing rooms while I tried on numerous outfits. Sometimes she would adamantly say, "Take it off immediately" and other times say, "I don't care how much it costs, you look stunning."

She was my fashion guru. And each Saturday, I made sure that she was well compensated. She loved carrying the shopping bags throughout the mall and I was grateful because I hated it. But now, it was her turn. She was about to graduate from high school and she needed a white dress. I wanted to go shopping with her for it, but I had way too much work to do. I had to work the weekend she was going graduation dress shopping. I thought *this is not right. She only graduates from high school once in her lifetime.*

Heather graduated in a class that was not her own. She had pulled it off and was graduating as a junior, barely seventeen years old. Rebecca became the family photographer and took numerous pictures of her sister walking up to the podium to receive her diploma. I sat with William who resembled a ragamuffin. He had not had a haircut since his father died. Many parents commented how disheveled he looked and I thought *if this is how he wants to grieve, leave him alone. Just leave him* alone. *It's simply a haircut.* But Heather was stunningly beautiful and conducted herself with grace and elegance. Her white dress fell off tiny spaghetti straps swishing down, conforming tightly to her petite waist. She wore her grandmother's pearl necklace. Her blue eyes sparkled brightly with life.

I thought *I wonder if my husband sees how beautiful his daughter glows today.*

———⟶•◆•⟵———

The renovations began in late May and continued through June. Each night when I returned home, Heather, William and I inspected the work that had been completed during the day. Almost every night, there was another problem with the construction. First, it was the type of nails the workers used on the deck. They were of poor quality and would eventually rust. Each nail had to be taken out and replaced with the proper nail. Then it was the concrete foundation for the hot tub. The foundation wasn't tall enough. The hot tub had to sit on a foundation parallel to the deck flooring to access its drain on its bottom side. The foreman had told me the lower foundation was satisfactory. I could climb under the deck to access the drain. We argued on that topic for at least thirty minutes. And then there were days that the workers just didn't show up. I would call the foreman and he would tell me that he wasn't sure where they were, as if he were Little Bo Peep and had lost his sheep.

During these times, I didn't know who I missed more, my husband or my father. I began to be aware of being a woman navigating solo and I began to understand the concept of a partner in a way I never had. I thought *how I had taken for granted everything my Dad and husband had done for me: all the things they had fixed, all the things they had put right without me having to think of it. I never knew what an allen wrench was. I barely knew the difference between a phillips head and flat head screwdriver, but now…. Now I am learning. I don't want to learn this. I never want to take anything for granted again, ever.*

But it was still exciting to see the old windows in the dining room being replaced by French doors that entered onto a cedar deck. Heather and her good friend were painting the living room a hazy, light peach color and the dining room a pale cream. We bought a billowy brown leather couch, which we positioned on an angle in the corner of the living room as if to greet the person entering the front door. Behind the couch stood a narrow rectangular table that my dad had built with a large, rust colored vase filled with flowers. A new green flowered oriental carpet lay in the living room, exposing the hardwood floors on the perimeter. New standing lamps gave the living room a warm glow in the evening.

We bought a new buffet cabinet for the dining room and gave the old crowded furniture to a friend. A rich dark green carpet lay under the walnut dining room table. A modern group of picture frames hung on one side of the dining room, filled with the red poppies of Corinth and the wildlife outside of Nafplio and a large standing glass vase filled with pussy willows separated the living room from the dining room. We installed glass doors from the kitchen to the dining room so kitchen sounds would not be heard from the dining room. The hot tub was delivered and was placed at the end of the deck by the den's sliding glass doors. We secured bird feeders on the new deck railings. We finished by buying new deck furniture with sangria colored umbrellas.

And in the garage, we bought outside carpet and laid it over the concrete floor so that William and his buddies in their band could practice. We installed new garage doors, which were more durable and hopefully, more sound proof. And when the renovations were completed, we had a party and invited everyone. The four of us couldn't believe what we had done. This was the beginning the of revolving door policy. Our front door never was locked. Our house became the safe haven for any of William's or Heather's friends and mine too. It was a home where, when you walked through the front door, you entered a different world: a world of tranquility and peace.

Mid-August, it was time to drive my baby girl to college three thousand miles away. Upon my recommendation, Heather had bought a small car to drive across country and to have while in Southern California. I knew that if she didn't have a car, she would become stir crazy. Public transportation was almost nonexistent where she would be and she was not the type to stand still. We were to take off on a Tuesday afternoon. I did my usual routine and rose at four-thirty in the morning, walked the dog, showered, dressed, listened to the songs my husband played for me in the car. I was sitting at my desk at seven in the morning.

At noon, I began organizing my desk and files so that my assistant could locate anything she needed in my absence. The director walked in and instructed me to follow her into her office. The look on her face astonished me. Her lips were pressed firmly together. They reminded me of that red line which reliably depicts anger. I entered her office and sat down by her small round conference table. She sat opposite and leaned back. She said, "You said 'bla bla bla' to another staff member and that was very inappropriate."

I looked directly into her eyes and said, "If I had said 'bla bla bla,' you are correct. It would have been very inappropriate. But I did not say 'bla bla bla'." I continued, "Let's call the staff member to meet with us so that we can resolve this miscommunication."

The director replied, "I didn't hear this from that particular staff member. I heard it from someone else."

My brain swirled and I thought *let me get this right. You are accusing me of saying something to someone, but you did not hear it from that someone. You heard this from someone else— a third party. And you believe this third party. You haven't even asked the person to whom I supposedly said this. Wow. Talk about not wanting to go to the primary source.*

I then replied, "Okay, let's get all the people in question into one room and discover if this miscommunication happened and how." "No," she replied. "You go on your vacation and think about your inappropriate comments."

I stared at her incredulously. She was adamant about not furthering the discussion. I left and finished organizing my desk. I closed my office door and shook my head.

When I arrived home, Heather had the car packed and was ready to go. I dashed upstairs to change my clothes and grab my bag. Rebecca and William came out to the driveway and we hugged goodbye. They were going to hold down the fort while we drove across country. I began the drive for the afternoon. We were going to try to get past Pennsylvania by nightfall. Once we were in the car and established a rhythm of driving, my mind kept reenacting my last conversation with the director. The more it swirled through my head, the more absurd it became. I thought *did she really say this? Did she really believe a third party? This is hearsay. I can't believe it. I have never met anyone professionally who acts in such a way. The dean and his meaningless handshake. He had hired her. I stand corrected. I know that my kids even in elementary school would not believe a third party. They had been taught to go the primary source, whether it was gossip or research. Is this what I have to look forward to on a daily basis?*

Then the traffic started. It was evening rush-hour traffic and it was stop and go. I shifted from first to second gear and sometimes stalled out. Heather could tell I was agitated and upset. She knew better than to ask why.

When I ground the gears, she said firmly, "Stop the car. We're switching drivers."

I told her no, that I was fine. I told myself to relax and stop thinking about the director's behavior. We pulled into a crummy hotel on the trucker highway just before the border of Pennsylvania. It was past nine o'clock at night and I was exhausted. I sat in the restaurant and being so tired, I couldn't eat. I needed sleep to drive tomorrow. Our plan was to drive the three thousand miles in three and a half days. I would begin driving by five in the morning and then we'd stop for lunch at noon and switch drivers. I would sleep in the passenger seat and my daughter would drive until about five in the afternoon. Then, I would take over and drive until nine in the evening. That was our plan.

We were driving through Oklahoma and making good time. It was in the afternoon and Heather was driving. I rummaged through my backpack and found my grandfather's memoir book. He had grown up here and had written his history about his life near Soonerville. His mother and father had been full-blooded Cherokee Indians. I asked my daughter if she knew what the Cherokees believed in and she shrugged her shoulders.

I read from my grandfather's book, "The Cherokee believed that everything was round. The power of the world worked in circles. The sky was round. The earth was round. The birds made their nests in circles for theirs was the same religion as the Cherokee. Bird feathers were the messengers between earth and heaven."

I stopped and looked out the window to the flat brown earth and thought *back to a psychic telling me that bird feathers were important to me. I should pay attention to them. They would lead me in the right direction.* I had started consulting psychics about six months after my husband died upon the prodding of Rebecca's boyfriend. He very much believed in a higher order. He believed in the Divine. It was uncharted waters for me, but I decided to be open to it. I only knew that psychics may or may not posses something of the unknown and in this unknown, I may be brought closer to my husband and dad. My cleaning lady had said that my behavior was not unusual for someone in my situation. When she had said this, it reminded me of the despicable word "widow." Nevertheless, for some reason I took my bird feathers to heart and paid close attention when I saw one.

I continued to look out the window to the brown flat earth and then she caught my eye. I quickly pointed to it for Heather to see and she gasped. Through the passenger side window in the distance was a hawk. Her black and white patterned wings outstretched to what must have been four feet. From her white head to her white tail, she must have been two feet long. Magnificently, she flew solo in the sky.

Then the memory. I was in elementary school and in the summer after dinner, my dad and I would play ping pong. He would begin my score at eighteen so that I only had to earn three more points to win. He would begin his score at zero. In this way, he taught me to play aggressively and competitively. Afterwards, at sunset, we would drive to the town pier and turn off the car. Sometimes we would get out. Sometimes we stayed in the car. I always thought each night my father was checking on our small sailboat moored off the end of the pier. But he wasn't. He liked to look at the seagulls flying, soaring in the evening sky. I remember one particular night, he commented that if man could understand the mechanics of how birds fly, as he watched one glide over our heads without moving a muscle, then the entire technology of aerodynamics would be transformed. Because he was a mechanical engineer by trade, I didn't think too much about the comment. I remember the beauty of the white bird, but I didn't really understand. Now, watching this gorgeous hawk soar above the flat plains of Oklahoma, it makes perfect sense. Yes, bird feathers. They will show me the way. What my dad was saying was that when something is unharnessed or something is unexplainable to man and if we can't understand it, we can at least very much appreciate the beauty of it. Yes, bird feathers make sense.

Heather broke our silence and said, "Continue, please."

I read on. "The Cherokee valued order and harmony in interpersonal relationships, with nature and with spirits. To live otherwise was a violation. Sin did not exist in the Cherokee religion until the Christian missionaries came."

Heather asked me what percentage Cherokee she was. I told her that I was something like twenty-five percent, so she was twelve and half percent. She asked me why her grandfather's father left Oklahoma and became a schoolteacher and then a doctor. I replied that his back had hurt so much when he picked cotton that he vowed there was a better way to live.

———

Once in the college town, we began the task of cleaning her dorm room, acquiring the various things she would need for the coming year. We met her roommate and her roommate's mother who was a psychologist and on her third marriage. We stayed two days and on the last night, we had dinner together. Driving Heather back to her dorm, I suggested that she should begin to think about her eighteenth birthday trip to anywhere in the world other than the United States next summer. Since she had graduated from high school when she was seventeen and coupled with my overwhelming workload, we had agreed to take the trip next summer. Driving up to her dorm in my rented car, I parked to get out and give her one last final embrace. I wouldn't see her until Thanksgiving. We hugged and I thanked her for being my fashion consultant, interior designer, cook, and best friend during the past year. I didn't know how I could be standing here without her and all she had offered me.

She smiled at me and said, "You had better begin your research. I want to go back to Greece next May." I smiled and hugged her strong shoulders firmly. Driving back to the hotel in the darkness of the night, I thought *I can't believe it. Ellas in the spring with the smell of her wildflowers. Nostos.*

———◆◆◆———

FALL – WINTER
2004 – 2005

Back at home, William entered his sophomore year of high school. When I returned to work, I immediately found the director. I insisted on a meeting with all parties involved regarding this so-called miscommunication. She agreed and several weeks later the meeting was scheduled. Only the third party, from whose lips the director had heard this heresy, was not asked to attend. The meeting consisted of the director, the staff member who purportedly told the third party of my remarks and me. The director asked me to conduct the meeting.

I thanked the staff member for attending. I wanted to clarify that everyone was on the same page and that if I had misrepresented something, I wanted to make clear what my intentions had been. The staff member nodded. I continued that I had not meant to say 'bla bla bla.' I had intended to say 'xyz.'

The staff member with a surprised expression, said, "But you did say 'xyz'."

I breathed a sigh of relief. I knew I couldn't trust myself completely. I knew the death drug was still in my system, but I had been trying to be really careful. The staff member repeated herself, "But you did say 'xyz'."

I thanked her. The director intervened and said, "But don't you see how the staff member thought you could have said 'bla bla bla'?"

And this is how it continued until 2007.

Our family in our home now consisted of my son, our seven-year-old golden retriever, our ten-year-old cat, and me. William and I were like two ships passing in the night. I left the house before he rose in the morning. This was the beginning of communicating by notes left on the kitchen counter. I would leave him a note in the morning as to what I forgot to tell him the evening before and he would leave one at night and tell me what he forgot to tell me. I always left money in the top drawer so that if I didn't make it home from work due to an evening meeting or too much work, he had money to buy dinner at the local deli. This was the beginning of his friends hanging out at our house all the time.

I spent the weekends in the yard during the fall. The yard had been neglected for the last three years and I loved being outside. Each Saturday, I filled the bird feeders and watched the sparrows fly from the forsythia branches to the bird feeders. When we sat outside in the twilight on the weekends, William and his friends kidded me that I was making the birds fat. On some occasions, we would see one bright red cardinal with a robust chest. I decided this cardinal was really my father. We had never had a cardinal visit us in our backyard before.

One Sunday in late October, I drove out in my usual routine to see my mother in the country. I left early so that I could see her for the morning, but be back in the afternoon to be with William. My cell phone rang and I searched in my bag for it. I heard the ex-director's voice. He wanted to know if my family would like to join him and his family for Thanksgiving. I hadn't considered Thanksgiving yet, probably because I was dreading it. I thanked him and said that would be great. I appreciated it. To some people we weren't contaminated and it was refreshing to be included. When I arrived at my mother's, I told her and she was delighted. We wouldn't have to sit around, looking at each other, being reminded of who was no longer here. I was grateful to him and his family. Everyone was invited, including my brother, Rebecca's boyfriend – everyone.

During the fall and winter, our home became the established haven for the lost boys. On the weekend nights, when I went to sleep, I asked them to keep the noise level down and they did. They played video games in William's room in the basement with the door closed. Our golden retriever played the nanny and kept them in check. In the morning, when I rose and walked downstairs, I knew who had spent the night by whose shoes were by the front door. I marveled at the different shapes and sizes. Sometimes it was only one pair of shoes, some mornings, it was several pairs.

Every Friday night after grocery shopping, these boys greeted me. They came to the back of the car and carried in the many, many bags of groceries. They put them on the kitchen counters, took out the food and asked where things went. They carried in the bottles of water, the large bags of dog food, the fifty-pound bags of salt for the water softener and put them where they should go. Afterwards, they sat around the kitchen table talking about Nerf gunfights and girls. There were two house rules: no one was allowed to go hungry and there was no violence. I no longer kept up with the friends I had before my husband died. I was too busy with work, and besides, these boys were my new friends.

My other new friend was my next door neighbor. She was eight, and my constant companion. She liked to play the drums in the garage when the band was taking a break. She helped me cook dinner for everyone on the weekends. She taught me how to make Rice Krispie treats from scratch, so I didn't have to buy the store-bought variety. It was a huge success with the boys.

During these months, William competed on the high school swim team and I tried to make each home team meet, after work. It was here that I saw people from my life when my husband was alive. It was here that I stood alone. One woman whose son had swum with my younger daughter talked to me, but the rest of the people gave me wide berth. This was fine with me, as I didn't know what to say to them either. I mostly talked with parents from the opposing team and noticed the glares from the parents on our team. William was usually on the third block, reserved for the fastest swimmer, as he still retained his speed for a high school team, even though he had taken a year off from swimming. Each time he climbed onto the block for his race, his buddies, maybe six or seven of them and his girlfriend all lined up by the glass railing separating the spectator seating from the pool deck and yelled, "GO" to him. He always turned towards them, smiling, and gave a thumbs up.

During one meet in which the score was touch and go and the opposing team was the arch nemesis, William took the block and his friends yelled their encouragement. It was necessary for him to win if our team were to tie. Then it would be up to the last relay to determine the winner. This was the 200 IM. On the first leg, the butterfly, my son swam several seconds behind the opposing team's top swimmer and the entire team started screaming for him to swim faster. When he flipped to do the backstroke, while his arms were pulling strongly and his legs kicking white water, he still lagged behind the opposing team's fastest swimmer. The parents on our team joined in yelling for him to swim faster.

I stood with my back against the wall in the overheated spectator area on the top row and smiled. I didn't need to yell. The breaststroke was next and sure enough, at the turn as he flipped off the wall and zoomed under the water, he executed the underwater pullout. He and his dad had worked for years on this. When he was young his dad instructed him that this was key. You could glide faster underwater and there was no rule as to how far you could glide underwater, unlike the backstroke. He made his son use every once of muscle in his thighs and calves to propel his body off the wall in a perfect streamline position. He made his son practice the pull technique with his arms until he had perfected it, and here tonight, his underwater pullout was performed to perfection. Many of the parents gasped because all the other swimmers were already on the surface of the water, swimming the breaststroke, but not the guy in lane three. When he emerged from under the water, he was a half body length ahead of the fastest opposing team member. Everyone screamed to go, but they really didn't have to. When he flipped on the wall to swim the freestyle to finish the race, I said quietly, "Come on, guy, bring it home" and he did. Everyone was jubilant. He climbed out of the pool and gave a broad smile with a thumbs up.

The medley relay was next and William swam the breaststroke. He repeated his stellar performance with his secret weapon, his underwater pullout.

When he was eight years old, I had asked him why he liked the breaststroke so much, why not the backstroke or freestyle. He had replied that he liked the way the water felt between his toes. I had loved his reasoning. After winning the meet, I suggested to his buddies that we all go out to dinner to celebrate. We went to a local favorite restaurant and the boys were boisterous and radiant. The amount of food they consumed amazed me. At home, the boys congregated in the den to watch TV and I sat down next to William's best friend. He had been quiet during dinner and I asked, "What's up?"

He replied, "I don't get them."

I asked, "Who?"

He muttered, "Girls."

I put my arm over his shoulder and said, "Don't worry. They don't get you either."

My son was still with his girlfriend from eighth grade, but his friend was having issues with a girl whom he wanted as his girlfriend. I thought *I'm glad I'm past this age of uncertainty with the opposite sex.*

SPRING 2005

When I had my time on late Sunday afternoons, I researched our impending Greek trip. Heather and I would take three weeks and she wanted to see a lot. She hadn't been back to Greece for seven years. The last time we went together was in 1998. She wanted to celebrate her eighteenth birthday on the island of Paros, but she wanted to visit Crete and many sites on the mainland as well. I had learned from our previous trips that if you did your research, you could create an affordable vacation and see the important as well as the remote sites. It was during one of these sacred afternoons that my mother called. I heard it in her voice and I remained still. She said, "I need you. I need you to come now."

I knew I would go, but I wanted to know why. It was late in the afternoon, almost time to start dinner. A condominium had come on the market today and she wanted to buy it and move there. The geriatric crowd in her town sought these out and she wanted my advice. I told her I would be there in an hour. I left my research and told William we would eat when I got home. He was with his buddies and didn't care. Driving the hour stretch, I thought *why does she want to move? She and my dad had searched and searched for the perfect retirement house. It was a one story ranch, wheelchair accessible, a beautiful private yard, and an oversized two-car garage. It had been perfect, and then it hit. Right. He's not there. The house is too big. She sits at night and is constantly reminded. She didn't gut her house. I visualize my home with the natural wood floors, earth colors and the warmth. I get it.*

She was waiting when I arrived, sitting on the bench next to her front door. She climbed in the car and directed me to a different section of town. When we pulled up, I saw a row of condominiums all looking like each other and I shuddered, but I didn't say anything. As the realtor opened the door, I realized this was going to be a horrendous move. This was a very small two-bedroom condominium. The basement in my mother's house was filled with my dad's tools, three work benches which he built, his DeWalt power saw, over eighty screwdrivers, a screw to fit any hole and every possible tool known to mankind. He could fix anything with his tools. We walked throughout the condominium and I could tell my mother was more than interested in securing it. When we finished, she told the realtor she would call tomorrow with an offer and that's exactly what she did. She would move during the summer.

<hr />

May 2005: Athens, Greece. Heather and I successfully landed. We were breathing the rich, toxic fumes of the motos buzzing throughout the center square of Athens as we checked into the hotel. We threw our bags into the room and went immediately to explore what was new and what had remained the same. I could navigate this city blind. I had studied her topography for years at Berkeley and had walked her streets endlessly. We meandered up the hill towards the Plaka and gazed up to the imposing rock with the north side of Athena's temple towering majestically towards the sky. No other word but breathtaking, in the truest sense of the word, could describe our view. We both stopped walking, stood and stared.

Out of my mouth, the words flowed, "Who are you, Athena, goddess of wisdom?"

Athena represented the transformation from the mysteries of the female earth powers to the male dominated sky god, Zeus.

I thought *try to imagine the power she wielded over her people in order for them to create such an incredible temple. What did they feel in their hearts towards her? I want to know her. I want to know her secrets.*

We told ourselves that we would visit her tomorrow, but this afternoon, being jet lagged, we walked the Plaka streets. As evening descended, we sat at an outdoor taverna, eating our dinner, watching the Athenians perform the evening promenade. We sat and watched the Greek families, the mothers, fathers and their various children clamber up the Plaka streets as if they had somewhere important to go. But each time I had watched their promenade, I could never exactly figure out their destination. The promenade itself was what was important to them. The warm spring evening air with the local wine was a soothing tonic as we headed back towards the hotel. We would explore the Acropolis, the Agora and Keramikos tomorrow before heading up to Delphi the following day.

Early next morning, we walked through the flea market on the way to the Keramikos, the ancient cemetery located beyond the city walls that once encircled Athens. Being out of the main tourist route and so early in the morning, we had the entire site to ourselves. As we left the small museum, we strolled down the long dusty path and gazed at the enormity of the graves commemorating the various people. Huge marble slabs depicted in bas-relief the deceased waving goodbye to their relations. All seemed to have a look of serenity on their faces and then I thought *of the grave stele in the Metropolitan Museum, showing a small girl, maybe ten years old. I had been so spellbound by her when I saw her after the Met had opened the New Greek Galleries, I had bought a poster of her, had it framed and hung it in our bedroom. This young girl, wearing a long robe that rested on her toes, was holding two doves, one in each hand. She nestled her left hand, gently holding a dove next to her breast while her head tilted toward the bird's head, about to kiss its beak. Her right hand with the second dove was slightly in front of the first. I always wondered which dove she would miss the most, but her overwhelming countenance reflected serenity, a tranquility that transcended time. It wasn't as though she embellished or was resigned to death, but she gave an impression of an acceptance filled with an unusual understanding and peace. And her doves emitted the same aura. They were not agitated. They wanted to stay close to her heart if only for a moment longer. Unlike the grave markers we are seeing now, she stood alone, without any mother or father or siblings. Alone with her two doves, she exuded an internal calmness.*

The evening before we left for Delphi, as we were preparing for bed, the phone rang. We both looked at each other terrified. I thought *no, nothing can spoil our trip. Maybe we shouldn't answer it. Maybe it's a wrong number. Don't answer it.* Then reality hit and I picked up the phone. It was our rental car agency. They had left our car in the garage down a side street with the key atop the right front wheel. This was Friday night. They didn't want to get up in the morning at eight to bring us the car. They had left it tonight so they could party. The paperwork was in the glove compartment. I sighed with relief and thought *relax just a little more. Bring it down a notch.*

The next morning, we found the car and the key and I handed Heather the map. We had asked the gentleman at the hotel desk how to get out of Athens, but he told us that Greeks don't know the names of their roads. He made some lines on a piece of paper to illustrate how to get onto the National Road. I told Heather to translate his lines onto the map and tell me where to drive. She looked at me as if I had nine heads, but I knew she was up for the task. We were lucky as it was Sunday morning and there was little traffic in downtown Athens. My daughter skillfully navigated through Athens until we saw the National Road, but then she instructed me to take a right. As soon as I turned right, I knew that this was the same mistake I had made before on a previous trip. I pulled the car off to the side ramp. I told her we needed to continue on the same road for another kilometer and she agreed after scrutinizing the lines and the map.

I tried to shift into reverse. The gearshift wouldn't budge. No matter which way I tried, the gear would not shift into reverse. I could shift it into first, second, third, fourth, but for the life of me, it would not shift into reverse. Heather said that this was a defective Greek car and that we should take it back. I stared at her as if she now had grown nine heads. I opened the glove compartment and found the owner's manual. It was in Greek and I neither read nor spoke the language, but this was when I developed a new appreciation for pictures. I looked at each page and came to the one with the picture of the gearshift and I saw a ring at the bottom of the rod. I looked at our car's shift and saw the ring. I pulled it up and then it shifted easily into reverse. We gave each other a high five and reversed the car ever so cautiously back onto the road and proceeded.

The drive to Delphi was long, but spectacular, climbing slowly up eighteen hundred feet into the mountains. We rolled down the windows to smell the wildflowers and to allow the morning sun to warm us. Once we arrived in the small town, both the navigator and I became turned around. We were trying to locate our hotel, but we drove around the town in circles. I pointed out to my daughter an elderly Greek woman sitting on her doorstep with worry beads. I had only seen men with worry beads before. This was my first time seeing a woman holding them. The fourth time we saw her, I waved and said "Yassas."

I said, "This woman probably thinks we are completely nuts."

Heather replied, "And she would be right."

After five complete circles through the town, I saw a small sign on a rock wall with our hotel's name on it and an arrow. I drove in its direction up a long hill and we finally located our hotel. Upon checking in, the gentleman behind the desk realized somehow that we had stayed here before. He greeted us by saying "Welcome Home."

This felt right to both of us as we both remembered it vividly from our previous trips. We left the car behind and walked into town to explore. We would rise early tomorrow morning to see the archeological site before the tourist buses with the gawky tourists arrived. Delphi was a small town with many tourist shops, hotels and small tavernas, located on the southwestern spur of Mount Parnassus in the valley of Phocis.

As we walked down the main road, we looked into the different gift shops, but didn't go in. We came across a building with huge glass windows that didn't blend in with the rest of the shops. We peered inside and saw that it was a small museum documenting the archeological excavations of the site over the past one hundred and fifty years. Intrigued, we opened the glass door and entered. A gentleman was sitting behind a metal desk and we introduced ourselves. Heather admitted to him that we had been here before three times, but something kept pulling us back.

He replied, "Delphi is the navel of the universe."

We smiled, knowing this to be true. It was here that the two eagles landed. The two eagles, which Zeus sent in opposite directions to find the center of the universe. It was here that the oracle foretold of man's future with its ambiguous responses. I scanned the room and saw a map entitled, 'The Transfiguration of the Hellenic Cosmos' depicting in triangles the distances from other sacred sites to Delphi, indicating that Delphi was the center. I stepped closer to the map, inspecting the various locations, such as Pylos and their distances from Delphi.

The gentleman inquired, "Would you like it?"

I turned around and looked at him with surprise.

"I only have this copy and it is in Greek. You may not understand it," he apologized.

Pointing to the various sizes and shapes of the triangles, I said, "But math and geometry transcend all languages. Math is its own universal language. I love this."

He walked over to the wall and removed the thumbtacks that secured it, rolled it up and put a rubber band around it. He handed it to me. I began to ask how much and he replied, "It is a gift. You should feel like you're home."

I smiled and thanked him and we headed back to the street.

The next morning, we dressed warmly and arrived at the archeological site when it opened at eight-thirty. We parked the car on the main road and leaned back looking up to Mount Parnassus, which ascends seven thousand feet into the sky. We saw several remaining Doric columns of Apollo's temple thrusting upwards on a small plateau and then upward, the orchestra carved into the mountain and further; we saw the retaining wall of the stadium. Breathing the thin mountain air, we stared at its formidable peak and then turned around and gazed to the valley below where Athena's temples from various ages were located as well as the gymnasium. I pointed to a small band in the distance and reminded my daughter that was the road we were on yesterday.

Turning around again, I stared at the earth's majestic creation. I said, "I remember reading in college that wherever the symbols of the old chthonic goddess of the earth are most remote and most difficult to travel to, where she seems to open up her interior secrets, that is where the Greeks built the temple to the young god, Apollo."

I pointed to some caves above the stadium. "The earth goddess was worshipped there since 4000 B.C. It wasn't until the 8th century B.C., when Apollo slew the goddess's guardian python that Apollo gained power. As we climbed, I calculated that Gaia was worshiped here for about seven hundred years and Apollo less than four hundred years. Entering, we strolled past the treasuries and the statues commemorating a village's thankful contribution to the oracle. Each village or polis outperformed the other by contributing a more beautiful offering. The various offerings became overwhelming and I thought *this is the same concept as in America. Each neighbor wants to be better than the other. This is just the ancient Greek way.*

As we passed the small but beautiful Athenian treasury, we spied the conical white rock, which symbolized the omphalos or navel of the universe. It was an unpretentious rock rising only about two feet. We stood next to it and again our eyes were diverted to the peak of Mount Parnassus. Hiking the inclined path, we arrived at Apollo's temple whose axis orients with the midsummer sunrise and the midwinter sunset and we marveled at the mathematical exactitude. Gazing at the limestone columns, I explained, "It was in the vestibule where Apollo's famous saying was inscribed: 'Know thyself.' Apollo, the complex god of light, sun, and the arts was the god to whom Zeus gave the gift of prophecy, which had come from the earth. He symbolized the rational, the civilized values."

"Remember his other motto?" I nudged her.

Heather quickly replied, "Yes, 'Nothing in excess'."

"Bravo! People traveled far and wide to receive answers from the oracle in Apollo's temple. Here, the priestess sat on a tripod over a fissure in the earth, inhaling the gas emitted from two fault lines, which lay under the temple. She became intoxicated by the fumes and uttered words. Then priests translated what the priestess had said and rendered the oracular answer."

Then it hit me. I touched her arm and exclaimed, "What an irony! Apollo thinks he's taken over the site, but yet it is still a priestess who hears or feels the oracle from the earth."

She glanced towards me and said, "Yeah, but the priest interprets it."

In a nanosecond, I shot back, "But the priest doesn't have the ability to communicate with the earth. Only the priestess has the ability. It is the woman to whom Gaia, the mother earth goddess, speaks."

"Wow, you're right. Woman to woman. I wonder what the priestess really thought after she muttered her words. I wonder what she felt? Have you ever read up on that?" she inquired.

"No, but you know I will, now that the question has been asked," I said continuing to gaze.

We trekked to the stadium in silence.

We were alone save one photographer. We noticed him taking a picture of us as we sat down and drank from our water bottles.

Heather asked, "How high up do you think we are?"

I smiled and thought *she is her grandmother's grandchild. Both of them like their numbers. Math makes them feel safe.* I pointed to the stadium and told her it was about six hundred feet above where we parked. She continued, "How cold do you think it becomes in the winter if we're about twenty-four hundred feet in elevation?"

I said, "It gets cold. That's why Apollo left every winter. It was too cold. Dionysos took over for the three coldest months. His was the way of the raw, wild passion. He was the mysterious god behind his mask who radiated raw, sexual energy. He was the breaker of boundaries who liberated his followers through wine, dancing, and unrestricted sex to the realm of sacred ecstasy. Moving between earth, sky and the underworld, he was linked with crops, the harvest, the changing season, life's changes. I always remember him on the vases, wearing his flowing robe, his long hair cascading down his back, yet his symbol, the phallus, was seen as a weapon and fertility. I think he combines both male and female qualities."

She asked, "Why would Apollo put up with such a guy on his awesome site?"

I responded, "I think both Apollo and Dionysos offer what is necessary in order to live a rich, full life."

She looked slowly at me and said, "Tell me more."

"Reason, moderation, music and poetry are essential ingredients to a person's life, but so is the passion. The unrestricted sexual freedom, the knowledge that things change, not only in seasons, but in a person's life, things change and this is to be embraced. When your sister and I were visiting Iria on Naxos, the caretaker said that it was the liberation from the routine, mundane tasks that Dionysos evoked. The dance between both of them is difficult. The balance between rational moderation and passionate liberation from the routine is the hard part. Balance is essential. So, what they're telling us is to combine our lives with three-fourths of Apollo and one-fourth of Dionysos. Live in the ratio of seventy-five percent knowing yourself, being true to yourself, living with reason and moderation, healing your soul with music, poetry, but then in that sacred twenty-five percent, lose yourself to your unbridled passion and in doing so, find yourself. Make any sense?" I asked.

She smiled. "I get it."

I took her hand and we hiked around the stadium. I asked, "Do you want to run the length of it?"

She replied, "I am no longer nine years old and besides this is not Olympia."

I smiled and was glad that she remembered running the Olympic stadium with her brother and sister as her father took pictures of them.

The sky turned gray and it began to drizzle as we made our way down the mountain, past the road, to where Athena resided in the small valley below. We found the foundation of Athena's first temple built in the seventh century B.C. of porous limestone and just a few feet away, spied her modern temple built in the fifth century B.C. Standing under an olive tree to escape the rain, we looked at the two foundations and discussed the transfer of power from the earth goddess to Apollo and how Athena fit into the equation. We figured she embodied this transfer by both her energies being invoked as a mother nature goddess outside the polis, while in the polis she made man civilized. Man received through her wisdom the ability to establish ethics and thus, laws by which to live.

It was well into the afternoon and our stomachs growled. We headed back into town in search for some comfort food. As I climbed into the driver's seat, my daughter bent down to look at the ground. I rolled down the passenger window and told her to get in. I was starving. She pointed to the ground and said, "The ants are huge. I have never seen such large ants. What kind are they?"

I quickly replied that I didn't know. We would figure it out later, but she was mesmerized by their size. Impatiently, I turned the key and started the engine. She climbed in and insisted that I should get out and look at them. I told her to name them and she did: the Delphi Ants.

We continued our trek over the bay of Corinth on the new suspension bridge and wound our way down to Pylos to see Nestor's palace. Heather wished to see Nestor's wife most beautiful bathtub painted with frescos equipped with a footstool. Nestor was the eldest and wisest of the Greeks who fought at Troy. The wind through the pine trees cooled us as we entered his sweeping site with its spectacular view to the bay. An inner calmness overtook me, as I slowly understood that only a kind man could have created this palace. We marveled at the throne room and the large storage rooms, which had held numerous containers of olive oil that catapulted the fire, destroying the palace. Upon slowly meandering back to the car, my daughter was taken again with the ants. These ants were a fraction of the size they were in Delphi. I took her hand in mine and lead her back to the car, shaking my head.

Instead of staying in Pylos as we had planned, Heather wanted to drive the three hour stretch to Nafplio, one of her favorite villages in Greece. She, the navigator, took us through the middle of the Peloponnesos, a route neither of us had been on before. The drive through the afternoon sun and the verdant greenery, the smell of the wildflowers was soothing.

She spoke of her first year of college and her unknown future. She didn't know what to major in. I reassured her not to worry, to take a variety of courses. She would find her way. I continued that a liberal arts college degree was not a vocation and that she should follow her heart. She was smart enough to learn anything after college in order to secure employment.

I spoke about my unknown future and how I wanted to leave my job as soon as William graduated from college. I didn't know exactly what I would do. Heather softly mentioned that she drove the hour from her college to her father's grave at least once a month and talked to him. I glanced at her, surprised. I never knew this.

She quietly said, "I sit by myself next to his grave marker in the afternoon sun and draw. Sometimes, I bring my paints. Sometimes, I bring my pastels. My fingers decide what to draw. Sometimes, it's a landscape of the sloping hills overlooking the Pacific. Sometimes, it's a portrait of how I remember his face when I was young. One time, I drew his grave marker. You know, he really likes what's written on his grave marker."

I smiled as I continued to drive. I thought *I don't need to see his grave marker to remember him. Then the memory. A dinner conversation one Sunday afternoon after church, when I was in middle school. My parents, brother and I sat around the dining room table and for some reason we were talking about death.*

My father said he didn't want a grave marker. He wanted to be cremated. My brother was concerned and said that he wanted to have a physical location to see him by which to remember him. I didn't think much of the conversation then, but now, yes. I get it. I'm in sync with my father. I don't need, no, I don't want, to look at my husband's grave marker. He's not there. He's flown. But this is important for Heather and I am glad the special words on his grave marker: 'Lover of Knowledge' came to me in that split second. He may not have always been a lover of me, but he was an authentic and genuine lover of knowledge. This was his truth. And I am glad my daughter visits her dad's grave. It must give her comfort and I know he's appreciative. My dad's ashes? What about them? They're in a rectangular box in the bottom drawer of my dresser in my bedroom. Okay, yes. Someday, when my mother joins him, they'll sail into the wind together, somewhere in the Aegean. And how are you going to pull this off? I don't know. No clue, but they both loved the Aegean and they both loved sailing.

She broke our silence, "We need to bring our lives down a notch. Our adrenalin needs to subside. It's been two years since he died. My blood is not on fire the way it was, but it still percolates. It does not flow smoothly. How about yours?"

I nodded. "I know. The death drug still swirls, still creates havoc. Just when you think you're doing okay, it rises from nowhere."

We pulled into the large hotel parking area outside the village of Nafplio just down the road from Tiryns. We entered the hotel and felt as though we were walking back in time to the refined Victorian age. Marble floors, huge vases with beautiful wildflowers, the spacious lobby, the comfortable bar off the lobby and the library rich in the history of ancient and modern Greece were magnificent. We rode the elevator to our room and opened the shutters to the balcony and gazed out to the bay. I imagined Agamemnon's ships sailing from Troy with his Achaean heroes. I felt as though I had entered another time, another world, and I liked it very much.

The next day, we toured Tiryns, a huge colossal fortification that felt and looked like a huge ship gone aground. The site dated back to the Neolithic period, but was famous for its Mycenaean palace built in the fourteenth and thirteenth century B.C. Legend had it that the Bellyhanders, a family of the Cyclops, built these massive walls that were between four and seven meters thick. These walls caused much admiration and were considered built by supernatural beings– no human force could have constructed these walls. Both of us agreed as we surveyed the formidable entrance. When we ascended to the megaron, the throne room, and viewed the base of the throne, Heather was again looking at the ground. I reminded her that we needed to hurry up and drive to Athens to catch our flight to Paros. But she was scrutinizing the ants. I walked over to her and looked down. The ants had a greenish color to them. She said that maybe she would get her Ph.D. in Greek ants. I thought *that's it. I've helped to create the most abnormal children on the face of this planet.*

Once on Paros, we found our small hotel situated by a small cove and introduced ourselves to the dogs on the beach. We named them, Mamma, Pappa, and Junior. Junior had a friend who was a smaller yellow dog. We fed them at breakfast and afterwards threw sticks on the beach for them. Heather brought her father's camera and spent hours taking pictures of her new friends and when she was finished with them, she turned the camera towards the sea and took beautiful pictures of the vastness of the Aegean.

We celebrated her eighteenth birthday on this island, but on that day, neither of us could rise out of our funk. We drove the perimeter of the island and spied a sandy beach on the south side with clear waters and clearer skies. We lay on the beach, listening to the waves, but barely spoke. We reminded one another who was missing. Later we drove into town for an early dinner. We selected an outside small taverna and enjoyed the souvlaki in silence.

The last leg of the trip would be on Crete in a town just east of Agios Nickolaos, not far from where my other daughter and I stayed three years ago. We took the high-speed ferry from Paros to Heraklion, the main port of Crete, and arrived after nightfall. Heather hailed a taxi to drive us the forty-five minute stretch. The evening light had become pitch dark by the time we found our hotel. The driver drove up a long hill and I saw our hotel's name, but every window was dark. He took our bags out of the trunk and we climbed out. He told us that he would not leave us here until we found the owner. I had no idea what we would do if we didn't find the proprietor.

Standing there dazed, Heather grabbed my bag and retrieved the cell phone. She scrutinized the carefully compiled itinerary and called the owner's number. Sure enough, he answered. He was at a taverna down the road and would be right there. He had assumed we would arrive tomorrow since it was so late. We waited for a while and eventually saw a dark Mercedes sedan drive up the hill. I tipped our wonderful taxi driver who had stayed with us and thanked him. The owner introduced himself and immediately hauled our bags up a flight of stairs to our room. The overhead light bulb had burnt out and he went to fetch a new one.

Upon returning, he looked at me and then to Heather and then back to me. He looked directly into my eyes and asked, "Where is your husband?"

I felt as though someone had just thrown a glass of cold water in my face. I thought *you are on a need-to-know basis. You don't need to know if he's dead or alive. I'm tired of having to explain that yes, I have children, but no husband. I'm me. That's it. What you see is what you get. Me. That's all you need to know.* Heather looked at me as if I had grown nine heads, but I couldn't answer his question. My mouth wouldn't open.

Heather replied calmly, "My dad passed away two years ago."

He looked at her and nodded and then climbed on a chair and unscrewed the dead light bulb and screwed in the new one. He asked if we were hungry. He wanted to take us to the taverna he had just come from. Another group of guests from the hotel were there. They were in the middle of their dinner when we had arrived. We agreed and piled into his sleek Mercedes and wound down the coastline in the darkness of the night. When we arrived, there was another woman and her daughter about the same age as my daughter, but there was no man with them. I sat down and wondered if the hotel owner had asked her where her husband was. He ordered more food and the table was completely full of an assortment of every Greek dish imaginable. When we returned to the hotel, it was way past two in the morning. We caved into our beds.

The following few days were spent touring the eastern section of Crete. We drove up to the Laisthi plain in search for the cave where Zeus, the mightiest of the Olympians grew up. It was a chilly, overcast May day as we drove the plain. The rain began a steady rhythm and the air grew cold. When we arrived at the cave, there were two tour buses parked in the parking lot with many German tourists milling around. They had just finished the tour of the cave.

I didn't like caves. They were slippery and had weird stuff growing on their walls. I didn't like the way caves smelled, but I reminded myself that this way my daughter's trip. Heather took the lead and entered the cave. She said, "Why do guys have such issues with their fathers? I mean in order for Zeus to live, he had to grow up here because his dad would have eaten him, thinking his son was going to overthrow him. Was it just his mother who saved him by giving her husband a blanket full of rocks, thinking it was his son?

"No, I think her mother, Gaia, helped Zeus's mother hide him in this cave," I answered as I shuddered, walking along the narrow, circular carved path on the side of the cave. "I can't imagine growing up here, can you?"

My daughter, watching her feet as her flip-flops scooted along the slippery stone, said, "Yeah, it wouldn't be bad. Nice and cool in the summer. Look below at the stalagmites. How cool is that?"

I grabbed her waistband. If she slipped, I might have a fighting chance of saving her. My adrenalin kicked in and I felt my heart racing. I replied, "Very cool. Have you seen enough?"

"No, come on. You like Gaia, the mother earth. She's protecting us. She wouldn't let Zeus grow up in a dangerous place. We're fine. Just one more level."

I reluctantly followed her while the cool darkness gave my entire body goose bumps. I thought *of the bronze votive plaque my husband had pointed out to me in the Heraklion museum when we saw the Phaistos disc. It had been found in this cave. The plaque was incised with a religious scene showing the sacred tree, a bird, a fish, the sun disk and a half moon. The whole scene had been interpreted as depicting the basic elements of cosmogony. My husband had said it symbolized the divine epiphany to him. It was beautiful and simple. But, why would someone come way down here to offer the gifts to the gods?*

Heather, as if reading my thoughts, said, "Caves are safe, mom. Relax. They're like a special room hidden in the earth. It's nature's way of hiding you from her violent elements. It's not raining in here like it is outside. We're dry and warm."

I thought *she is right. We are protected here. The mother earth is protecting us. Listen to your daughter more. She's on the mark.*

After descending to the lower strata of the upper cave and looking into the bottomless abyss, Heather had seen enough. We made our ascent slowly and silently watching the sunlight as it became brighter and brighter. When we exited the cave, we rubbed our eyes, adjusting to the bright Aegean sun in the misty rain. We made our way over to our small car and drove back to the northern coast, stopping along the way to buy honey from a sweet Greek lady on the side of the road.

We ended up at a small village on the coast with one taverna and one small supermarket. The taverna was on the beach and we sat down in the warm sun, looking out to the Aegean. We ordered wine, a Greek salad and saganaki and ate leisurely, enjoying the fact that we hadn't plummeted to our deaths in the slimy cave.

Heather pointed and said, "Maybe that's your sign."

I looked up. A realtor sign advertising several homes for sale on the north side stood on the taverna's roof.

"You've always wanted to move to Crete," she said. "Maybe you should write these down."

She and I had become firm believers in signs during the past two years. My signs continued to be bird feathers. Whenever I saw one, I stopped and said thank you, knowing I was going in the right direction. I smiled at her and replied, "Maybe."

She was right. I loved Crete. I felt home here. There was something about the island. While I loved all the land in Greece, somehow, I liked the ruggedness of her islands in a different way. I looked out to the sea, but didn't see any seagulls and I scanned the beach. I told her that there were no bird feathers, here. She smiled and told me that I should continue to look. The wine, the sun, my satiated stomach relaxed my body. It was ready for a welcome siesta. We headed for the car to drive back to the hotel.

The last evening on Crete, we decided to eat dinner late in town. Returning to our hotel, Heather took her pastels from her bag and began to draw the cove our balcony overlooked and beyond to the Ha Canyon. She sat, drawing, as twilight faded into the evening sky. I had finished the two novels that I brought. I rummaged through my backpack for more reading material. I found one of my husband's journals that I had discovered when cleaning out his desk. I remembered packing it. Picking it up, I thought *maybe the distance from Greece to the States is going to give me the strength and perspective to read it. Should I really read it? Why not? Because this isn't right. It was his. These were his private thoughts. Maybe they weren't his private thoughts. Maybe they were just his thoughts.* I held his faded green journal in my hands. I put it on my bed. I poured a glass of white wine and returned to the bed. I sat down next to his journal and ran my hand over its cover. Putting my glass of wine on the nightstand, I picked it up and opened to the first page. His entries were before we had children, back twenty years ago. I tried to remember what we as a couple were like twenty years ago. I turned the page and barely breathed.

September 28, 1984

A follow up to our conversation on the beach
at Itea. Something bothered me after I finished
explaining to my wife my understanding of
Plato in his Phaedrus. I knew my understanding
was not complete, but now reading Burkert, he
elucidates far better than me and it is so true.

The Greek Mathematical Astronomy: The
cosmos obeys unchangeable intelligible laws
that are mathematically formulated. Two
conclusions result: the cosmos is eternal since
in the many centuries of observation no change
has been discerned, nor does the mathematical
admit change. The old cosmogonic hypotheses
that the cosmos had risen at some time and
is open to decay in the future must be false.
Second: mathematically exact movements are
rational, thus the cosmos is rational. It has a
moving mind. The soul now receives a cosmic
status. The movement of the cosmos must be of
a psychic nature.

Plato in the Laws repeatedly emphasizes this
important turn in the history of philosophy.

It is no longer possible that any single mortal
man will be god-fearing for long if he has
not grasped these two principles mentioned;
that the soul is the oldest of everything which
participates in coming-to-be (and that it is
immortal, and that it rules over all bodies),
and moreover (secondly) he must grasp, as has
now been said many times, the intelligence
of being which is in the stars, as mentioned,
and in addition also the necessary preliminary
mathematical sciences. Astronomy becomes the
foundation of religion.

Stunned and shaken, I threw the journal down on the bed. I thought *he never said a word about this to me. This should have been our continued conversation from the beach at Itea. Why didn't you want to continue the conversation when we returned, when you had read Burkert? You knew I would have been interested. You never brought the topic up again. Why? Did we just get too caught up with our routines? Was it easier for you to sit in your office and read and write what you thought was important rather than to engage me? I would have loved to continue the conversation. Was it that I appeared too busy with my work? Was I too remote? Was I sleeping while you stayed up in the wee hours of the morning? I want to talk to you. I want to talk to you now. This isn't fair. I want to know why. You left without an explanation. You left me not knowing. I want to know why. Twenty years ago, you didn't continue our conversation. How many other conversations didn't you continue? Do I dare continue to read your journal? No, this is enough for now. I can't. Maybe sometime later.* I rose and walked out to the balcony and gazed across the bay to the Ha Canyon. A feeling of sadness, not anguish, not soul pain, but a depth of sadness I had never known crept throughout my body. I didn't share this with Heather. She was continuing to draw. I watched the ascent of the full moon. I thought *I first came to Greece with my husband, then with my parents, then with our entire extended family, then with William, then with Rebecca, and now with Heather. The next time I come, I will come alone. I will come alone and have the courage to read the rest of his journal.* I told my daughter I was going to take a walk. I would be back in a while and then we should get ready for dinner.

SUMMER – FALL
2005

My mother was moving from the house that she and my father had lived in for the past twenty-five years. I couldn't take off any more time from work, so Heather and her good friend since fifth grade went out to help. Her friend was a strapping 6'6" man made of muscle, a kind heart and sharp wit. I had unofficially adopted him since meeting him when he was ten years old. Because I was so indebted to them, I told them I would fly them to London for a vacation when they had finished this horrendous move. Every day for three weeks, they drove the hour out to the country to decide what to pitch, how to pitch it, where it to pitch it and then slowly began to box things up.

One Sunday morning when the move was actually finished after three weeks of enduring work, I drove out to visit my mother in her new condominium. When I walked in, she was sitting in the den in her reading chair. She looked sad. I told her how wonderful her new home was and that she should be very happy. She didn't respond and I asked, "What is the matter?"

She replied, "I can't find him here."

Rebecca began her junior year at college in the city. We still didn't see her. She was with her boyfriend now twenty-four hours a day and stayed mostly in the city or at his beach apartment. People in town asked me how she was and I thought *my oldest daughter– do I have one?* Heather, after her trip to London, had returned to California to embark on her second year of college. William entered his junior year at the high school with an attitude.

He decided to return to the swim team where he began his swimming career at age five. The head coach whom my husband had known and admired would coach him. This was a complete circle. But I was happy he would be swimming again. Not only would it help keep him out of trouble, but this was his time to shine, being a junior. He had worked hard and was a talented swimmer. I understood that the little life I had to myself would be forfeited for the next two years because swim meets all over the northeast states would consume that time. I continued to leave money in the drawer as I rarely saw William during the week. Some nights, he came home as I was going to bed. But on the weekends, he and his buddies played their music in our garage and lived in the basement.

———••———

WINTER – SPRING
2005 – 2006

It really started back in 2005, but I did my best to ignore it, hoping it would go away. But by March 2006, I knew I had to take care of myself. Each month, my menses did not become unpredictable the way they should in a woman who is entering the stage of perimenopause. They became torrents of blood, copiously flowing, zapping my strength, and depleting my iron reserves. I swallowed vitamin pills and ate more spinach than Popeye did in all his cartoon episodes. It was March 23rd when I knew I faced a serious situation.

I was driving to pick up William after swim practice and I stopped at the liquor store to buy a bottle of Merlot. When I pulled into the parking lot and opened the car door, I was horrified. In the dark night, illuminated by the overhead van lights, lay a pool of red blood about an eighth of an inch deep on the floor mat. My eyes looked down to my lap and it was the same. My head felt light and I held on to the steering wheel. I breathed in slowly, but my heart was racing.

I fumbled in my bag for my cell phone and when my trembling hands found it, I called William's assistant swim coach. I knew he would still be coaching swim practice and be on the pool deck, but I also knew that he would answer when he saw it was my number. He was one of William's solid guardian angels and he knew I was eternally grateful to him. He answered and I asked him if he could drive my son home tonight. In keeping with his status, he replied, "Of course." He didn't ask why.

I drove home. I entered the front door and climbed the stairs slowly, feeling faint and queasy, and stepped into the shower. After changing into loose fitting clothes, I lay down on my bed and called my gynecologist. I listened to her voicemail instructing me to call another number if this were a true emergency. I hung up. I thought *what is a true emergency? Is this one? What is the definition of a true emergency? I don't know. Why doesn't the voicemail give examples of what is an emergency? Am I bleeding to death? No. You are going to be fine. Call in the morning. You will be fine. Breathe deeply.* I didn't call the second number.

The following morning, I tried to get out of bed, but the room kept spinning and I lay back down again. I called the director's line and left voicemail that I wouldn't be in today due to illness. I dozed on and off until eight in the morning when I called the gynecologist. The secretary answered. She knew me well and I told her my situation. She patched me immediately through to the gynecologist. After repeating the particulars to her, she instructed me to come in to the office immediately, but not to drive myself. She assumed my hematocrit was dangerously low which meant I could easily pass out while driving. I said I would. I slowly, slowly rose and holding anything in sight to steady myself, made my way downstairs. William was in the kitchen, making breakfast and I asked him if he would drive me into the city. Being a junior in high school, he was happy to forego his classes and we both went to dress.

As we parked the car in the all-too-familiar medical center's parking garage, he put his arm around my waist to help me walk up the hill. At the gynecologist's office, she saw me immediately. After the examination, I sat in front of her desk and we discussed the situation. She was a woman, perhaps a little older than me, with a genuine heart and a head full of intelligence and wisdom. She told me that massive fibroids had grown throughout my uterus and that the largest one was sitting atop my cervix causing my torrent. In order to resolve the condition, a hysterectomy should be performed, but that would send my body into immediate menopause. I should consider estrogen therapy to ease the symptoms.

I inquired if it was only the uterus causing the problem, then couldn't only it be removed, leaving the ovaries and their waning estrogen and fallopian tubes. In this way, menopause could proceed in its natural way. I was not keen to intervene in a natural process that might or might not have its challenges. I remembered my mother telling me that she and her mother had no problem with "the change" as she called it. It was, in fact, a liberating experience. I liked the concept of liberation, of not having to think on a monthly basis. I had no husband and even if I did, I would never want to have any more children. Reading glasses were more important to me than a uterus. I thought *I want to move on in life. What do you want to move on to? I don't know. Possibilities. I want all my possibilities. I want possibilities I don't even know about. I want them. Then, I'll figure out what I want to move on to. Maybe. Maybe I will. Maybe I won't.*

My gynecologist interrupted me by saying this was a good idea, of allowing Mother Nature to proceed on course. We then discussed the different ways the uterus could be removed. The most common method was to extract the uterus through the vagina, but in doing so, the cervix would be removed as well. She saw the shock on my face. A cervix, my cervix, could yield enormous pleasure during lovemaking. I asked her for other options. The only other option was more invasive. It involved an incision about four inches below the navel though which the uterus was extracted. The recovery was more painful and longer, but I kept thinking of my cervix.

I thought *back to the day when the woman who slammed her hand on the table, after my husband died had said it would be years before a widow could enjoy life's satisfactions again. This is one of life's satisfactions. I want to enjoy this life's satisfaction again with passion. Yes, twenty-five percent Dionysos's unbridled passion. I want this. To lose myself, to be liberated from my mundane routine of life through his frenzied madness. Yes.*

I told her that I preferred to have my uterus surgically removed. She agreed full-heartedly, understanding without words my motivation. She forbade me from working until the surgery was performed as physical movement could dislodge the large fibroid sitting on my cervix. Surgery would be scheduled in the next two weeks as the operating room schedule dictated. Recovery would take about eight weeks and I should take everything very slowly, paying close attention to a nutritious diet. I thanked her and she said her secretary would call me with the surgery date.

As William drove me home, I thought *I am not yet fifty. I have the rest of my life before me. I have no idea of what it will look like. It's a mystery. I will be a woman, a woman without a husband, a woman without a husband and without a uterus, but still very much a woman. My uterus does not define me as a woman and neither does my husband or lack thereof. I'm me. What will the rest of my life look like? No clue. But I will have possibilities.* William asked me how I was feeling as we drove and I said, "Eh."

He continued, "I've qualified for the National Swim Meet in Fort Lauderdale, Florida in two weeks. I qualified in four events: 200 IM, 100 yard Breast, 100 yard Back and 400 IM. After that, my friend's parents invited me on their Mexican vacation during spring break. This is maybe right after your surgery. Maybe I shouldn't go."

"Don't be ridiculous. Go. This isn't worrisome. I'll be fine. I'm just sorry I can't come to Florida and watch you."

For the next two weeks, I stayed on the couch or in bed until the day of surgery. I had to be at the hospital at five-thirty in the morning and I remembered back to my husband's surgery when he had to be there at the same time. This time, I would drive solo.

I rose at four to take a shower, went into the bathroom and turned on the light switch. On the mirror above the sink was a note from William. I took it down and slowly read it. The stationery had my dad's letterhead on the top of it with his name and address.

> *Mom,*
>
> *I know the stationary might have thrown you off, but this is your son. I'm saying hello and I hope you had a great night's sleep. I'm one hundred percent sure that your surgery will be a huge success and you'll be the best patient ever. I had a lot of fun tonight with you and my girlfriend. I'm also really glad we have been getting along better and we are hanging out more. I forgot how*

much fun you are! Anyways, I'm lazy and forgot to do
my college testing stuff. But with you going in for surgery
tomorrow, it really puts life in perspective. Qualifying
for the National Swim Meet isn't a big deal to me. You
are though. And everything that is meant to be will be.
Any mom even with a uterus cannot compare to you!

I love you so much.

Your son

I smiled and tucked this into my journal that lay on the
bathroom shelf and climbed into the shower.

Upon entering the pre-surgical area of the hospital, I was
instructed to change into a hospital gown and to remove all
jewelry. I went into the changing room and followed the orders.
Sitting, waiting in the cubicle for surgery, the nurse entered to
take my vital signs. She frowned and scolded me that all jewelry
must be removed. She pointed, and my hand instinctively
fingered my neck. I had not removed my necklace, the necklace
with the replica of the Phaistos Disc hanging from its golden
chain. I didn't consider it jewelry. I considered it part of me. It
hadn't been removed since my husband clasped it around my
neck twenty years and four months ago. I unclasped it and asked
where I could retrieve it after surgery. She told me to check at
the nursing station. It would be there. I thought *I may never*
see it again, and then Dionysos appeared. Things change, seasons
change, lives change and then I was wheeled into surgery.

Surgery was a success and the following day, my gynecologist
told me that as soon as I could walk to the bathroom that was
at the far end of the room and back, I could be discharged. I
raised my eyebrows. That entire morning, my total focus was on
getting out of bed, pushing my IV stand in front of me, taking
one step in front of another to the bathroom and back. I was
going to do this. I was going to be discharged today.

Ever so slowly, I took my legs out from under the blankets
and placed them on the floor. I held onto the guardrail of the

bed and steadied myself as I stood up. My stomach felt as though I had swallowed an elephant and was extremely tender. I stood up and took one step. I was light headed. My body perspired from head to foot. I had no idea why. I didn't care. I was going to make it to the bathroom. I took another step and breathed in deeply. The next step, I exhaled. Feeling more confident with each step, the patient in the bed next to mine clapped. I smiled and told her I was going to walk. I was going to walk to the bathroom and back. Slowly, one foot in front of another, I made it to the bathroom. Exhausted, I sat down on the toilet.

I sat for quite awhile and thought *I have had the operation. I no longer have a uterus. I remember my William's note: any woman with a uterus cannot compare to me. This isn't true, but it is true for him. It does make me feel better.* I stood up and took the step to the sink and looked in the mirror at my face. I thought *what will it look like when I am my mother's age, approaching eighty? Do people consider my mother's face ugly because it is old? Why don't people find the beauty in age? Old women are beautiful. Wrinkles – it all depends on how you look at them. They depict character. They depict wisdom. The strength and passion of life are found in wrinkles. They show that you have fully lived.*

I looked at the bathroom door. I put one foot in front of another and walked back to the bed. The total exhausting walk took me more than two hours, but I had done it. I had walked to the bathroom and back and my witness was the patient lying in the bed next to me. When my gynecologist returned in the late afternoon, I told her of my accomplishment and my new friend lying next to me confirmed the success.

My gynecologist smiled and said, "Why am I not surprised? Call your son. I'll sign the discharge papers. Tonight, you may go home."

———◆•◆———

When I returned home from the hospital, William and I continued to be like two ships passing in the night. He was in the middle of packing for the National Swim Meet and then on to his vacation in Mexico. Maneuvering ever so carefully so as not to disturb my stomach that still felt like an elephant resided in it, I helped him assemble his swim gear and then his vacation clothes. The following week, I gingerly drove him to the swim team's parking lot where the swimmers met before boarding the bus for the airport. A team picture was taken of the handful of swimmers who had qualified. I looked at William. Three years had passed since his father died, but the sadness in his eyes remained. I thought *how his father would have been so proud of his accomplishments. Are you here? Can you see? It's your son. It's your son who you named.* I drove home slowly and eased carefully out of the car.

I opened the front door. I was going to live alone for the next two weeks. It was the first time I would be alone, live alone since college and I thought *in a year and half, I will live alone for good when William goes to college. Is this what it will feel like, living alone?* I put on my jacket and went outside to the backyard. While I had tried to maintain the yard since my dad's initial illness five years ago, it sorely needed much attention. Brown bare spots appeared through the grass. Bushes needed pruning. Leaves behind the bushes and in the flowerbed needed raking. Everything needed to be fertilized. I thought *this is how I will recover. Slowly, but surely rejuvenating the backyard.*

The next morning, I made a list of all the gardening supplies I needed. With great caution, I made my way to the nursery. When I returned midday, two of William's friends were sitting at the kitchen table. Surprised, I told them William was at the National Swim Meet. They nodded. They knew. They were here to see if I needed anything, if there was anything they could do for me while I was recovering. I smiled and sat down with them and told them of my plans to resurrect the backyard. They were enthusiastic about helping and went to the car and brought in the supplies. I sat at the kitchen table in a stupefied state. I knew that these boys and I had become friends, but it had been only when William was around. It slowly dawned on me that these boys were my good friends as well. They actually cared for me and I remembered I hadn't felt like this for a very long, long time.

We assembled in the backyard to discuss the various projects. Each one of them wanted their own job. They wanted to be responsible for one project. They told me that they would come after school during the week and in the afternoons on the weekend. One boy was in charge of reseeding the grass that constituted about one third of an acre. The other friend was in charge of raking all the leaves from behind the bushes and flowerbeds throughout the yard. I was going to tackle pruning the small bushes. Together we worked, sometimes commenting on our progress or congratulating someone else on theirs. I took many more breaks than the two boys. Each time I sat down on the deck stairs, one of them would come over to see how I was: did I need any water, did I want to go in and lie down on the couch, could they get me anything to eat?

I was genuinely touched by their kindness and knew William was incredibly lucky to have these boys as friends and, yes, I was lucky as well. By dusk, we had made a dent in our respective projects. I was totally exhausted. We cleaned up our gardening tools and went inside. I collapsed on the couch and told the boys to find whatever they could to eat. While I dozed, one of the boys, the caterer's son, prepared chicken and rice. When I woke up, I smelled the home cooked meal. He came over with a plate of dinner and told me to eat all of it. I needed the nourishment. I smiled and thanked him and asked him if he would join me, but he needed to go home to his family. I sat up and ate slowly while I heard him clean up the dishes. Then the front door closed. I put down the plate on the coffee table and lay back down and slept. I didn't wake up until the sun was well over the horizon.

Our schedule continued for the next two weeks. Each afternoon, one or two of William's friends came over. Sometimes it was the same two friends. Sometimes it was different friends. But each day, I was not alone while William was gone. Each day, we tackled more of our backyard projects and each day, the boy whose mother was a caterer prepared dinner for me. At the end of the two weeks, not a leaf in the yard remained, the flowerbeds were replanted, the bushes pruned and the entire yard reseeded. When William returned home in the afternoon, his friends and

I greeted him and displayed our accomplishments. He was like I had been: stupefied and surprised at their wonderful generosity.

For the next six weeks, I moseyed around the yard and house, acquainting myself to a life I had never led before. I rose when I wanted to, ate when I was hungry, rested when I was tired, went to the nursery to acquire more seedlings to adorn the flowerbeds. One day at the nursery, a workman who had assisted me many times before said, "I see you more than I see my own wife."

I laughed and said, "I am a temporary phenomenon. I will be returning to work next week and will not be around, except on weekends."

Leaving him, I thought *this is wonderful. How I wish I did not have to work. I love my time alone. I love the quietness of the air. I love the smell of the flowerbeds. I love the feel of dirt in my hands. I remember the therapist who asked if I might crumble if I had time alone. No, I am not crumbling. This is my time, my time to heal.*

After eight weeks, I returned to the gynecologist. My body, while permanently altered, was in excellent shape. I could return to work next Monday. As I left her office a heavy, debilitating wave overcame me. I was returning to my recent past life.

SUMMER – FALL – WINTER
2006 – 2007

One June evening, I made the boys a gourmet dinner and the lingering smell of cooked beef permeated the house as I descended the stairs the next morning. Opening the kitchen windows over the sink to allow in the early summer breeze, I saw the note.

> *My Dear:*
>
> *The shredded beef you cooked last night is very good. You must give me the recipe. I was sorry I was not here to eat it with you for dinner last night. I came over late. I shall make it up to you.*
>
> *Farewell, my dear.*
>
> *Your son's best friend*
>
> *P.S. Your son had sex.*

I thought *of the level of communication these boys had developed with me. My husband would never have tolerated this. I am not sure I want to know that William had sex, but maybe this is the consequence of the past three years. Maybe this is the result of us all trying to do whatever it takes to forge a new life, to forge a new life together. I would never have discussed this sort of thing with either my father or mother. God Forbid. There had been strict boundaries of conversation, but today we are in uncharted waters. I don't have a husband. The kids don't have a father. We are living day-to-day, making up the rules as we go along. And this is the result. It is better to have this than anything else. Yes, it is good to have this.*

The next weekend, William's friend who had left the note stopped by and I saw in his eyes that something was terribly wrong. I asked him how he was doing. He told me that his dad was sick and I nodded. I remembered his mother, Sandra, who was a caterer, had told me months ago that her husband was no longer capable of working. I didn't know the particulars.

He continued that the hospital discharged his father yesterday because there was nothing more they could do for him. He was home, in bed, and their dog of nine years lay beside him, not allowing his mother in bed. I was shocked and then upset at myself for not having stayed more in touch with Sandra. I asked him if there were anything I could do. He shrugged his teenage shoulders, dropping them into a slump.

He left to the garage where William's band was practicing. I immediately went over to the kitchen phone and called Sandra. When she answered, I heard the automatic pilot voice. I asked her if there were anything I could do and she told me that he lost control of his bladder this morning. I thought *of that horrible day when my husband lost control of his as Rebecca sat with him on the black couch. How I wish she never experienced that. How long does her husband have? One more week of quality life? And then the life you know is over. It's not only that he is not here but your life as you know it is not here as well.* I told her that I would bring some disposable bed sheets over now and she thanked me.

When I arrived, she greeted me and said, "I don't know what I'm going to do."

"We'll figure it out. We'll make him comfortable," I said.

We went into the bedroom and tried to slip a disposable bed sheet under him, but couldn't pull it to the other side because of the dog. Their dog did not budge. The dog would not move from her master's side. She redefined the word determination. We abandoned the idea and sat in her living room and spoke about her husband's condition, about her daughter and her son. I thought *why is this happening? Why is William's best friend's father dying? Why? I don't understand. Why is this happening? This man is younger than my husband was when he died. I don't know why. This is more than a coincidence. Pay attention. Pay attention to what? I don't know, just pay attention.*

She said, "Do you really think he's going to die?"

I didn't know how to respond. I thought *when you're in the thick of it, you don't think straight. You think death only happens to other people. Not to one of your own kin. How am I to comfort this woman? I don't really know her. I don't know what she believes.*

I said quietly, "If he does, he will die with you and his children. He will be at home. He will have peace. There won't be nurses or doctors making a last valiant effort to prolong his life when probably all he wants is to pass in peace and with love."

She nodded, but I knew she wasn't convinced. I didn't know how long her husband had been sick. I didn't know if she had prepared herself for the day when the life she knew would no longer be hers, ever again. I thought *did you prepare? No, but I knew that he was going to die. I know I did. And when he died? You couldn't believe it, right? You couldn't believe that he actually died, even though he lay in that hospital bed for three days unconscious. And when he died? You went on automatic pilot. Look across the room. This is you those two days before he died. Remember how you felt. Remember how you didn't know what to do. Remember the helpless feeling. Remember the stark fear of the unknown.*

I crossed the room and sat down on the bench next to her. I spoke softly, "We will stay in much better touch than ever before. You know that you can call me anytime any day, any night. There's nothing anyone can do or say that will alter what will happen. Everyone experiences situations differently, but know that I'm a phone call and a five-minute walk away. I'm not sure what I can do, but I'm good at just sitting and listening."

She rose. We hugged each other. I peered into the bedroom before I left. Their black pit bull lay next to his master's motionless body.

The funeral was held on the hottest afternoon in the month of July or so it seemed. The funeral home where the body lay in an open casket was air conditioned and people formed a line to view the deceased. William, Heather and I joined the line as the song "Spirit in the Sky" by Norman Greenbaum played through the speakers in the ceiling. I listened to the lyrics.

Never been a sinner. I never sinned
I got a friend in Jesus
So you know that when I die
He's gonna set me up with
The Spirit in the sky

As I stood in line, listening to this song, I thought *I wonder if I have ever sinned? What exactly is a sin? Is it not following one of the Ten Commandments or are there other sins as well? Who actually defines what a sin is? Is it the priests, the ministers who read and interpret the Bible for the believers? The Cherokee religion did not have the concept of sin. Did my ancient Greeks believe in sin? They believed in their twelve Olympian gods, but who interpreted their religion? They had no Bible or scripture. These gods and goddesses gave messages to man through signs and these signs gave guidance, sometimes in cryptic form. These signs were the main form of contact with the higher world. They had many signs. One of them was in the way a bird flew. If the bird flew from the right, it was a good omen. If she flew from the left, it was a bad omen. The seer or wise man sometimes interpreted signs. The ultimate seer was Apollo who was given the art of prophecy by Zeus. I remember back to Heather's conversation at Delphi when we discussed how Apollo had usurped the mother earth's power and it had become his site. What signs did she, the mother earth goddess, use to guide her people? I know I have my bird feathers, but what did she use? What signs did she use to show direction? The statue of the Snake Goddess in the Heraklion museum, the hot mamma, as Rebecca had called her. Snakes. That's it. Through snakes, the mother earth goddess gave man his messages. And the first healer, Asklepios knew it. He used them to heal his patients. Snakes they shed their skins and grow new skins. They renew themselves.*

William, who had ducked out of line returned, startled me when he tapped my shoulder. He was requested to be a pallbearer and was scared to death. He thought his hands might sweat so much that he would drop his end of the casket. I tried not to laugh and reassured him he would be just fine. I said I was going to drive with my daughter to the cemetery and if he wanted a ride home, to find us after the burial. He agreed and left to find the other pallbearers.

The cars followed the hearse down a long straight road in the height of the midday sun to the massive cemetery. In the cemetery, amidst a vast array of grave markers, a square canvas tarp, held in place by four poles, shaded the large hole in the ground and the fortunate people who arrived first. The rest of us stood outside the shaded area and watched as the pallbearers, including William, carried the casket to its final resting place. They set it down by the large brown hole. Their faces streamed with sweat. William's best friend had rigged a music system and the same song continued to play. A line formed and each person in the line approached the casket and placed a flower on top and then moved on. His wife greeted each person after they left the casket, but I ducked out of the line. As I walked away, I thought *why are you walking away? I don't know. This is disconcerting. My body is agitated. You're like the rest of them: the people you saw in the grocery store who, once they saw you, shunned you. Remember? You made them uncomfortable. Well, this woman standing by herself needs the touch. She needs to know that her life will continue. Offer her this.*

I retraced my steps and stood in the scorching sun until it was my time to offer my condolences. Perspiration pouring down my face, I hugged Sandra's small body as tightly as I could. I whispered in her ear, "You will have a new life. It won't be easy, but we will compare notes and we will stay in each other's lives."

Heather found me and we walked to the car. Neither of us said a word to each other. We climbed in the van and I turned on the air conditioner to high and drove home. I climbed up the stairs, unzipping my black dress. I took out a loose undershirt I had saved from my husband's clothes. He had always worn soft, white cotton undershirts and I liked the feel of them against my skin. I turned on the overhead fan and lay down on my bed and closed my eyes. I couldn't think of anything. I was numb.

I stayed in close contact with Sandra during the following months and it was during this time that she discovered she could no longer afford to keep her house in our town. She was going to move to an adjacent town. On the weekend of the move, all the boys and I helped her cart her furniture, bicycles, boxes and more boxes to her new house and settled her in as much as we could. Afterwards, we ordered pizza and bought cheap beer. We sat on her new back porch and I thought *at least Sandra will not have to gut her home. She's moved. I hope she can find her husband in her new house. My mother couldn't find my dad in her new condominium. Wow. Have I found my husband in my renovated house? No, he is not there. He doesn't belong there. It's not his home anymore. It's mine.*

———◆◆◆———

Heather flew home from college for Christmas break in early December. At the same time, Rebecca was preparing methodically for a yearlong sojourn in India with a good friend of hers. Her boyfriend was sponsoring their quest, as he was a staunch advocate of internal growth. I was not quite sure what I thought of this trip, but I knew I had no say in her life anymore. She was guided by her own compass, whose magnetic north was unknown to me. She was going to India and that's all I knew.

As Heather and I decorated the house for the holidays, she asked me why I was not dating anyone. Surprised, I blurted out that I didn't have the time. My work schedule was too demanding. But I thought *dating at my age. How do you do it? My grandmother's husband had died in his fifties and she never dated after he passed. This is fifty years later. How do I date? How do I meet men? Remember life's satisfactions? Remember them? If I don't date, how will I discover this life's satisfaction? But, I don't know how. Where do I begin?*

She continued that it was coming up four years since her father died and that I should move on with my life. I should find someone. Her brother would be away at college in a year and a half and I should find someone. I didn't have to marry anyone. She wasn't keen on sharing her inheritance, but I should have a man by my side. It wasn't right that I live alone. As I hung the wreath on the front door and felt the cold air, I confessed to her that I had no clue as how to begin. All the men where I worked were gay. We laughed and she told me that there were many online dating sights and she would fix me up. We finished with our decorations, but I changed the topic of conversation. I wasn't sure I wanted my eighteen-year-old daughter giving me advice regarding men.

The next morning, as I rounded the doorway into the kitchen, Heather sat at the computer in the den. I asked what she was doing and she replied, "Last night, I set you up on several dating sites and I'm checking how many responses you received."

Quickly, I replied, "Oh my god. What have you done?"

I walked over to the computer and froze. Dozens of responses with pictures of men from all walks of life stared at me from the computer screen. I shuddered and thought *if this is what is out there, better to stay in my cocoon.* I went back to the kitchen to start the coffee and told her that I wasn't terribly impressed.

A few minutes later, she said, "Come here and check this guy out."

I walked over and glanced at the screen. A photograph of a man with long hair pulled back in a ponytail looking upwards into the sun was on the screen. He had a gentle looking face with what appeared to be genuine eyes. Underneath his picture, he had written a brief introduction to me.

Heather turned to see my reaction and said, "This guy would like you in your comfy jeans. Write him back."

I looked into her blue eyes and thought *why does she want me dating?* I replied, "I will think about it. Okay?" I returned to the kitchen to drink my coffee.

Later that night, while the kids were out with friends, I returned to the computer and opened up the dating site to the man with the ponytail and thought *why not? Why not just write him back? What is your problem? It is an email, just an email. Stop being nervous. Being with a different man is unnerving. It's scary. Just do it. You have nothing to lose. You don't have to go out with him if you don't want to.* I wrote him back and hit the send button. Afterwards, fifteen emails popped up. Fifteen other men asked me to respond to them. I thought *if I am seriously going to date, I need to research. I remember in high school and college, I met guys and we would just hang out. We didn't ask each other, "Do you want to have dinner at a restaurant at a specific time." We just met up casually and if there were an interest, the relationship would be pursued. This online dating scenario is weird. What, you email a few times, perhaps have a phone conversation? If that goes well, actually meet the person? The jury is still out on this.*

I began to research the dating scene for women in the year 2006 and then I became distressed. Some books said that men were hunters. They enjoyed the chase. Make sure you played "sort of hard to get." Other books said you had to know the man's astrological sign. Men with certain astrological signs did not enjoy the chase. But it was important for your astrological sign to be compatible with his. Yet other books said that in order to attract a man's attention, a woman should drop from her lips a provocative, sexy word like 'panties.' I was confused. I hadn't known my husband's astrological sign. I hadn't known any guy's astrological sign.

I had lunch with one of my staff members who was a single woman and we chatted about my confusion. She told me that it just boiled down to sex. That was really all a man wanted. She told me to forget the rest. It was just sex that a man was after. Walking back to my office after lunch, I thought *of my husband and sleeping with him the first night we met. There was no chase and while there was sex, it had been because of the way we knew we felt. It had been an expression of our immediate affection for each other in a way that could only be communicated nonverbally. It seems as though today men are really a different species, according to all these books. Have men really changed this much in the past twenty-three years?*

The man with the ponytail emailed me back inquiring if I wanted to meet him for dinner and I sent a positive response. We met the following evening in front of a statue in the park and introduced ourselves to each other. His name was Stephan. He took me to a vegan restaurant nearby and we talked effortlessly, sharing many things in common such as music, dancing and sailing. He had an inquisitive, intelligent brain and what seemed to me a gentle heart. After dinner as we walked to my car, in the middle of the park, he bent his tall body forward and kissed me passionately and I returned his kiss. Driving home, I thought *all the research I have done should be thrown out the window.* Pulling into the driveway, my cell phone rang. It was Stephan. He asked, "Did you feel what I felt when we kissed?"

"Yes."

We made arrangements to see each other the following Saturday at the museum in the city. When I told my cleaning lady about my experience on Saturday morning while we were cleaning, she was adamantly opposed to Stephan after looking at his photograph on the computer. She said he didn't look conventional and I thought *another instruction on whom I should date.* I dropped the subject.

When I met Stephan in the afternoon, I was still unnerved by my cleaning lady's comment and I told him what she had said. I thought *where is your social filter? Why did you just say that?* He smiled, though, and put his strong arm around my shoulder and we began to walk through the various exhibits.

When we entered the Egyptian section of the museum, we stopped in awe of the magnificence of the Temple of Dendera. I stood in front of him and he pulled me back into his large muscular body and wrapped his arms around my torso. I felt his heart beating through my back. I thought *I haven't felt a man's warmth or his heart for what seems eternity. I want time to stop. Just for a while. I want to feel this warmth, this inclusion. Please, time, just stop for a while.*

That evening, we began our lovemaking in a most seriously passionate way. Subsequently, we saw each other over the next month, but William was displeased about the situation. In fact, it was not only he, but his friends joined in with their dissent. One boy told me that if the gentleman came to the front porch, they would form a blockade and not allow the man to enter. I didn't know how to navigate around their disapproval, but I continued seeing Stephan without letting William or his friends know.

A few weeks later, one afternoon at work, my cell phone rang, but I couldn't pick it up. I was in the middle of reviewing the budget. In the car, that evening, I looked at my missed calls and saw that it was Stephan. I listened to the voice mail. He asked me to call him. When I arrived home, William was at swim practice. I put my bag on the kitchen table and called Stephan. When he came on the line, he said he couldn't talk. He was concerned for the number of cell phone minutes he had left. Click. Dial tone. As I sat there with my cell phone still by my ear, I thought *why did he call me first? Leave the voicemail? For me to return his call? And then when I do, I get this? Is this the phenomena of a guy asking you to call him so he can hang up on you? Was it a test to see if I would return the call? What the hell? I don't get it.*

I became angry. Then I became really angry. I went over to the computer in the den and opened my email and wrote "One question, sir. Why call me if you didn't want to talk with me?" I hit the send button.

I went over to the kitchen and poured myself a glass of white wine and looked out the kitchen window into the blackened night. After several sips of wine and remaining quiet, I retraced my steps back to the computer and reread the email. I stared at it for quite a while. I thought *why not give the guy the benefit of the doubt. Maybe something came up. Maybe it has nothing to do with you. Why did you react so strongly? Slack. Remember the concept? Why don't you cut him some slack? Who wrote that email? I don't like the person who wrote that. I don't like that person filled with anger. Whoever that person is needs to do something. That person needs to do something about the anger. Slack. Give the guy some slack.*

This was when I began my research on self-improvement programs from psychic healing to Akashi readings to numerology ad nauseam. Nothing I researched seemed right to me. Nothing seemed as right to me as my bird feathers. Undeterred, I kept typing in a new word for the computer to research, but nothing grabbed my attention. I stopped and thought *what is wrong with me? What do you want to change in yourself? Why am I so angry? Nothing is wrong with you. Your heart hurts. Your heart is still in pain.* I entered into the computer the words, 'heal my heart' and clicked the send button. The screen displayed, "Movement towards a Heart Centered World through Kundalini yoga."

I had never heard of Kundalini yoga before and then I thought *of when I was a girl in elementary school and my mother took me to our village's art center where we were to learn yoga, every Tuesday evening for twenty weeks. I loved to perform the Sun Salutation and the exercise in which you stand on your head by making a platform with your elbows. I could keep this position the longest in the class by focusing on an object. But the thing I loved most was at the end of the class, lying on my yoga mat with my eyes closed. The instructor asked us to think of gentle thoughts while she played sounds of waves lapping against the shoreline. We remained like this for ten minutes. When I slowly stood up, I was relaxed, at peace with the world. All the playground arguments, all the fights with my brother, they had gone away. Heart centered. Yes, I want to be heart centered. I want my heart full of love, again. I don't want my heart to be filled with this pain, this pain that bursts into anger.*

I opened the web site and read about opening your heart, healing yourself and experiencing peace and joy. These words drew me in. I learned about the chakras that comprise the Lower Triangle.

> The Root Chakra makes us comfortable and secure with earthly things. The Sex Chakra insures creativity. The Navel Chakra bestows strong character and sustenance. Develop these as a strong

base before working on the higher chakras. The heart center is the seat of love and compassion. It is called the first human chakra. Opening this center can be a profound experience of compassion for others and self-love. Surrender the analytical head and allow the heart to be the focus of decision making.

I stopped reading and thought *perhaps I should explore this. I would love to operate from serenity and clarity. My head is my guide to all decision making. No, it's not. You use your heart. You could never have done what you did for your husband if your head governed your actions. But you still use your head way too much. You don't actively listen to your heart. Your heart is on automatic pilot. You need to turn off your heart's automatic pilot and see where it will take you. Let it sail itself without your head's interference. It may have a life of its own that you never knew. Kind of like what Rebecca told me about. The dakini. I like her. She's like Athena except she swirls around in Tibetan Buddhism. Unlike Athena who is steadfast and strong, Dakini is the spiritual process of surrendering expectation. She is the fertile symbol of the heart of wisdom. She is the sky dancer. What did my daughter say? The dakini's breath is that unknowable twilight of imperturbable bliss? Something like that. I hope she feels a dakini while traveling throughout India.*

I gazed out the bay window watching the sparrows fly from the forsythia bushes to the bird feeders, their wings twittering in midair. Mesmerized, I walked out to the deck and surveyed the birds that flew into the bushes and saw on the Japanese Elm tree, the robust cardinal who frequented our backyard for the past several years. I whistled and he sang back to me. As I walked closer, he watched me until I stood underneath his tree. I thought *seriously why not try Kundalini yoga?*

This became my new religion. Instead of walking the dog, I rose at four-thirty in the morning and performed the wake up and stretching exercises in bed. Then, I dashed into a very short cold shower, toweled off and performed the warm up exercise set on the rug in front of my bed, followed by a set aimed at strengthening my heart center. After relaxing, I lay on the rug and instead of meditating, I thought *of the place past the sky, past heaven, where Plato's ideas and all the souls lived. I imagined different souls from different time periods bumping into one another and what fun it must be.*

When I returned home from work, I went directly upstairs and changed into comfy clothes and performed two more exercises. It was during this time that I noticed my shoulder muscles easing into a relaxed posture. Each time I started to say something critical to William, I kept my mouth closed. I waited and thought *is this what you want to say? Is this how you want to say this?* It was during this time that I slowly but surely abandoned my desire to be with Stephan. And it was during this time period I began to become more aware, more perceptive of an inner calmness. I did not relent performing my Kundalini exercises until April when we left for Fort Lauderdale, Florida. William had qualified again for the National Swim Meet. This time I was going. This year, I was going to participate in my son's life and I was going to bring my mother. This trip was my birthday present to celebrate her eightieth birthday. We were going to stay in a lovely, comfortable hotel and I was going to treat her like a queen. We were going to celebrate her eightieth birthday on April 3rd and we were not going to think that three days later, I would celebrate the fourth anniversary of my husband's death.

SPRING 2007

April 2007: Fort Lauderdale, Florida: When we arrived, I rented a car and a wheelchair at the airport as my mother couldn't walk any real distance. We drove to our luxury hotel and checked in. We had the penthouse suite and our balcony looked over the blue Atlantic Ocean. Two queen-sized beds, dressers, a large writing table and a large marbled wheelchair accessible bathroom would be our home for the next three days. My mother was happy.

The following morning, I ordered room service for breakfast; hot, very hot black coffee, one egg over easy, one piece of toast with lots of butter and a small glass of orange juice. When it arrived, it was perfect and my mother was thrilled. She was particular about what she ate and her black coffee had to be almost scalding hot.

When we left the room, I pushed her wheelchair to the elevator and rode down. The concierge had retrieved our car. It was waiting outside the lobby door. We drove along the coast to the meet a few miles away, marveling at the expanse of the Atlantic Ocean. When we entered the massive site, the cashier and entry guards were not accustomed to seeing an elderly person, let alone in a wheelchair. At first, there were scowls of how are we going to get her inside into the cramped spectator area and where is she going to sit. One security guard beckoned us to come to a different gate. He opened a large gate and instructed us to park the wheelchair behind the swimmer's block in lane five. I couldn't believe our good fortune. We had an unobstructed view of the meet. The other parents were way up in the bleachers, but here we stood on the very pool deck. This was unheard of at any swim meet I had ever attended. No one other than officials, coaches and swimmers were allowed on the pool deck. I remembered thinking this is a very good sign. We stayed during the morning, watching the various races and all the heats associated with each event. My mother counted the number of strokes each swimmer took to swim the length of the pool. She determined that the swimmer who took the least amount of strokes always swam the fastest.

William's head coach, the man whom my husband had admired, walked over to greet us during the meet. My mother, with her southern charm, thanked him for not only being such a great coach, but also being supportive of her grandson over the many years. They spoke about the number of strokes each swimmer took in the various events, the fly, the backstroke, and the freestyle. After quite a lengthy discussion, the coach offered my mother a job as an assistant coach for the team. She laughed and told him that she had never seen so many naked men before. He responded that while they were small, the swimsuits were called Speedos.

After the meet, I pushed my mother down two blocks to an immense beach. It stretched for as long as you could see with its beautiful soft sand. There were no piers, no obstructions, just beach and the Atlantic Ocean flowing to the horizon. The air was warm with a slight offshore breeze.

My mother said softly, "You can just leave me here all afternoon. It's gorgeous."

In the afternoon of the third day of the meet, April 3rd, my mother and I went to the swim team's hotel to visit with William so that he could give her his small present and card. She was delighted.

Afterwards, I surprised her with a paddleboat ride through the Florida Keys as her birthday gift. On the boat, the crew was especially accommodating to my mother and her wheelchair. One large, muscular crew member picked up my 80 lb. mother while another crew member folded the wheelchair and brought it on board. They secured the wheelchair on the bow of the boat with various lines and blocks. They brought me a chair. We had the best view on the boat. As the boat motored away from the pier, the views of the various homes and wildlife were spectacular. I had purchased a small carrot cake, my mother's favorite, to celebrate while on board. As we ate our cake, enjoying her birthday afternoon, my cell phone rang. I dug it out of my bag and looked at the number. It was the director. I thought *I am on vacation. Can't you deal with whatever? You are the director.*

But I answered it. I heard her voice and visualized the tight red lips of anger. She sternly told me that I would have to reschedule an important meeting, which I had previously scheduled for her. She, the director, had a conflict with the meeting time. I had checked the director's calendar before scheduling this critical meeting. In fact, I had double-checked because I still knew the death drug could rear its ugly head at anytime. Her calendar had indicated no conflict. She continued that she had forgotten to update it. I told her I was on vacation and that I couldn't reschedule it from here. I closed the cell phone and thought *she just wanted to see if she could make my vacation a little miserable. No, no you can't. This is my mother's celebration of her eightieth year of life. You're not invited.* My mother asked if everything were okay. I replied, "Everything is peachy."

We continued our cruise through the keys until sunset, soaking up the warm sun, enjoying being on the water. That evening, we ate her birthday dinner in the hotel dining room. I had whispered to the concierge it was her birthday and much to my surprise, they brought us a complimentary bottle of champagne with strawberries. My mother was thrilled, but I thought *back to the last time I had a sip of champagne. It was in the fancy resort on Crete with my daughter where our lives changed forever. And today would have been my husband's fifty-sixth birthday as well.* For dessert, they brought a small chocolate cake with vanilla icing and one candle. It was simple, but elegant, just like my mother.

When we opened our hotel room door, my mother looked back to me from her wheelchair and thanked me for the special birthday. She hadn't had such a nice birthday in years. I agreed. I'd had a great time as well. She was exhausted and wished to retire. She walked into the bathroom to change and once tucked into bed, we began to talk of William's swimming career and how proud she was of him.

I said, "I think swimming has not only given him invaluable time management skills, but the opportunity to meet kids from all walks of life as well. I believe this is important."

From her bed, she responded, "What ever happened to his friend whose family was so wealthy? His mother always made me feel uncomfortable. I never knew what to say when I saw his mother at your house."

"Oh, she's wonderful. She's just like the rest of us. Remember she was the one who came to the front door the day after my husband died? She didn't bring flowers or food. She brought herself. She brought us hugs. That transcends money."

My mother said, "I can't treat her like the rest of us. She's not like everyone else. She's terribly wealthy. You don't understand me."

"Mom, but she is a human being. We all have one-way tickets on this planet. She's no exception. Treat her like you would anyone else. We're all in this life together."

"She's different. Wealth and power alter a person. They live in a different world than you and me."

I breathed in very slow and exhaled slower. The anger towards her limited view was not going to rise in my chest. She was a depression baby. She had worn cardboard in her elementary school shoes when the soles were almost bare. I went over to her bed and said, "Yes, I do understand. Money does funny things to people and sometimes rich people may act quite differently than the rest of us. But now, this segment of William's swimming career is over. Don't give it any more thought."

I folded her blanket and kissed her goodnight. I was going to the piano bar to have a nightcap and listen to the jazz pianist. More than ever I missed my dad's music filling our home.

——— ❖ ———

When we returned from Florida, it was springtime and everyone's mood was upbeat. The trip had rejuvenated my mother and she glowed. After the past few years and two serious operations, this was just the tonic to make her feel whole again. At work, I rescheduled the director's critical meeting and emailed her the particulars. I took a moment to check my personal email and discovered an email from Stephan. He apologized for falling off the radar. It wasn't because of me. He wasn't ready to deal with a seventeen-year-old boy. He had appreciated our sexy times together and remembered them fondly. His falling off radar had nothing to do with me, he reiterated.

I stared at this and thought *I really do not understand men. My husband was a man and I understood him. Did you? You would never have known that he read Burkett and what he wrote in his journal if he hadn't died. Maybe, you just don't. Maybe you really do not understand men. Why does Stephan think he has to have a relationship with my son? He's my son. The relationship is with me. It has been three months since I heard from him. I don't get it. I don't get it at all. Does he want to continue to see me? Did he just want to explain his rude behavior? Leave it alone. Right now, it doesn't matter if you don't understand. Come back to it later. Later.*

That afternoon, I left work early. Tonight was William's swim team dinner at a fancy restaurant in a town about half an hour away from ours. When I walked in the front door, I asked my son if I could catch a ride with him in his car. I hated driving to this town. He was driving an old Volvo that the retired director had given him. He quickly replied, "No," as he passed me in the front hall. "I'm taking my buddies. There's no room for you. Don't be late. The awards will be presented before dinner."

I thought *how rude. Don't say anything. Maybe it's just his adolescent anger. Maybe it's his anger about his father. It doesn't matter. It is still rude. Don't feed it. Don't feed the anger. Be still.* I took the directions and program off the magnet on the refrigerator and scrutinized them. I always got lost driving in this town. When we first moved to this house, I took the kids on an exploratory trip and ended up in this town. It took me hours after stopping at many gasoline stations to find my way out. It was an industrial blue-collar town with a high crime rate, but the restaurant where the swim team dinner was held was elegant.

I put on my coat, climbed into the car and drove. Pulling off the main highway onto the ramp into the town, I switched on the reading lights to figure out the various turns. After many turns, I was going around in circles. I glanced at my watch. It was ten minutes before the program began. I stopped at a convenience store to ask directions and hurriedly wrote them down. Driving down a hill, I spied the restaurant and saw the sign for valet parking. This was not my custom as I felt it wasted money, but tonight since I was already late, I would pay it. When I entered the driveway, the sign read "Valet Parking Full."

A wedding reception was taking place in an adjacent facility. I drove out of the parking lot and drove up and down side streets, trying to find a parking place. After several streets, I found a space large enough to park the van. My hands were sweaty. I felt my heart pound. I was now twenty minutes late. I ran in my high heels down the hill and stopped short. I stooped down and slipped off my shoes, looking at the spiked heels. Barefoot, I raced down to the restaurant. Just before arriving at the facility, I slipped on my heels and breathed in slowly. I walked slowly to the front door, catching my breath and breathing deep. My heart pounded into my ears.

I opened the door and stopped dead in my tracks. I felt as though a semi truck had hit me. Inside, round tables covered with elegant white linen tablecloths adorned with flower arrangements and candles filled the room. Around each table sat four couples, dressed in their formal dinner attire. Each couple I had known from the past fourteen years. The problem was that I had not seen any of them for the last four years since my husband had died. It was if I were entering my previous life. It was as if I were entering my previous life alone. There was not one vacant seat. I walked slowly over to the coat rack and tried to back into it, just long enough to get my bearings. This was setting me over. I didn't know if I were going to throw up, cry or tremble. I felt no connection with my body. I felt no connection with these people. This was no longer my life. I backed further into the coat rack.

William walked over with a look of disgust and said, "Would you sit down somewhere? You're embarrassing me." He turned and abruptly walked away.

I stared at his back as he walked away and all the Kundalini yoga in the world could not stop me from walking out of the restaurant in record speed. Out in the cold, dark night air, I retraced my steps to the car, but my mind was fixated on the white linen tables with all the parents sitting around them. I thought *they were all couples. There was not one single parent. Would that have been my life if he hadn't died? Would I have looked like one of the conservatively dressed ladies, sitting next to their conservatively dressed husbands? Would that have been me? Our relationship was on edge before he became sick. It needed to change dramatically if it was to live, but I can't imagine myself looking like that. I cannot go back to that life. That life is gone.*

I kept walking. I didn't know where I had parked the car. I was lost. I took a deep breath and thought *stop. Do you remember the name of the street you parked on? No. Okay, be systematic about this. I remember the crumpled map my husband gave me showing me where he had parked his car.* I walked methodically up and down each side street, becoming colder and colder until I passed one man. He looked at me from head to toe and said, "You shouldn't be walking in this neighborhood dressed like that."

I thought *shit. Where is the car? An idea. The car's been stolen. Okay, go back to the reception and tell them the car's been stolen.*

The receptionist called two police officers who happened to be there due to the magnitude of the wedding. They questioned me endlessly and wrote down the information. They asked me why I was here and I told them about my son's swim team dinner. They went in to the restaurant and found William and brought him out. They asked him if the information I had given them was correct. I was shocked. I thought *I should get their badge numbers and report them. I am the adult here. He is my son and a minor. What is wrong with them?* After William verified the information, he went back to the restaurant. The policemen said they were going to canvass the area for the car before reporting it. They returned in less than five minutes and told me to come with them. They had located my car.

We walked in the opposite direction than I had previously. Down two side streets, I walked with a police officer on each side of me until we reached my van. They asked me if I remembered parking it here. I tried to explain to them that I had become one hundred eighty degrees turned around. I told them that I was sorry. It had been a long day. They instructed me to drive the van back to the restaurant and wait in the reception area. When I walked into the reception area, William was standing there with the two policemen. They asked him if I had been drinking, if I were on any anti-depressants or any other medications that would alter my mental state. I was incredulous. I thought *scream at them. I am the adult. No, be quiet. Don't open your mouth.*

After it was verified that indeed I had just become one hundred and eighty degrees turned around, that I had not been drinking, that I was on no medication, William returned to the restaurant, shaking his head. The officers told me I should go home and get some rest. But I didn't know how to get back to the highway to take me home.

Reluctantly, one officer agreed to drive to the highway in front of me. I followed him and merged onto the highway. My body trembled as I pulled into my driveway. I opened the car door and threw up onto the spring grass, clutching my stomach. I entered the kitchen and drank a glass of water, sat down on the kitchen floor and the tears flowed. I thought *I got confused. Isn't a person allowed to be confused? And what was with William? He needs to be angry with someone else, not only me. When will this death drug dissipate from my blood? When? Would that have been my life with all those people? Would I have continued to be a stay-at-home mom? What would you be doing, with only one kid at home? Would my husband have continued to work? He would be fifty-six years old this year. Would our relationship have changed? I don't know. All I know, it was awful to walk back into that life without him tonight. That is a life that belongs to couples, not single people. It was awful.* My arms encircled my knees and my knees were my head's pillow. When my breathing became quiet and my mind relaxed, I opened my eyes and looked at the clock. It was past eleven. I climbed slowly up the stairs and felt something in my stomach. I hadn't eaten anything today.

The next morning at work, Stephan called me at seven-thirty. No one was at work yet. I answered the cell phone. He said he had been thinking about me and wondered how I was doing. I was dumbstruck. He immediately heard the tension in my voice and he asked how I was. I reiterated a shortened version of the previous evening. He responded that now it was over and I should look forward to the day.

I hung up and I thought *yes, I do look forward to this day, but last night reminded me of a life I used to live. A life that I don't own anymore. And William's anger, my son's anger cut. It cut into my heart. I cannot just forget an experience like that and think only of today. Its memory does not fade into the newness of this day.*

<hr>

April 2007: "How do you do it?" A tall woman wearing a long, black dress coat, and a black fur pillbox hat, golden hair spilling down to her shoulders stood on the sidewalk inches away from me. I was in our front yard, cleaning out the winter debris from the flowerbed under the magnolia tree, preparing to plant seeds. My knees cold and damp as the moisture from the ground seeped through my torn jeans. At first, I thought she was referring to cleaning the flowerbed. "I mean with your husband?" she continued. I slowly rose, taking off my soiled garden gloves, rubbing the dirt from my sweatshirt and looked into her piercing blue eyes inquisitively.

I responded the only way I knew, "One step in front of another."

Dear Reader,

What you have read thus far is a narrative of how I put one foot in front of another during those four years leading up to April 2007, but now it is October 2009. From this vantage point, I can tell you that during those four years, I began to see a glimmer of a solo life. I began ever so slowly to build a life, a new life for me. While many times my brain operated on automatic pilot and my body functioned in overdrive, there were moments when I saw the future of a new life filled with contentment and perhaps, even happiness. And now in October 2009, I have developed a steadfast, solid core in my heart. I have gained a rich understanding of what I consider to be the real heart and entrails of life. I know this process will forever continue, but it seemed to become even more heart centered after I heard the voice. A voice I had never heard before.

On Memorial Day weekend, William asked to have a party at our house for a large group of his friends. He had less than a month of his high school education left. He and all his friends were feeling the giddiness of the moment. I agreed, but told him to first decide on his trip abroad. I needed to plan it, as it was only a month away. On the spot, he blurted, "Italy."

He had studied Latin for six years with the accompanying history and literature. He wanted to travel to the topographical primary source. Quickly, I replied, "Okay, then. We are going to Italy."

It was raining cats and dogs as I drove in the early June morning to work. Six in the morning, there were more cars and trucks than usual. Everyone began their commute early on inclement weather days. I arrived at work, drenched from head to foot. As I took off my raincoat, I saw a note from the director on my desk, requesting my presence at a meeting with her and the dean at one-thirty in his conference room. The agenda was the reorganization. I stared at the note and thought *reorganization? What does that mean? She wants to reorganize the department? I remember back to when I began here and how Human Resources and the dean used that term. Reorganization was how they described the staffs' layoffs. She's actually going to lay me off. I never doubted that she would. I had felt her animosity towards me since day one. What will the severance package be? Calculate it. Do the math.*

When my assistant came in, I showed her the note and told her what I believed was going to happen. She and I worked in simpatico with each other, knowing each other's strengths and weaknesses. We made a phenomenal team, performing what it would probably have taken four other people to perform. She looked horrified. I assured her it would be fine. Things happened for a reason and when you look back at your life, you realize it has been perfect. She sat at her desk all morning, looking despondent. When one-thirty approached, I strolled up the hill to the dean's building and rode the elevator. I thought *back to his handshake years before and wonder if he'll shake my hand goodbye.* When I entered his office and the conference room, the director was sitting at the front of the table.

She instructed me to sit down. The dean was delayed, but he had given her permission to begin the meeting without him. She pulled out papers and said that due to a reorganization, I was being laid off. I smiled to myself. We reviewed the severance package and the director asked me to sign the paper, indicating my acceptance of the layoff.

I read the terms of the layoff and noticed I had forty-eight hours to sign the paper. I told them I would mail the paperwork after I considered if I would accept the layoff or challenge it. I thanked her and on the way out of the conference room, the dean entered the hallway.

I looked down at him and said, "Thank you for the opportunity. I appreciate it."

He replied that he had hoped he had helped me out over the last few years. I left and as I rode the elevator down. I thought

I am grateful for the income. I didn't have to sell our home. But at what price, what sacrifice? I gave them four years of my life. Four years of my life I gave so that this department could function. I didn't have to sell the house. Our house is now a safe haven. I created a sanctuary for myself, the boys, everyone. Four years. Be grateful. Be grateful, it's over now.

When I entered the office, I showed the letter to my assistant. I saw the tears well up and I hugged her. I reassured her that things would be okay. She wanted to know what I was going to do. Would I be okay with my kids? Where was I going to find work? I told her I would be fine. My kids would be fine. I didn't know anything beyond that.

The director entered with brown boxes and said she was going to help box up my things. I gazed around my office. I had brought from home pictures of my kids, my carpet, paintings, a vase my mother had given me, candles, lamps, plants and the evil eye. I took the pictures of my kids in one hand and my mother's vase in the other and said, "That's it. You can keep your boxes."

I kissed my assistant goodbye and walked out the door. Driving home, an enormous sense of relief enveloped me. Someone was removing fifty pounds of bricks off my shoulders. I didn't know what I was going to do. All I felt was liberation.

When I entered the house, William was sitting at the kitchen table. It didn't dawn on him that I was home earlier than usual. He was talking to a friend on his phone. When he hung up, I told him my news. He said he didn't believe it. I showed him the letter and he was upset as if I had done something wrong, that I had failed. I told him this was a silver lining, that I would find another job. This wasn't the only job on the market. He was unconvinced and began worrying about money. I told him that the income was my concern. This was not his problem. We would still go to Italy as planned. He wanted to delay the trip. I insisted that we go. I went upstairs to change. As I climbed the stairs, I knew that I must explain this layoff to my mother in a much more positive way than I had explained it to William. She would go off the deep end thinking that we would end up in the poorhouse.

———⇒•⇐———

My son graduated from high school with his buddies on schedule. On the afternoon of graduation, my second daughter was the designated photographer and she clicked away. As William walked up to the podium to receive his diploma, wearing his white tuxedo, I didn't feel my husband. I wondered why he didn't show up. I watched William returning to his seat after receiving his diploma. He was one handsome young man. He combined the looks of both my husband and myself in the most balanced masculine way. He was no longer a boy, as his father had last known him. He was a man. For the last seventeen years, my mother always said that neither I nor my husband were exceptionally good looking, but we had turned out three exceptional children and I always agreed with fifty percent of her statement.

———⇒•⇐———

SUMMER 2007

Rome, Italy. When we arrived at the airport, we waited for our luggage on the carousel. I noticed the aggressive Italians pushing each other to get their bags first. I told William to wait. I didn't care if we were the last to retrieve our luggage, I didn't want to be in the midst of mayhem. We took a taxi to our hotel located on the outskirts of Rome and checked in. We wanted to go back into Rome, but the taxi was expensive. William told me not to worry. He was going to figure out the bus schedule and that's exactly what he did. We waited at the bus stop and right on time, the bus came. Once in Rome, we ate at a local restaurant on a side street beyond the congestion of the city center. Sitting outside, we ordered an early dinner and while waiting, William went to the nearby kiosk to buy a map. His next task was to figure out the city.

I glanced to my side and my eyes wandered up the wall of a massive concrete structure with an incredible dome. When William returned to the table, I told him to hold down the fort. I wanted to walk up the alley to discover what this enormous building was. As I rounded the bend, I saw the portico with the tallest, most ornate Corinthian columns leading to massive bronze doors. I was standing in front of the Pantheon: the temple to all gods that Agrippa had built in the early years of the first century. I remembered years ago attending a lecture on the Pantheon at the Metropolitan Museum with Rebecca. It had the largest dome built of unreinforced concrete in the world and in the middle, an oculus, a round opening, allowing the only natural light into the building. I read the sign. It would be open until nine in the evening.

When I returned to the table, I excitedly exclaimed that we were eating dinner next to the Pantheon. We must check it out after dinner. He looked over to its wall and grinned.

"You know what? We're in Rome. We're not in Greece. You're looking at your new cruise director and yeah, we'll check it out. Your cruise director will give you the low down."

I smiled and leaned back in my chair and relaxed. He was right. We were not in Greece. This cruise director was off duty. After dinner and after my son grilled the waitress on various and sundry facts about the city and safety, we strolled up the alley. When we stood in front of the portico, William took my hand and we stopped.

He paused, "Just look at this. This temple is for all the gods. It was not built for just your Greek gods, not just the Roman gods, but all gods. Every god that has ever existed has a home and you're looking at it. Amazing."

As we walked between the Corinthian columns and through the massive bronze doors, we both paused again. I pointed to my arms. I said, "This is the definition of awe."

He looked at my arms and I at his. Our arms had their hair raised with goose bumps running the length of them. Slowly, we entered into the center of the temple and gazed up to the evening sky through the hole in the dome. He told me that the oculus was twenty-seven feet in diameter and that the floor was sloped, allowing the rainwater to flow to the side drain. I was looking at a perfect sphere resting in a cylinder. The huge dome was a perfect hemisphere. There was a choir harmonizing beautifully in Latin to one side of the round building. He pointed to the seven alcoves which each had a statue within. He said that even though this was a temple to all the gods, these seven deities had given their names to the seven planets in the Roman State Religion. Until the invention of the telescope, only seven planets were visible to the naked eye. He went on to list them; Saturn, Jupiter, Mars, Venus, Mercury, Diana, and Apollo. As he was reciting the planets, I thought *of my conversation with my husband at Itea when he pointed out the constellations and planets in the night sky and then of his journal entry, his conversation with himself. Two years later, this still makes me sad. Shake this off. This is your son's trip. You're going to have a blast.*

I put my hand on his back and said, "Wow, I'm impressed. Six years of Latin. Good stuff."

We remained in the center for some time and eventually circled the entire building. When we were at the door to leave, we both looked back and took in a deep breath. We didn't move. Yes, this was a temple to all gods and I was glad Agrippa had the idea. I thought *maybe I should have an attitude adjustment regarding these Romans. Maybe I should be more inclusive. It's not just the Greeks that got everything right.*

Firenze, Italy: We rented a car and successfully managed to drive, unharmed, out of Rome to Firenze where we stayed in a small pension. The Italian drivers were like no other, ruthless with their high-speed antics. We parked on a side street and looked up to our small hotel. The elevator, which had no walls, just iron gates around it, took us to the fourth floor.

"Where are you taking us?" William inquired.

"I don't really know. I didn't have time to research this trip. I only had a month. Let's just see. We're in Firenze. No problems here," I replied.

We checked in at a small reception area. Our bedroom was up two more flights of stairs and we climbed with our bags bumping behind us. We had a small window in the bedroom, which looked out to the Cathedral of Santa Maria Del Fiore. She was massive, much more so than the Pantheon. I asked William if he knew anything about her and he shrugged. She was too modern for both of us. She was built in 1296. I suggested that we walk down to the square and see her. He agreed. We took the elevator back to the street level and walked towards the center of town. The more we listened to the conversations of the people we passed on the street, the more English we heard. This was an English-speaking student town.

We window-shopped as we passed the stores, but the replicas of the Renaissance art were again too modern for our taste. In high school I used to like the art, but today it didn't attract me. We came to the main square and were confronted by the largest church I had ever seen.

"Why would someone want to build such an incredibly large church? More people could fit in it than Firenze had living here," I asked.

William read from his guidebook. "The dome designed by Brunelleschi was a feat of engineering. It was forty-six meters in diameter at the base. He had to lift 37 thousand tons of material including 4 million bricks to build the dome. He invented hoisting machines, which was his main contribution to architecture. Brunelleschi looked at the Pantheon for solutions, which was a single shell of concrete, but the formula had long been forgotten."

I interrupted, "That's like the place where I used to work. Progress is defined as doing the same thing twenty years later."

He didn't look up. He informed me that I should look at Giotto's famous campanile, or bell tower, and I gazed up. I thought *back to the born-again Christian church's tower in Southern California. Both of them want to get as close to the sky as they can. Plato is right. The souls are beyond the stars, past heaven.* As we were about to enter, William ended his lecture by reading out loud, "The Santa Maria Del Fiore is one of the most important religious buildings in the world."

I asked, "Why?"

He looked in the guidebook. "It doesn't say why."

Walking through its doors into this cathedral that is bigger than a football stadium, I felt the vastness, yet sensed an immense emptiness. I asked, "Do you feel the god here?"

He shrugged his shoulders and picked up a pamphlet by the door. "The Gothic interior is vast in order to give an impression of emptiness."

I nodded in agreement. He continued, "The relative bareness of the church corresponds with the austerity of their religious life." We toured the length of the church and exited.

We strolled over to a small restaurant and took a seat in the afternoon sun, looking at the cathedral. We ordered our drinks and I said, "That church gave me the creeps." He agreed. A band was setting up to play in the square and we stayed to listen. As we were watching them set up the backdrop, my eye caught Michelangelo's statue, the David. I knew it was a replica. The original was in the Galleria dell'Accademia, but David's replica was impressive. I pointed to it. William glanced up. He told me that it looked as if it were modeled after a Greek god. It reminded him of Apollo's statue in the frieze in the Olympian Museum. I stared at him with eyebrows raised.

I asked, "You remember that? You were ten years old. That was the last trip with the grandparents."

He replied, "I remember sitting on the bench in the museum and in front of us stood the frieze. You told me to be quiet and to just look at the statues. You told me to think whatever thoughts come into my mind. I remember Apollo stood in the center, towering above the other statues. His right arm was raised, commanding all the others to behave themselves. His head was turned in the direction of his arm. His chiseled features were strong, handsome and distinguished. He had a calm, but determined presence. He knew the right way. David has the same thing going on."

"Wow, I'm impressed. Good memory. I like Apollo. Maybe Michelangelo also saw Apollo at Olympia. We're going to see the David in the Accademia tomorrow."

I thought *of his memory. It was as if it were yesterday that we all sat on the marble bench looking at the frieze in Olympia. William sat between his grandmother and grandfather. We rested and gazed at the frieze for a long time. It was if time stopped then and there. It is one of my favorite memories. We felt Apollo's silent strength. None of us wanted to move.*

We relaxed, soaking up the sun, listening to an Italian rock band. After some time, we were ready to leave. We meandered back to our pension. William walked ahead of me along a very narrow sidewalk crowded with various students, and I kept track of his back so not to lose him. I thought *he is going to turn eighteen years old tomorrow. Where was I when I turned eighteen?*

Where was my husband when he turned eighteen? My husband, upon graduating from high school, bought a one-way ticket to Italy and explored Europe for six months on a shoestring budget. His son is walking the same streets at the exact same age as his father did.

The next day before we drove to the Amalfi coast, we visited the museum housing the actual David, where a tour guide escorted us through the museum informing us of the salient features of each piece of artwork. She was an enthusiastic advocate for her town and it was refreshing to have such an exuberant guide. When we came to the David, she made it abundantly clear that the reason the statue's head and hands were distorted in size was due to the fact he was to be placed on a building sixteen feet high. Because of this, Michelangelo had sculpted his hands and head disproportionately to his body. I looked at the statue. My eyes gravitated towards his head and I thought *William is right. He does look like Apollo in Olympia.*

After the tour ended, we headed towards the exit and then I stopped. I saw two large marble slabs and gasped. I pulled on my son's arm to wait. I made my way over to these slabs through the tourists. The marble slabs were rectangular about six feet by three feet. In each slab was a figure trying desperately to escape. The bodies were writhing in pain. One body had his arm above this head, trying to free himself. In each slab, both faces were contorted in pain. Their feet were trying to push away the stone. The emerging figures and the marble constraining them were beyond forceful. Immediately, I saw my husband lying on the bed during Interleukin treatment. Michelangelo nailed it. This was it. I went over to read the placard. The title was "Slaves." "Commissioned by Pope Julius, but when he died, his relatives decided that such an expense was too much. They have been left incomplete, unfinished." I thought *no, they're complete. They say it all. The pain, the desperation in struggling to get free, to get free from what is constraining you. Unbelievable. Nothing describes better the man I saw lying on the hospital bed being injected with the drug that was going to save him: the drug that made him writhe in pain.*

My Journal:

July 1st, 2007:

Amalfi Coast, Minori, Italy: William, the age of majority as of two days ago, drives us from Florence to Minori, a small village on the Amalfi coast. My son, a man, buys his own drink, navigates through swarms of vespas, incoherent Italian road signs, lectures me on the events that went down in the forum. A full moon cascading her light down to and across the calm Tyrrhenian Sea to where we are standing on the small village beach. Dories secured in a straight line going out to sea. "Past what boat and how many skips?" he asks. "Second boat, seven skips," I reply. Studying the stones carefully, discarding the ones that don't have the feel, he flicks his wrist. Past the third boat, eleven skips. He doesn't remember his father teaching him how to skip rocks. I remind him of when and where. He doesn't remember. He only remembers always being able to skip rocks. He has the art. It is in the wrist. I watch. A blonde haired little girl runs up out of the beach darkness. She approaches William. Her hands are cupped together with a load of stones. She wants to see him skip more. Her brother, diapered, swaggering with chubby legs, waddles up with more stones. He claps and giggles each time another stone is cast, skipping past the second, and third dory into the dark water. I can see the smile on William's face. I haven't seen his smile so wide since elementary school. Arm hurting from throwing so many stones, William turns and bends down to give the little girl a stone. He takes her wrist in his hand

and flicks it. The stone skips twice and plops
into the water. She takes another stone and
William takes her wrist again. This time, past
one dory, five skips. Her brother jumps up and
down and claps, giggling. We see their mother
approaching, calling them. The little girl,
smiling runs up to William and throws her arms
around his waist and then runs to her mother
with her brother. As William and I walk up the
beach, he tells me that he'll never forget this.

Pompeii, Italy: This was our last visit before returning to the
States. I knew that while the trip had been a good one, William
was missing his girlfriend and his buddies. He was ready to be
back with them. I bought him a book on Pompeii illustrating
the different erotic paintings on the various brothels, baths
and homes. The paintings on the brothels were either a form of
advertisement for the services performed inside or to heighten
the pleasure of the visitors. In any case, they were explicitly
sexually charged and were painted with great care to detail. I
figured he would have fun sharing the book with his buddies.
At the site, we were overwhelmed by its vastness and I reminded
William that the population was 25 thousand people. One
sensed immediately that it was a vibrant, close-knit community.
We didn't have the time to do the site justice, as we had to drive
to Rome, return the car, and catch our late evening flight home.
I had always wanted to see the House of the Faun, so we headed
in its direction.

On the way, we stopped to take in as many paintings as we
could find especially those on the brothels. William commented,
"These paintings make anything in Playboy look conservatively
frigid."

I nodded. I suggested, "These Romans were not afraid of
life's pleasures. They embraced them."

"Why does our society view sex in such a puritanical way?"
he asked.

I replied, "You've answered your own question. Puritans. It is like the cathedral in Firenze. The religious emptiness inside reflected the austerity of their everyday life."

He added, "The Romans had their State Religion that was mimicked after the Greeks. So why this unabashed sexual freedom?"

We walked in silence for a while along the brown, dusty path. Slowly, I said, "Anyone who builds a temple to all gods is open-minded. He's not scared of insulting one god over another. He is embracing all possibilities. It is a temple for all gods, the gods that man has not yet created. Agrippa is saying yes to everything the universe holds. He is saying yes to everything that life holds, held and will hold. It stands to reason that a person who builds a temple like this would embrace his sexuality passionately and the society that endorsed a temple to all gods would also endorse their sexual passion."

He stopped and looked at me, but I kept on walking and thought *what a great man Agrippa was. I would have liked to have known him.*

<hr />

One morning, a few days after we returned from Italy, I was carting the trash barrels to the curb when I saw my neighbor Dorothy, from down the street, with her new chocolate lab puppy. She crossed the street with the puppy pulling her all the way. I bent down to play with the puppy and as I looked up, I saw Dorothy's face beaming with pride. William walked out of the garage to see the puppy and lay down on the grass. The puppy licked behind William's ears, his nose, his cheek, his neck and William couldn't stop laughing.

Dorothy explained that the breeder had two puppies left and that she needed to give them away immediately as the breeder had to fly to Italy to care for her ailing mother. William pleaded that we should take one puppy. Dorothy pulled a card out of her pocket with the name and phone number of the breeder.

William became passionate with his pleas. I sternly told him that I would think about it. We congratulated Dorothy on the new addition to her family and wished her well.

Later in the morning, I was cleaning the kitchen when the phone rang. I still always looked at the phone, wondering if I should pick it up or just let it ring. Today I picked it up. It was the breeder. She had heard that we might be interested in adopting one of her last two puppies. She was desperate to find them good homes. Dorothy had told her that we were exceptional dog lovers. William, realizing who was on the phone, was in my face now with his hands in the prayer position. I caved. "All right," I said.

I suggested that we drive to the breeder to see the puppies, but that I didn't promise anything. Before I knew it, William was in the car with the engine running. I didn't believe his enthusiasm. As we drove through the lush green valleys, I asked William why he wanted a puppy. He was going away to college in two months and I would be stuck with the dog. He assured me it was the right thing to do. He would take care of the dog every chance he had. Besides, I needed a dog. I would be living alone for the first time in twenty-three years.

When we arrived at the breeder's farm, she brought the two puppies out from the barn. William sat on the sprawling hill. Both puppies romped and tumbled all over him. One ran over to the large water dish, climbed in the dish, splashed around, drank copious of amounts of water and then with water dripping from his mouth scampered back to William and jumped into his lap. William said this was his new puppy. I caved. The breeder and I went into her kitchen to complete the paperwork, while William played with his new puppy. Finishing the paperwork, the breeder asked me how Dorothy's husband was. She didn't think he was doing very well. He hadn't been healthy enough to make the trip to pick up their puppy. I told her that I didn't know. I didn't know either of them very well. She asked me to give them her best. She was thinking of them. I told her I would and we piled into the car with the new puppy sitting on William's lap. As the hum of the engine took over and the cool evening air swirled through the car, both William and his puppy slept. William's hand was draped on his puppy's stomach. I smiled and said, "Welcome to your new family, puppy."

At home, William immediately left to fetch dog food and supplies. I walked the dog over to Dorothy's house so that he could meet his sister. When I rang her doorbell, Dorothy smiled. In one split second, the two puppies were all over one another, frolicking, tumbling over one another. We laughed and I suggested that brother and sister had missed each other, even though they had only been apart a few days. Looking from the puppies to Dorothy's face, I saw something was wrong. I asked her if everything were okay. She told me that her husband was back in the hospital. His condition had dramatically worsened. He had the very best doctors from around the world, who specialized in his disease, but nothing was helping. He was going to come home in a few days, but she didn't know for how long.

She offered me a drink and we sat watching the puppies play. I thought *what stage of death is her husband experiencing? This is why I have this puppy. She and I are going to become good friends.* A few days later, I was walking our puppy down the street when I saw Dorothy's husband walking down their driveway with their new puppy. He looked emaciated and gaunt, but he didn't have the skin tone I remembered from my husband or father. I stopped and congratulated him on his new addition to his family and he beamed. He told me that I would be impressed with how smart these dogs were. He had researched and researched to find the top of the line chocolate labs and he was convinced that he had found them. I agreed, but offered that puppies were still a lot of work. He laughed and walked slowly back up his driveway.

I watched this tall handsome man whose clothes hung off of his back walk the little puppy up the stairs and into the house. He looked like a skeleton.

The following week, Dorothy called and asked if I could watch her puppy. Her husband had been taken back to the ICU of the local hospital in an ambulance. In a heartbeat, I said I would be over to pick the puppy up. I told her to get ready to go to the hospital. The adrenalin pumped through my blood and I thought *this is not your husband. Slow down. Your husband is already dead.*

———◆◆———

One afternoon, I returned from grocery shopping and the boys were playing badminton in the backyard. They quickly stopped to help bring in the groceries. As I was unloading the bags, I glanced around and didn't see our puppy. I asked William's best friend where the puppy was. He didn't think the backyard gate had been left open, but he didn't know. The boys and I looked everywhere, but no trace of the dog. All of a sudden, without a knock or the sound of the doorbell, Dorothy entered through the front door, carrying our puppy in her arms like a baby. A gentleman accompanied her. Putting the puppy down, she explained that when she had driven into the driveway, the dog catcher was trying to catch our puppy. She had immediately taken him inside and explained to the dogcatcher it was hers. She apologized that the dog was off leash.

I thanked her and said I would figure out how the puppy had escaped. Wiping off puppy fur from her pantsuit, she introduced me to her brother. I noticed how smartly dressed she and her brother were and asked where she had been. Without batting an eye, she explained that the oncologist had removed all life support from her husband this afternoon and that he died. Shocked, I told her how sorry I was and asked if there was anything I could do. She interrupted me and said that there was nothing. She would be fine. They turned around and left. I held on the puppy's collar so he wouldn't bolt out of the front door and thought *this woman is in shock. She can't feel anything. She's not even on automatic pilot yet. She's in irons in the storm. Time has stopped for her. And I remember when time stopped for me.*

The memorial service took place in the lobby of the pediatric wing of the hospital where he was chairman of the board. There was no funeral service. There was no church. There was no graveside service. There were no cremains. There was no casket. Inside glass sliding glass doors, people congregated in a lobby. I attended, not knowing anyone, and listened to her husband's various friends stand in front of the people and eulogize him. Her husband had a special place in his heart for sick children and had donated extensively to this wing. After the service, Dorothy stood, dressed in a navy blue suit, surrounded by her husband's friends and greeted everyone. I looked at the line forming to meet her and I looked at her. I just couldn't stand in another line at a service for someone dead. I didn't know this woman. This woman was operating on a high level of adrenalin. I thought *I will find another time to offer the touch, the feel of human contact. If I do it now, she won't feel it. She doesn't have the capacity to feel now. She's in an out-of-body experience.* I waited and caught her after the line was over. I told her the service was beautiful. She asked me to come to her house for the reception.

I didn't really want to, but I made myself go to take her puppy back to our house for the night. There would be way too much commotion for a small puppy. It was a warm summer evening and there was no escape from the heat in her house built in the mid-1800s with no air conditioning. I stayed in the kitchen and helped the caterer as more people came than had been expected. In the middle of the evening, Dorothy came into the kitchen and said she had forgotten to feed the dogs their dinner. I told her not to worry. I would feed them and went to retrieve their food. I thought *the death drug is beginning to infect her.*

I spent the remainder of August 2007 mostly with William buying things, and packing his stuff for college. My baby was going to college about four hours away. He was right. This would be the first time in twenty-three years that I would live alone. The boys were at our house 24 hours a day, 7 days a week, during the last few weeks of August as everyone knew that while they would see each other again, life as they had known was ending. It was during this time, that Dorothy and I began our tailgate parties in the evening on her driveway while we watched the puppies play in her fenced-in backyard.

During one of our tailgate parties, she looked quite upset. She was going to have to sell their Cape Cod summer house immediately. She had believed it might be a possibility, but her husband's accountant confirmed this. Her blue eyes looked at me inquiringly. I understood. I would help when the time came.

When I returned home that evening, I noticed voicemail on my cell and I looked at the number. It was my niece from California. I returned the call immediately. Her daughter had recently been accepted into a prestigious graduate program in the city, which began in two weeks. She didn't have to ask. I told her by all means her daughter could stay in our home and take the train in to her school until she got her feet on the ground. The city could be overwhelming for its residents, let alone for a California babe.

I didn't really know her daughter very well and was actually happy that I would have a chance of building a friendship with her. Heather especially was fond of her and I looked forward to this new experience. I was having a lot of new experiences: unemployed, a new puppy, William going away to college, a new friend who just lost her husband, not knowing what I was doing with my life and now the opportunity of getting to know my niece's daughter.

She arrived a few days later, and a few days after that it was time to pack the car and take William to college. Driving up to the college, William slept most of the way, as could be expected since he had stayed up most of the night partying with his buddies.

When we arrived at the college, we hauled his gear up to the dorm room he would be sharing with one of his buddies from town. His buddy's parents were there organizing everything. We went to the store to buy things that he needed, but seeing that his buddy's parents had everything under control, I decided to leave. I preferred to get home before midnight. William walked me down to the car and said, "I don't believe it, mom. You are really going to cry."

I hugged him and got in the car and backed the car out of the parking lot. Driving away, with blurred vision, I thought *yes, I am going to cry. You mean the world to me.*

FALL 2007

Being unemployed had its advantages. I loved having the time to myself. My niece's daughter was consumed during the week with her classes, but on the weekends we made plans to see different parts of the city. She had an angelic countenance about her. With her long blonde hair, her soft but vibrant deep blue eyes, and soft, quiet voice, there was something infinitely calming about her. One warm early September afternoon, we found ourselves in Soho and hungry. We stopped at a small restaurant that had tables outside on the sidewalk. We were taking the afternoon slow. We ordered a main dish to share and a salad with a carafe of wine. I liked this pace. I liked taking it slow. We had no timetable. My friend was watching our puppy.

After leisurely eating our meal and relaxing with our wine, she asked me about my husband and his death. She wanted to know because her father had died of the same cancer. He had been a Southern California boy as well, but he died when he was only forty-six years old. I didn't know how close she was to her father and I didn't know the particulars of his death. My niece's daughter began to tell me slowly and quietly that she had always stayed close with him, that even after he had remarried and had two sons, she became close to her half brothers and stayed closer to him.

We spoke of the overwhelming, time-consuming process of death and then the numbness that sets in afterwards. She stopped and told me to wait and dug around in her bag. She found her wallet, opened it and pulled out a picture. She handed it to me. It was a black and white photograph of her father. He had his head tilted to one side, with his long curly hair covering his ears, and a smile that would melt any girl's heart. He looked like a man with a kind heart. She smiled and I smiled back and said how very lucky she was to have had a father like this and she agreed. We both sat, soaking in the afternoon sun, sipping our wine, each of us consumed with our own memories.

When we came home, Dorothy came over with both puppies.

It was time for them to play, a.k.a. destroy my back yard, and time for me to play hostess. Dorothy and my niece's daughter got along famously. They were both in the same career field. We sipped our vodka tonics, watched the puppies play, admired the cardinal feeding on the birdfeeder and spoke of how grueling city life can be. Dorothy decided it was time to take her puppy home and feed her dogs dinner and she left rather abruptly. I remained on the deck with my niece's daughter enjoying the last remnants of daylight. During the last month or so, Dorothy had been indoctrinated into one of our house's policies. No one rings the doorbell or knocks. If you heard the doorbell, you considered twice about answering it, trying to figure out who it may be. It was the same thing with the phone. Sometimes, we would answer it. Other times, we would look at the ringing phone and walk away from it.

Suddenly, we heard the front door open and we both looked at each other, stunned. It was Dorothy. She marched out to the deck, and stood in front of me. She said, "All you can do is say no, if you don't want to come. But I am going to invite you. My husband and I have a timeshare in Bermuda and next week is our week. Would you like to go with me?"

I was tongue-tied. I didn't know what to say. I didn't really know this woman, but I knew that she would be returning solo to a place that she and her husband had vacationed together. She didn't know that the death drug was in the process of ramping up its toxins in her body.

I replied, "Sure."

She smiled and she gave me her flight information. I told her I would book my ticket tonight. We would leave on Monday, in two days. She left smiling and I turned to my niece's daughter.

She smiled and said, "You did the right thing."

She knew that I was concerned about money, but I knew my severance pay would carry me through Christmas. I went in to book my ticket.

Bermuda: When you entered the complex where she and her husband had a cottage, it was as if you were entering a different world. This world was one with crystal blue water, warm, clean air, luxurious accommodations and a staff of men that were accommodating and cheerful in every way. There were no cars, only motorized golf carts. Dorothy wanted to take me to the beach and the way to get there was on a motorized golf cart. We found her cottage and she showed me my bedroom. It was the luxury of Bermuda. No want was not met. I changed into my swimsuit and a cover up and met her outside by the golf cart. She had to drop off some paperwork at the outside concierge across the way before going down to the beach. I was along for the ride, so anything was fine with me.

She drove across the parking lot area and stopped to give the paperwork to a tall, lanky Bermudian gentleman who had a smile that went ear to ear, showing his pearly white teeth. He told her to wait for a minute and went inside the concierge booth. He returned with a vintage bottle of wine.

Handing it to her, he said, "This is for you. I know that your husband loved his good wine, but this is for you. You only. I hope you enjoy it while you're here. And you know, if there is anything any one of us can do for you, we're here."

Immediately, I saw it in her face and thought *it is the random acts of kindness that bring you up short. When you expect someone to act in the bereavement way, you prepare yourself. You are there for them because it is they who have come to tell you how much they are hurting and how much they will miss the deceased. But when you least expect it and think I am just going to drop something off at the concierge, something like this happens. You receive a beautiful bottle of wine and it is given to you, for you, because the giver is thinking of you, thinking of only you and your pain. He does not ramble on about what a great husband you had, how your husband loved wine. He is giving this to you because he cares about you. These random acts of kindness derail you. They cut right through your strongest protective shield and you succumb to the wonderful feeling of someone cares, someone cares for you and then you remember how deeply your husband cared and then you cave.*

I told her to move into the passenger seat. While I hadn't driven a golf cart for along time, I knew I could manage. We didn't say anything on the ride to the beach. I wanted to give her privacy. I wanted to honor her feelings by not intruding.

Once we were at the beach, we walked down to the ocean and wiggled our toes in the warm sea. The sand was the smoothest and finest I had ever walked on and the view to the horizon across the sea was unobstructed. We ordered drinks, which a waiter brought down to the beach for us, and we spoke of geographical facts about Bermuda.

Dorothy finally looked at me and said, "I don't know the answers to all your questions. I never thought about what longitude or latitude Bermuda is."

I told her I was sorry for pestering. "I always have too many questions," I replied.

I thought *if you want to know, look them up for yourself. Be quiet. Let her take the lead. This is her world.* After finishing our drinks, we meandered down the beach. She pointed to a small beach down the coast and told me that she and her husband called that beach Sandy Pants.

I smiled. I stood there on the beach with her, when she said, "Why couldn't someone else have died? Why did he have to die?"

I thought *back to when I would take my dad into radiation treatment. I would see a man on the street and think, why can't he die instead of my dad?*

I turned toward her and said, "I know, I felt the same way when my dad was dying. But then you slowly realize that you were going to have to face his death someday and it just happens that the day is now. It doesn't diminish how much you miss him. It doesn't diminish the ache. It just makes you understand that it is today and not a future experience."

I thought *I didn't have this thought when my husband was dying. Maybe it has something to do with the first death you experience. By the second death, your subconscious kicks in and helps you understand your powerlessness and you come to understand all you can do is comfort and love the dying. You slowly discover that all the research in the world is not going to alter the process of death.*

———◆———

It was a chilly fall October afternoon when a friend of mine said he would stop by after touring the country hills on his motorcycle. This was his annual fall ritual. He loved his bike and he loved the fall foliage. He would arrive around sundown. I had known him since before my children were born. When I returned to work after my husband's death, this friend went out of his way to call me, to make sure I was doing okay. He came and took me out to lunch every month or so and we would talk books, concepts, history. He made my routine bearable.

As I was preparing dinner, waiting for him, my cell phone rang and I looked at the number. It was Stephan. I answered it and he told me he was training people where I had worked. I told him that was great, but I didn't work there anymore. I told him I had to go and hung up. I thought *why did he call? It doesn't matter. You are not going to continue.* Just then, my friend walked in, his face windburned and chilled. I offered him a glass of wine and told him dinner would be ready in a few minutes. We ate slowly, talking about his various and complicated projects at his work and compared notes.

Afterward, we walked outside and he inquired if the hot tub was working. I responded affirmatively. He asked why hadn't I asked him to get in. He was still chilled from his bike ride through the autumn air. I opened the top of the hot tub and turned on the jets. I told him I would go down to William's room to find him a suit. I ran downstairs and started opening drawers, but only came across Speedos and decided no, that wouldn't do. I finally found a pair of mesh gym shorts. When I climbed back upstairs and went out on the deck to give them to him, he was already in the hot tub, naked. I looked at him as he watched the stars in the night sky and I thought *okay, when in Rome, do as a Roman*. I undressed and gently eased in. He pulled me to his side and with his left hand turned my face toward his and kissed me. I said, "I'm taking your lead on this."

He told me that he remembered the first time he saw me. I had opened the door to a conference room in a huge exhibition hall. He was sitting at the head of the conference table. He told me he remembered thinking he had never seen such a beautiful woman.

We spoke of how we had always felt about one another, but never acted. He was married and I had been married. I looked up at the night sky and couldn't find the North Star and asked him if he knew its location in the autumn sky. He pointed to it and my eyes followed his finger and there she was, hiding behind the end of the roof of the house.

After a while, warmed and soothed, we climbed out and as he was bending over, tying his shoe by the kitchen table, he said, "I'm Catholic. This is all that I can offer."

I nodded. He kissed me goodbye and I climbed upstairs. I took off my clothes and put on a comfy T-shirt and climbed into bed. I couldn't sleep. I kept thinking of the events during the evening. I turned on the nightstand lamp and went over to my desk and wrote the following:

Polaris

In one gesture
His arm encircles my waist,
pulls me through the water to him.
Side by side, suspended in, suspended by water,
his hand finds its way to my breast,
securing softly and then the other to the other.
He scans the night sky for Polaris and
points to its direction.
Concealed by darkness, cloaked in warm water
a release of roles past
an introduction to how we always felt.

Polarity

I understand the concept
"The Good Married Catholic Boy"
and
in the middle of the night
my body aches for your hands.

I didn't hear from him during the next few weeks. He had been a good friend and because of the hot tub experience, he fell off the radar. I thought *back to my staff member's remark. With men, it all boiled down to sex. A heavy lead weight rests in my chest. I refuse to believe this. I have no idea what to believe, but I don't want to believe this. What do you believe? I don't know anymore. While it is flattering to feel his affection and be told that I am a beautiful woman, his absence leaves a hollow space. Another rejection by a good friend. Death is a type of rejection to the living. But why do the living reject the living? Embarrassment? Shame? I would rather have his friendship, but this hot tub experience removed our friendship from history. Perhaps, only temporarily. I love the passionate embrace, but the steadfastness of friendship nourishes me more than the moments of physical ecstasy. It is nourishment that feeds that which needs sustenance. I don't know what to call it. How can a romantic gesture negate an established friendship? Fear? Fear of the unknown? Fear that normalcy is no longer normal or not of the known established routine? That friendship may turn into something else that is unknown? Is the unknown that scary?*

After this experience, I forced myself back into the dating scene. Perhaps my daughter was right. She wanted me to have a man by my side. William wanted me to have a dog by my side. I was not sure which was right, but each morning, I scanned the various dating sites and chose the man of the week. I must have dated at least fifty men during this period: Lawyers, financial gurus, Italian Mafia, engineers, a guy specializing in inventory systems. And then there was one guy who was up front and just asked to have purely a sexual relationship, which we did for a short while until I became bored. On some dates, I'd excuse myself from the dinner table and en route to the ladies room, would tell the waitress that if the bill were on the table and paid when I returned, I would give her this and flashed her a twenty dollar bill. Not one of them intrigued me like Stephan. Dating took time, a lot of time and after a while, I decided it took too much time. Discouraged, I turned my attention towards my consulting work with Rebecca's boyfriend and figured maybe this just wasn't meant to be.

———◆———

In the morning, I checked my email and saw one from Rebecca in India. She was in the Himalayas. I knew from her boyfriend that she and her traveling companion were having some difficulties after nine months of being in each other's constant company. They were planning on coming back to the States in early December, but nothing had warned me of the severity of the situation until I opened her email.

Hi Mom,

Sorry I've been out of touch for a few weeks. I hope you are doing well in your writing process and had a good time with Heather. I hope she is doing better.

I've been going through a beautiful process of dying. The last nine months in India has brought me deeper into my fears, disconnecting me with my body, my feelings, my boyfriend, my traveling companion and myself. Every time I have surrendered, let go of fears, fallen into the arms of the Divine, I have fallen on my face flat.

Almost like a reverse pregnancy of uncreating a self, I have been forced to let go of everything. The last week here culminated when I talked with my guides and they said that my experience here in India was entirely predestined, a life lesson my soul chose to experience so that I must shed everything before I can step into a place which is my destiny. I felt like dying. My body was at the lowest it's ever been nutritionally deficient, borderline hospitalization, very weak.

I couldn't feel anything. Now I am changing. Being unborn back into the Great Mother and finding a new life, one that I've never known. Alone and yet never more connected with Life and Love. I am Love, I am Divine and I am slowly opening the wings after breaking the cocoon.

Some things happen instantaneously. Others take time. Like a gradual instant, I am moving now.

I'll call soon when I'm able...just know I've been thinking about you...

Rebecca

The words– "dying, nutritionally deficient, hospitalization"– reverberated in my head. My fingers tapped the desk in an uncontrollable manner. I thought *I should go to her. Yes, I should fly to the Himalayas and find her. I don't know who she's become. Since her father died, she bolted from home. I know she blames me. I understand Joseph Campbell's concept that the father is the first intimate relationship to the male principle for the girl. When the father is no longer around and when the mother is forced to play both roles, the girl blames the mother. She thinks the mother has taken away the person who would have been her guide and messenger. Yes, I deeply understand how she thinks I have caused her this excruciating pain, but it has been four years and maybe time does soothe the soul. This is your daughter. This is your flesh and blood. It does not matter if she hates you. You are not going to let her die without her knowing how much you love her. And if she will allow, help her nutritionally heal. I will fly to the Himalayas. I will invade my savings. I will do it.* I wrote the email back to her.

Sweetums –

I am concerned for your well-being – both spiritually and physically. I believe that the greatest gift a person has is their own inner voice, their own intuition, their own compass. Seek your own voice. Be in a room by yourself and the answers will come to you.

I think the only advice I have is "Trust yourself." Do not be afraid of listening on a very deep level to your own voice and no one else's. Be true to yourself. You are an incredible, wonderful, human being.

And if you would like the companionship of your mother, I would love to visit you.

I love you, too.

Me

I immediately began investigating various flights to India and then how to travel to the Himalayas when my cell phone rang. I looked at the number and recognized my brother's number. He never called me unless something was up. I answered it. "Do you have a minute?" His voice sounded ominous.

I replied, "Yes."

I heard him breathe in deeply. He had ended up in the emergency room the day before due to severe shortness of breath. He was at work, sitting behind his desk when he developed trouble breathing. One of his workers called 911 and the crew hastily transported to him to the hospital. They ran extensive tests until the emergency room doctors established a diagnosis: narrowing of his major heart arteries. He was scheduled for an emergency quadruple cardiac bypass surgery tomorrow. The surgeon was concerned because he had diabetes and this could affect the survival and recovery rate. His cardiologist requested a family member be present during the surgery and through the recovery. He didn't know how long the recovery would be in the Intensive Care or Nursing unit, but once he was discharged, recovery would be from eight to ten weeks. Basically, during the recovery process, he would be dependent on someone else. He asked if I would be able to be present tomorrow for the surgery. In a heartbeat, I said, "Yes. Yes, I will be there."

I hung up and glanced out the window to the deck and saw my cardinal standing on top of the birdfeeder. I went to the sliding glass door and looked at him closely. He was a beautiful bird with his crimson feathers, his plume rising off the top of his head. I thought *who knew? Now it is my brother. What about my daughter? What do I do? Your daughter will be okay. Be there for your brother. Okay.*

I walked over to my desk and called my mother. In the most reassuring way, I explained the situation.

My brother's surgery was more extensive than initially expected. Several weeks later, he was still recovering in the hospital. He had been moved from the Intensive Care Unit, where he remained for three weeks, to the Nursing Unit. The plan was that he would be discharged before Christmas, but it was a day-by-day decision.

For Thanksgiving Day, my mother's driver drove her to our house. I had insisted that she no longer drive great distances and she had reluctantly agreed. I had cooked our dinner, complete with turkey, stuffing, mashed potatoes, a broccoli soufflé, rolls, cranberry sauce, and a salad. I knew the menu was not the best for a diabetic patient recovering from a quadruple bypass, but this would only be one meal and it was a special occasion. My second daughter remained in California for Thanksgiving this year, celebrating it with her boyfriend's family.

Driving into the city to deliver my brother's dinner, the highways were deserted. Everyone else was at home with their families, enjoying their company. I dropped William and mother at the hospital entrance and drove a few city blocks to the parking garage. As I walked up the street to the entrance,

I thought *when will this pattern stop, after everybody's dead?* I entered through the revolving door, signed in with the security guard and took the elevator to his floor. When I entered the room, my brother was sitting in a chair, still connected to various monitors and IV. William was sitting on the window ledge looking down to the city street.

My mother unwrapped the Thanksgiving Day dinner. The smell in the room was awful and my stomach immediately reacted. I felt nauseated. I prayed we didn't have to stay here long. My mother handed my brother his dinner and he devoured the mashed potatoes followed by the rest of the dinner. We spoke of Rebecca returning from India in several weeks, after being gone for an entire year. We all wondered who she had become. We wondered if we would recognize her. Later, I mentioned that after William returned to college in a few days, I would be heading up to Cape Cod to help my friend pack up her summer house. In a down market, she had sold it for the asking price. My mother commented that it must have been a beautiful home for it to sell so quickly. After my brother finished eating, he was tired and I suggested that we leave so that he could rest.

At home, I served dinner in the dining room. There were seven chairs equally spaced around the dining room table. Before sitting down, William told us to wait. He moved the two opposite chairs near the rear of the table closer to the rear chair. He insisted that the three of us sit close together. He said, "We have never had a Thanksgiving with only three members of the family before."

I softly reminded him, "We should be grateful for this. We should be grateful that the three of us are together. It is Thanksgiving."

WINTER 2007 – 2008

Dorothy rented a huge Suburban truck to drive to Cape Cod. I drove her Lexus SUV. I had my puppy and she had her puppy and massive black lab. She insisted on carefully packaging her husband's artwork. She would transport that herself. She didn't trust the moving company to handle such precious artwork. It was a five-hour drive to the Cape and as I was driving, I thought *this is my old stomping ground. This is where I grew up. How much fun I had as a kid, collecting salamanders from the river bank, building them a home in my mother's tin cooking pot, ice skating on a pond in the woods, playing pioneers in the deep, dark woods with my best friend, walking barefoot on the linoleum kitchen floor. This was my ritual every year, walking barefoot. It meant summer had begun. Sailing in the inner harbor and when I was older, venturing out to the outer harbor, flunking my father's sailing test to determine if I could take the sailboat out solo. I will go to my grave still being upset about that.*

When I was maybe six or seven years old, my dad, mom and I were sailing downwind as we entered the expansive outer harbor from the bay. Out of nowhere, the winds picked up violently. As the winds increased, my dad instructed me to take the tiller. He pointed to the red gong buoy, marking the outer harbor and commanded me to steer for it. The main and jib flapped in the oncoming wind while my dad scrambled to the bow and took down the jib in nanoseconds. Back in the cockpit, he immediately grabbed the tiller from me and eased the boat downwind. He glanced up to the main, but there was no time to put in a reef. The small sailboat rolled dramatically from one side to the other, sailing downwind. My dad yelled at us to put on our life jackets. As I secured the front buckle, I watched the seawater run through the railing drains and over the gunnels, my legs stretched out in front of me with my feet braced on the opposite bench. He looked down at me and sternly ordered me to stay with the boat if we should capsize. That was rule number one. Second rule, slip off your shoes and pants. I looked at my new sneakers. I didn't want to. They were my favorites. He told me to just do it. I was becoming scared.

I remember saying to him, "But you told me because the keel is made of lead, the boat can't capsize. How can she capsize?" He replied that an accidental jibe could capsize the boat. He pointed to the winds, indicating how volatile and violent they were. He was concerned about jibbing as he looked to the mainsail and boom extended way over the rail. The boat sailed at lightning speed. My mother descended into the small cabin. The afternoon sky became overcast and began to pelt rain. The whitecaps mounted. Sailing downwind, each wave catapulted the boat faster through the sea. My mom threw our foul weather gear to us. I slid mine over my head, but my dad did not put his on. He wouldn't take his hands off the tiller. I sat in the cockpit and took my sneakers off and put them in a hold where the docking lines were kept.

Five years later, I wanted to sail alone. In order to have permission, I had to pass my father's sailing test. Everything was going well. Winds were from the northeast, typical, about seven knots. I tacked, came about, sailed upwind, sailed downwind, purposely went into irons, eased out of irons, picked up the mooring, sailed into the wind and gently docked the boat at the pier's side. Then, the last test: perform a controlled jibe. I hated this. This was when the boat could capsize. I was scared. I took her out to the outer harbor on my father's instructions. He followed in the pram. I sailed the boat downwind and had the mainsail completely out. I felt the wind slightly shift and began pulling in the mainsheet until the boom was almost directly overhead. I began to release the mainsheet rapidly and then the boom smacked the top of my head. I stumbled and let the mainsheet go and scrambled to my feet.

My dad yelled, "That's too close to losing control of the boat. You'll need to perform the jibe again."

I was trembling. My head was throbbing. I can't. Next time, I will capsize. That jibe was almost perfect. I want to go home. I don't want to jibe again. I began sailing toward the inner harbor, to our mooring. My dad motored up along side and told me that until I did it again, there would be no solo sailing. I was a good sailor and I could do it. I turned away from him because I didn't want him to see my tears. I never did it again. I never passed his test. But on the weekdays, when he was at work, I would take her out and sail solo and not tell anyone.

When we arrived at Dorothy's summer house, it was dark and freezing cold. Dorothy showed me to the first-floor guestroom. I threw my bags into the guest room and escorted the two puppies in with their assorted toys. They immediately jumped on the double bed and began frolicking, making the bed a mess.

I asked her where she wanted me to begin. She opened a door that led to the basement and we descended. Against two walls were eight long shelves filled with paperback books. There must have been at least five hundred paperback books. She said this was her husband's summer library. She had come equipped with plenty of boxes. Would I mind dusting each book off and packing those in good condition in the boxes. She wanted to mail them to the hospital where her husband had been chairman of the board. They could use them in the patients' waiting rooms. It was a resourceful idea.

She went back upstairs to start packing the artwork. I walked slowly from one wall to the other, looking at these books and saw how organized they were. Each book was organized first by the last name of the author, then by the first name of the author, then by the title of the book, all alphabetically. I started, as I should, as he would have wanted me to, with the first book. I would not disrupt his meticulous order and I hoped that whoever unpacked the books in the hospital would understand and revere his great organizational expertise. I breathed in the damp, moldy air and began.

As I continued, I looked at the title and if I hadn't read the book, I read the summary on the back of the book. There were books on science, astronomy, troubadour poetry, wine books, trashy summer novels, and great literature. I was in the company of Ernest Hemmingway, Virginia Woolf, F. Scott Fitzgerald, D. H. Lawrence, William Shakespeare, Voltaire, Einstein. After several hours, I was halfway done when my friend called me. It was cocktail time. Before climbing the basement stairs, I scanned the packaged books. Smiling, I said, "It's been a pleasure getting to know you."

The next day, I finished dusting and packing the books in the boxes. I hauled them upstairs and put them in the car. We were going to the Post Office to ship them to the hospital. But first Dorothy brought me upstairs to the bedroom adjacent to the master suite. I peered in and saw on various tables half-finished models of whaling ships, sloops and clocks. By one wall numerous boxes of unopened models were stacked. She pointed to them and said that we needed to return them to the store. Her husband didn't have the time to start them. She told me he had bought them the last time they were both here, over the July 4th weekend, but had then succumbed to a bad spell and remained in bed for the duration of their stay. As we loaded all the models in the Suburban because they couldn't all fit in the Lexus, she turned to me and said, "If I continue to buy models, I won't die."

I smiled and thought *yes, she is getting this. She understands the death process while the death drug circulates through her system.* We climbed in and drove out into the gray, overcast afternoon: a grayness that is unique to the Cape in wintertime.

We spent four days packing, carting things to Goodwill, going to Staples to buy more bubble wrap. We boxed up the kitchen, dining room, living room, den, linen closets, and bathrooms. Dorothy was tackling her master bedroom and I was asked to pack up the adjacent room where he'd kept his summer clothes. I opened the dresser drawer and saw piles of polo shirts all folded in the same manner, organized by color. I smiled and remembered his books. I was not surprised.

Driving back from the Cape, my mind turned to Rebecca. She would be home in two days. I didn't know her anymore. She had asked me if it was all right if she moved back into the house. I was shocked at the request. Of course, it was. As long as I owned this physical structure, it was everyone's home, including the lost boys when they came home from college. My niece's daughter had found an apartment in the city and she was happily ensconced there. After the Christmas holiday, it would be just Rebecca and me in the house. William and Heather would return to their respective colleges.

———◆◆◆———

Rebecca's boyfriend met her at the airport and drove her home. When I heard the car drive into the driveway, I greeted them at the front door. My daughter, dressed in a flowing long Indian skirt, was emaciated, but her smile had not changed. I hugged her and felt her ribs protruding through her back, but I didn't say anything. Her traveling companion followed behind the boyfriend. She looked only slightly better. We sat in the living room and spoke with a formality I wasn't used to. After exchanging perfunctory remarks, the girls brought their luggage upstairs and were going to relax.

During the next few days, the two girls were constant companions. My daughter played Christmas carols on the piano and her traveling companion gracefully sang the lyrics. The actual Christmas holiday of 2007 was a blur as I focused on trying to understand how to help Rebecca regain her physical health. I had no idea of her mental or emotional state.

Then it happened, after Christmas– the explosion. Thank god it did not happen in our home. It occurred at Rebecca's boyfriend's house by the beach. After four and half years of being together, living with each other, being each other's best friend, my daughter decided that she wanted a platonic friendship with him. After her long, hard year in India, she no longer wanted the attachment of her girlfriend or her boyfriend. She wanted her freedom. He had asked her what she wanted and she responded that she didn't know. All she knew was she wanted the possibilities of life.

To say that he was heartbroken was an understatement. After their initial conversation at his house, they came home. One evening, the three of us sat on the brown leather couch in our living room. We spoke of my daughter and me continuing to consult for his company and whether or not it would be a good idea. While he was not reluctant for us to continue, he was unsure of our compensation, particularly mine. My usually reserved Rebecca became adamant, stating that I deserved a handsome salary due to my skills and expertise. I saw the red lines on her lips and then I saw his. That was when I left.

I called the puppy, who came obediently, and we left for his sister's home. During the last six months, Dorothy and I had forged an important relationship. I had introduced her to Sandra, the caterer who had lost her husband a year and half ago. I was closer to Dorothy than to Sandra, just as Sandra was closer to Dorothy than to me. The three of us formed a triangle, if you will, from all walks of life. Dorothy with her many homes, Sandra with a small home in a blue-collar town, and myself, somewhere in the middle. Yet we all shared the common denominator of experiencing firsthand, up close, the death process and the death of our husbands.

While walking my puppy in the night air, I thought *how unusual that these two women would come into my life and be my friends. I remember back to the caretaker on Naxos describing the Bacchoi initiation rites. Our similar experiences are the ritual that initiated us into this liberation of life without a husband. It is liberation, if not the most excruciatingly painful liberation and I am quite certain that these two women do not want to be liberated. Me, I'm not sure. I don't know. My husband's and my relationship would have had to change if it were to be sustained and grow. Over the last twelve years, the glue that held our relationship together for me was our Greek trips. Those trips brought us together as a family. Every day, time stopped during those trips and all of us were transported back twenty-five hundred years ago to a beautiful land. I do not know what held our relationship together for him. I do not know if he wanted our relationship to change, to move into safe, open and loving territory. A territory whose fundamental characteristics I now define as an almost desperate want to communicate, to disclose thoughts and feelings openly and honestly, to be vulnerable, to forgive, to make the relationship primary, to trust your love until your eyes shut forever. But the three of us, women, understand each other in a way that no one else can imagine. We don't have to talk about it. We simply know.*

Walking up the stairs to her side door, the puppies whined like babies. As soon as I opened the door, they began playing with each other immediately. Dorothy and I sat down at her wooden kitchen table. She told me of the renovations she was going to make on her house. The third floor was unfinished. She was going to make it into a warm, inviting office, lined with bookcases and wooden ceiling fans. I smiled and thought *of my own renovations after my husband died. Her timing is about right.* She explained that after the renovations, she wanted to sell her house and move south to where she and her husband had a condominium. It was on the beach and she loved being on the water. Both her dogs loved it there. She had established some friendships over the years when they had vacationed there.

Surprised, I told her that I would miss her daily companionship, but I understood. She had lived in her house for twenty-seven years and no matter how much she renovated, it was a constant reminder of who wasn't here. She and her husband had never had children and I could only imagine the loneliness that she endured each time she set foot in this house. She told me that the contractors would begin next week and that she hoped to have the house on the market by the spring. Walking home much later in the evening, I thought *nothing is permanent, nothing is constant.*

The following week, Stephan called me and asked to get together the following evening. Surprised by his request, I surprised myself further and agreed. When I met him outside his workplace in the city the next evening, he climbed into the passenger side seat and we kissed. Bewildered by his behavior, I asked him where he wanted to go. Neither of us having much money, we stayed in the car and debated our various options. My cell phone rang during this conversation. It was Rebecca. She wanted to know where I was, since it was past dinnertime. Not accustomed to being accountable to anyone, I was taken aback. William and I had been two ships passing in the night, but now that my daughter was home, she was very much trying to participate in my life. After four years of her being away from home, I discovered the adjustment unusual. I told her where I was and with whom. She continued that she had just made curried chicken and invited us to share the dinner. Stephan had never been to our house, since William and his friends had been opposed to the idea. We talked it over and agreed. When we arrived, Rebecca was still in the process of cooking and he took my hand and we climbed the stairs to my bedroom. He beckoned and I jumped into his arms with his large hands holding my thighs as he slowly walked to the bed and eased me down. Embracing every inch of my body, this man began to make passionate love to me. Allowing my body to receive warmth instead of concentrating on giving, made the warmth of both our bodies grow effortlessly.

Dorothy called me the next morning. I heard her agitation and anxiety. She said, "Tell me something good that has happened."

Dumbfounded, I blurted out, "I had great sex last night." She laughed until I heard her tears. Her contractor's crane, while lifting large wooden beams to her attic window, dropped them on her roof. Now a gaping massive hole adorned her roof. Now her lawyer would be involved. Now her timeline was derailed. She had told the contractor that it was a stupid way to proceed, but he ignored her advice and went ahead. This was the result. I listened to her frustration and I understood.

———◆◆◆———

SPRING – SUMMER
2008

April 2008: One year ago, Dorothy asked me the question, "How do you do it?" And now she was having to answer the question for herself. Everyone experiences the question uniquely and everyone lives the answer differently.

After Bermuda and through the last few months, I had gotten to know some of her good friends from bankers to real estate moguls to hot studs of contractors. She had a diverse group of people in her inner circle, but none of them, I felt, were stepping up to the plate. It was her birthday this month, the first birthday in her new life, without her husband. I knew that sometimes, significant milestones could set a person reeling, especially if you're accustomed to celebrating them with someone no longer around. While I didn't have a history with her as her friends did, I knew I had to do something. I knew that she had to forge new memories in her new life. I planned a surprise birthday party for her.

My now eleven-year-old friend from next door was terribly excited about this proposition. She was eager to help with the particulars, especially with the balloons and streamers. Sandra was on board as well, and promised to prepare the most delicious buffet dinner for the guests. Heather insisted on flying home from California for it and my other two children were equally excited. The trick was securing the guest names and phone numbers without my friend knowing. Making up excuses, such as I needed to have her friends phone numbers in case of an emergency, I easily obtained the information. Feeling slightly uncomfortable as an outsider in her life, I called her friends and secured a guest list of about twenty people.

As she entered our front door the day of the party and the guests shouted, "Surprise!" her face beamed with astonishment and gratitude. We immediately went to work on providing everyone with drinks and food as she sat in the center of the room and opened her various presents. Her face did not stop beaming as she wore her birthday hat and blew out her candles with the assistance of her new eleven-year-old friend.

As guests lingered on the new deck and relaxed in the living room, Rebecca took numerous pictures to capture the quality of the day. She later made a photograph album with these pictures and gave it to Dorothy as a belated birthday present. The pictures presented a day that was sustained by much laughter, love and camaraderie.

Afterward, she was ready to begin the immense task of spring cleaning. She wanted to go through each room, reviewing every sundry item. She wanted to streamline and simplify her life. It was during this time period, that every other weekend or so, it seemed, we hosted garage sales. Sometimes, they would be in her driveway. Other times, they were held in my driveway. And at each one, the boys carted all the items out to the driveways and at the end, hauled the unsold articles back into the garage. She was slowly but surely understanding the generosity of spirit inside each and every one of these young men.

Heather graduated from college in May and William, gramma and I flew out to California for the celebration. Rebecca had recently been hired at a prestigious consulting firm in the city and was unable to take off any time. She was excited about her new prospect and getting her feet on the ground in the city. Five months after returning from a hard year in India, she was becoming a young professional woman in New York City. I couldn't help but marvel how things changed.

My husband's niece met us in California, having driven down from the Bay Area. We stayed in a sprawling hotel on the Back Bay of Newport Beach. I promised myself to focus only on Heather's graduation this visit, but the truth of the matter was that William, my husband's niece, gramma and I were having a blast bunking into two adjacent hotel rooms. It was like a huge pajama party with pomegranate martinis in the evening and breakfast served in the room, late in the morning. Gramma and William slept in one room and my husband's niece and I shared the other room.

When gramma went to sleep at night, she told William that he could watch his porn now. I thought *how incredibly tolerant and outspoken we had both become over the past years. This never would have been the case with either my husband or father alive.* My husband's niece and I felt like we were in college, staying up late after everyone had gone to bed, sharing stories of funny dates, or miserable ones to be accurate. Then we would rise before anyone else and continue our stories. We had no limits on what we talked about.

The day of Heather's graduation was unusually cold and damp, and the program was held outside. While gramma sat in her wheelchair, we stood beside her on the lawn and listened to the various speakers present each graduate. William presented his sister and a newspaper photographer captured both of them on the stage. After the ceremony, I took gramma back to the car and started the engine to warm the car. She said that her bones were cold. I returned to find my daughter surrounded by friends of every type enjoying her newfound freedom.

Later in the evening, we enjoyed a celebratory dinner with the four of my daughter's friends and us. During the dinner, I thought *it has been five years, five long years, but I still feel you. I know you are here tonight.*

FALL 2008

By September, my feet itched to return to Greece. They hadn't felt her earth for the past three years. It was not only my feet; my insides yearned to be on her land again. I began to seriously contemplate a solo trip for only two weeks. Then I became excited. I wanted to go to places I had never been before. Northern Greece, the oracle of Dodona in Epirus, came to mind. This oracle was initially devoted to the mother earth goddess and was the oldest Hellenic oracle according to Herodotus. Barefoot priestesses listened to the sound of the winds swirling through a massive oak tree. They interpreted the sounds as signs and gave man his message. This made sense. I would explore Northern Greece and hike her mountains and visit Dodona. I investigated my flights and then I felt the butterflies in my stomach. I called them my Greek butterflies. I knew that my mother would be upset with my plans. The trip to Italy had upset her greatly even though William and I had called her every other night. She had become quite dependent on my weekly visits. During many visits, I did her food shopping and errands. She had become increasingly frail, but I reasoned with Rebecca working and living at home, she could act as a substitute if need be.

One weekend in September, I asked Rebecca to visit her grandmother with me so that we could both inform her of my impending trip. In this way, my mother could be reassured that Rebecca would take good care of her while I was away for two weeks. We drove through the chilly fall morning to the country where the leaves on the trees were already turning their spectacular colors of reds, oranges and browns. When we arrived, we sat in my mother's small kitchen and talked.

Rebecca broached the subject of my trip. You could see the furrow in my mother's face, but Rebecca continued that it would only be for two weeks and she promised to come to visit each weekend. My mother turned to me and said, "That isn't it. You should not be traveling alone, being a woman. A woman does not travel alone."

Reassuringly, I said, "Today, a woman can travel alone and be quite safe. There's no stigma attached to a woman traveling alone. I'll be fine."

She sternly reiterated, "A woman of class should not travel alone, ever."

Not knowing how to respond, I tried to reassure again that I would be fine. As we left that afternoon, I knew that she was still disturbed.

I continued my consulting work during the next few weeks and in my spare time continued to learn about Dodona. Never having been to this section of Greece, I began to think of what the land and climate would be.

The first weekend of October, I drove out to visit my mother. I brought groceries and staples that would last for the duration of my trip. I felt as though I were provisioning her as she had provisioned her family during the Cape Cod Nor'easters. When I entered the front door, she was at the kitchen counter, trying to cut up potatoes for potato salad. She was having difficulty in cutting. I went over to the counter and took the knife from her. She teetered to her kitchen chair and slumped over.

I glanced over to her, concerned about her weakness.

She said, "I haven't been feeling very strong recently. Sometimes, I become dizzy."

I replied, "It is time to see your general practitioner. I'll call him on Monday and make the earliest appointment. Maybe all he'll have to do is adjust your high blood pressure medication." She agreed.

On Monday when I called, he scheduled her appointment for that afternoon at four. I drove out to the country. At her doctor's office, I dropped her off at the front door and told her that I would be right in after parking the car. As I drove down to the parking lot, I looked in the rear window and saw my mother by the office's front door. I wondered why she didn't open it and go inside.

Having parked the car, I hurried up the driveway to the door where my mother still stood and looked at her inquisitively. She told me that the door was too heavy for her to pull it open. That was when the big picture began to form. She was too frail to live alone. Once inside the doctor's exam room, the doctor examined her from head to toe and began to type notes into his computer. I interrupted him by telling him that I was planning on being out of the country for two weeks quite soon. I asked him if he thought that would be a problem for my mother. He responded, "This is a wait-and-see situation."

I got it. My heart knew exactly what the doctor was saying. I thought *the Greece trip will wait. I need to be here. I need to be much more vigilant about my mother.* When we were driving home, I told her that I was going to postpone my trip. Spring in Greece was still my favorite season and maybe she would be stronger by the spring and we could go together. She smiled and said that she would like that. Then, I would not be traveling alone. I smiled and helped her to her front door and inside to her comfortable reading chair.

It was three days later, Thursday evening late, after ten. I had gone to bed and didn't hear my cell phone ring. William was hanging out at Dorothy's house with her. All the lost boys had now, over the past few months, adopted her as their surrogate mother as well. She had a comfortable den where the boys gathered and watched TV with her. William's cell phone rang and he answered it. It was my mother's country hospital. My mother had been brought there by the ambulance around six in the evening, but now was being transported to a different hospital, which specialized in neurology. We should go there immediately.

William raced home and bolted up the stairs, swung open my bedroom door and I was up in a start. He told me to hurry up, to grab some clothes. We had to leave immediately. He, breathlessly, told me about the phone call. I needed to use the bathroom first. He yelled at me that we didn't have the time. I walked into the bathroom, knowing that there was nothing we could do. There was time to use the bathroom.

He drove us to the hospital about an hour away like a speed demon, and upon reaching the hospital we waited and waited. We had arrived before the ambulance carrying my mother. After she arrived and had been examined by the neurologist, the neurologist asked me to come over to the nursing station where he was viewing a CAT scan of my mother's brain on the computer screen. He pointed to a section of her brain that was colored darker than the rest of her brain. He informed me that this was a ruptured brain aneurysm, causing bleeding into the brain. He continued to say that if this were a scan of my brain, I would be on the operating room table right now, but considering it was the scan of an eighty-two-year-old woman, he would not recommend surgery.

I concurred with him. I had promised my mother countless times since her last surgery that I would never let her undergo another surgery. He nodded in agreement. I asked if him if I could see her. He led me to her room and when I saw her, I thought *today she was to have her hair cut and then play bridge. She was going to be the driver today and escort all the ladies to lunch. How incredibly lucky her brain did not begin to bleed while driving the ladies to bridge and then to their homes.* I went over to her and took her hand and told her how beautiful her hair was. She lay motionless with her eyes closed.

I glanced around the stark hospital room and saw hanging on the wall a board that looked almost like a surfboard, which I supposed they used to transport patients. Looking at it closely, I saw in the middle of this red board, my father's initials. I didn't know what they medically represented, but I knew what they represented to me and I thanked him for being around her. William came in and when I looked into his eyes, it was as if I couldn't breathe. His grandmother had become his staunchest support and advocate during his high school years and I didn't know how he was going to survive the next phase of his life.

When we got home Dorothy and William's best friend were

sitting in the den waiting for us. We gave them the status report. It was really just a matter of time. It was well after three in the morning and I told everyone that they should get some sleep. The next few days would be a little trying.

Heather was scheduled to fly in from California on Friday for the weekend to give a bridal shower for her best friend who was to be married in December. I was not sure who would pick her up at the airport, as I was to drive out to the hospital to see my mother. When I walked into my mother's hospital room, the nurse told me that they had performed another CAT scan of my mother's brain. The neurologist would call me later in the evening to discuss the next steps in her care. I drove further to her house and opened the front door. Everything was just as she had left it, except she wasn't here.

I climbed upstairs and entered her bedroom. Her blue dress pants were hanging from a hanger that lay on the bed. Her coffee table in front of her small couch was disturbed as if someone had fallen on it. I went over to her desk and saw her journal. Her last entry was the amount of money she had spent having her hair done the previous day. I sat down at her desk. I thought *this had been her mother's desk and I remembered it from visiting my grandmother and watching her write in her journal. I had loved my grandmother with her old world charm and class. I wonder what will happen to this desk. Rebecca's middle name is my mother's maiden name. She will have the desk. She will cherish this desk.*

On the way home, from the car, I called the police to find out if there had been a police report. There was one, but I would have to come into the police station and fill out forms if I were to know its contents. I clicked my cell phone off and thought *it doesn't matter what the police report reads. It won't change the outcome.*

I drove home slowly as if I didn't want to get home. I didn't know where I wanted to be, but nowhere felt right. When I arrived, both of my daughters greeted me. We stood in the front hall and hugged each other tightly. William fell into this hug and said he had contacted my brother. He was on his way into the city to pick him up and drive him to see his mother. I was impressed with his compassion and thanked him for it. I was starving and suggested to my girls that we go out to eat. I didn't know why, but I couldn't stay home.

Rebecca recommended a restaurant in town that I had never eaten at and my second daughter chimed in that it would be perfect. It was a small restaurant with only about six tables. The pictures on the wall were from the *Wizard of Oz* and I thought *this was my father's favorite movie. He loved the music. He loved the plot. I had watched it so many times with him. Here, I am looking at the Tin Man, The Lion, and The Scarecrow, listening to Somewhere Over the Rainbow.* During our meal, my cell phone rang. The prefix was my mother's country area code. I answered it and walked outside into the chilly night air so that I could hear well. It was the neurologist. He explained that my mother's brain aneurysm continued to slowly bleed, but that he did not want to perform another CAT scan. The ordeal of putting my mother through this procedure was not worth the pain inflicted on her.

I thanked him and asked, "What is the next step?"

He replied, "This is a wait-and-see situation."

I thought *I have heard this term just too many times, now. This is enough. This is the new medical term of this century.*

I asked, "Is there anything that you are going to do for her in the hospital that I couldn't do for her at home?"

He answered, "Nothing."

I replied, "If that is the case, I'll arrange for my mother to be transported to my house in the morning."

"Are you sure?" he inquired in disbelief.

I answered firmly, "Absolutely."

He would arrange for hospice to come tomorrow. I thanked him and hung up.

The following day, the hospice representative came and

instructed me to purchase the box of medications from the local pharmacy. When I returned, the ambulance carrying my mother had arrived. The two ambulance attendants were having great difficulty maneuvering the stretcher with my mother up the stairs to the guest room. William intervened and instructed them to place the stretcher on the living room floor. They did so and he went over to the stretcher and unfastened the straps that secured my mother. He bent down and lifted her gently with his strong arms. He stood up and carrying her close to his chest, mounted each stair carefully. He entered the guest room, next to my room, and laid her on the bed.

The hospice representative brought an oxygen tank upstairs and informed me that my mother should have a face mask on to breathe in the oxygen. It would make her more comfortable. We watched my mother lying on the bed with her oxygen mask over her nose. She turned toward me and said, "She looks peaceful."

I walked the representative down the stairs and to the front door. Thanking her, I closed the door and went back upstairs to my mother. I opened the door and looked in. My mother had pulled the oxygen mask halfway up her face and kept batting it with one hand. Her eyes were completely closed. I removed the oxygen mask from her face and coiled the green cord connecting the mask to the machine by the end of the bed and turned off the swirling sounding machine.

Walking down stairs in a daze, I didn't know what to do. I started cleaning. I took out the glass cleaner and began cleaning the glass cook top, moving to the oven and then to the refrigerator. I took each shelf out of the refrigerator and ran them under soapy, warm water in the sink. I cleaned the walls of the refrigerator. I took out the side holders and was washing them when the phone rang. It was my brother.

He was upset that my mother was at our home. He was greatly concerned with how I was going to feed her. How was I going to give her water? She should be in the hospital so that she could recover. I tried to tell him that the neurologist had said there was nothing he could do for her in the hospital that I couldn't do at home. I asked him if he wanted her to die alone in a sterile room. I told him that our family's ritual of death was to die at home surrounded by those who loved them. He told me that I was forcing her to die. If she were in the hospital, she had a chance of getting better. I told him that he should contact the neurologist and gave him his phone number and hung up.

I put down my cleaning supplies and went upstairs to check on my mother. I knew that my mother should be with us, but my brother's voice made me momentarily doubt myself. I wanted to see her and make sure she was comfortable. When I entered the guest room, Rebecca was sitting beside her. I hadn't noticed that she had come home while I was on the phone. She had brought all the family photograph albums into the guest room and was turning each page slowly with tears sliding down her face. I pulled up a chair beside her, put my arm around her shoulder and began looking at the photographs with her.

After finishing one album, she picked up another one. My mother and I had compiled this album several years ago, after my father and husband had died. We had worked on this project together to divert our attention from where it would invariably wander: the death of our spouses. This album contained not only pictures, but also favorite quotes of hers and mine as well as newspaper articles we had found fascinating. At the same time, we had both been reading *Middlemarch* by George Eliot, thinking that the length of the book would sustain our diversion. On one page of the album, was a quote from *Middlemarch* that I had hand written on white paper and placed in the album. At the time I thought the quote poignant, and now looking at it, I said to Rebecca, "This reminds me of your grandmother." She read it aloud.

> *Her finely touched spirit had still its fine issues, though they were not widely visible. Her full nature, like that river of which Cyrus broke the strength, spent itself in channels which had no great name on the earth. But the effect of her being on those around her was incalculably diffusive: for the growing good of the world is partly*

> *dependent on unhistoric acts; and that things are not*
> *so ill with you and me as they might have been, is half*
> *owing to the number who lived faithfully a hidden life*
> *and rest in unvisited tombs.*

I couldn't sit anymore. I knew the feeling. They were coming, the flood of sad tears. I went into my room, into my closet where all my husband's clothes had been methodically removed years before. All that remained of his presence was on the dresser, a picture of a beautiful young woman in a long, white wedding dress with a tall, handsome gentleman dressed in a tuxedo standing beside her. The yacht club's pier, with the sparkling blue harbor's water, was their backdrop. The sun shone brightly on them as they stood on the brown summer scorched lawn. His right arm encircled her waist as she gently held her veil away from her face with her right hand as the soft wind blew. Their youthful faces beamed with their future ahead of them. I slid down the dresser, sitting on the floor, arms encircling my knees. I cried from the heart.

Early next morning, Dorothy came to the front door and inquired how I was doing. I asked her to come in for a cup of coffee. She wanted to know if my mother had arrived and I told her she was upstairs resting comfortably. It was a wait and see situation. She immediately told me that she had to go. She had many errands, but to please call if I needed anything. Out the door, she hurriedly left. I thought *she usually would have come in and had coffee. Why not? She seemed upset. Maybe, my mother's presence upsets her. Maybe someone dying in my house upsets her. But she's my mother. She needs, she wants to be with us.*

I went upstairs to check on my mother and while I was standing there, by her side, my cell phone rang. It was my neighbor next door. She and I had an unusual relationship. While she was perhaps fifteen years older than I, she sometimes acted like my mother and sometimes like an older sister. She knew my thoughts before I did and always gave me sound advice. She was a devout Muslim, waking up in the early morning to read her Qur'an, fasting during the week and attending the services at her mosque. Her garden was the envy of the neighborhood. She could make anything grow by simply touching it. She wanted to know if she could do anything and I told her that I was sitting with my mother, that if she wanted to come over and sit with me, that would be wonderful.

Several minutes later, she appeared, wearing her burqa. She hugged me and stood closely by the bed and began chanting an Arabic prayer, touching my mother's head, then her arms, stomach and legs and feet. Her voice was gentle and her touch was soft. I stood behind her and watched. After she finished, I watched my mother's tongue as it stopped moving and then one tear slid from her left eye, silently down the contour of her cheek. I never had before witnessed the actual moment of death. I never witnessed the grace, the elegance, the beauty of the actual moment and I wondered what the Arabic prayer had given her. Wrapped in each other's arms, I asked her what she said. She said that she prayed what was in her heart:

> O god, forgive our living and our dead, and whoever dies, allow him to die with faith. O god, do not deprive them of this reward for there is nothing greater than this. O god, forgive whoever dies and have mercy on him. Keep him safe and sound. Honor his rest and ease his entrance. Make his grave spacious and fill it with light.

My mother did not want a funeral. She had told me countless times over the years that she wanted a cocktail party with a full bar and live jazz music to commemorate her life. She did not want an obituary. She thought the journalists would spell her name wrong. She had told me that if I didn't abide by her wishes that she would come after me as a harpy in my afterlife. I never liked harpies in Greek mythology. They were ugly looking women with wings who punished and abducted bad people on the way to Tartarus in the underworld where evil people were sent after death.

After the funeral workers retrieved her body, this time, like my dad, in a body bag, and after I met with the funeral home director to instruct him on her cremation, I sat down around the dining room table and began planning the most wonderful cocktail party. I was going to host the most joyous, elegant cocktail party people had ever seen. It was going to be a true celebration of her life.

My children and I divided up the tasks. Rebecca was in charge of securing a live jazz trio. Heather was in charge of determining the food and hiring the caterer. Dorothy and I were in charge of purchasing the liquor for the full bar. William and his friends organized the furniture to accommodate the large number of people, the bar, and the jazz trio. The cocktail party would be held on Saturday from five in the evening until seven at my house and then a full dinner would be served at my best friend's house for those guests who traveled from out of town.

Before the party, in the evenings, my children, if you could still call them that, as they were actually young adults, sat around the dining room table and created a memorial book which we would distribute during the party. Looking through the albums, we selected the pictures. On the cover of her memorial book, Heather selected a picture of her grandmother at her fiftieth wedding anniversary after her husband had given her a simple, gold choker with a dolphin in the middle as if the dolphin would swim around her neck. My father had bought it the last time we were in Greece together at a jewelers in Olympia. He had been like a little boy, so excited about his surprise for her. My mother had loved the dolphins in Greece. I chose a picture of her standing in front of a bust of Herodotus, the father of western history in the Stoa of Attalos in the Agora in Athens, with the her wide-brimmed hat and sunglasses. The caption read, "The mother of western history." It was a fitting tribute. She loved history and all that it had taught her. She had said recently that if everyone would just read Thucydides, there would be no more war, ever.

I found an old album of my parents and our sailing cruises and saw a photo with her at the helm of the Concordia yawl. I was a senior in high school and lay on the bench with my head in her lap. There were other pictures of her with Rebecca sitting at the piano together playing a duet. Another one showed her sitting in a rocking chair reading poetry to Heather, on her lap. And another one with William atop the Venetian fortress, Palamidi, in Nafplio, Greece, after they had made the trek to the top. On the back cover, I told my kids that we should have her favorite song. My parents loved to sing together, while my father played it on the piano. My mother would stand by his side. Gershwin's "They Can't Take That Away From Me."

> *There are many, many crazy things*
> *That will keep me loving you*
> *And with your permission*
> *May I list a few*
>
> *The way you wear your hat*
> *The way you sip your tea*
> *The memory of all that*
> *No they can't take that away from me*
>
> *The way your smile just beams*
> *The way you sing off key*
> *The way you haunt my dreams*
> *No they can't take that away from me*
>
> *We may never, never meet again, on that bumpy road to love*
> *Still I'll always, always keep the memory of*
>
> *The way you hold your knife*
> *The way we danced till three*
> *The way you changed my life*
> *No they can't take that away from me*

The cocktail party was a huge success. I chartered a bus that brought my mother's friends in from the country. We had revolving trips to the airport to pick up the out of town guests and then there were our friends. The jazz trio played songs from Cole Porter, George Gershwin, Irving Berlin and others. The mood was upbeat, the food delicious, the music warmed our souls. Many of Rebecca's coworkers attended, people whom

I had never met. By the amount of her coworkers present, I realized what a success she must be. She introduced me to one of her coworkers who was an Orthodox Jew. I didn't know why I told him about the solo tear slipping down my mother's face as she left this world. He said, "You know why that one, single tear slid down her cheek?"

I shook my head, "No."

He replied, "Because she was grateful when she saw where her soul was traveling to."

I thought *of the conversation at Itea, my husband describing Plato. "The gods call on it to ascend. This ascent is a passionate undertaking that seizes the whole man, an act of love, Eros rising up to madness, mania. It is the beautiful which points the way. It touches the soul and excites it to a loving approach."*

I smiled and said, "You're right."

I left and made my way through the guests out to the deck through the French doors. The evening sky was descending, but it was too early to see the stars. I looked up and thought *did Plato really get it right? Was this really what happened? I don't know, but you actually witnessed the moment. How incredible. You witnessed the beauty of her soul leaving her body. Amazing. Never, ever forget this.*

As the end of the party approached, Rebecca asked the jazz trio to stop playing. She stood in the middle of the living room and addressed the guests. She said that her family had always called their grandmother "the giver of all good things" because she always was generous with her gifts. But the largest gift she gave to us was her love. She asked everyone to look at the back cover of the memorial book and to sing along. The jazz trio began the intro of "They Can't Take That Away From Me." My heart knew that my mother would have enjoyed her party immensely and that I would be eternally spared from the harpies.

WINTER 2008 – 2009

By January, I decided to gut the basement. I knew that someday I was going to sell this house. I didn't know when, but I did know that the basement was in derelict shape. After five years of the boys practically living down there, the main family room needed much help. My best friend gave me the name of a reputable contractor and I called him. When he came, he surveyed the basement and then we sat at the kitchen table and discussed the project. He recommended removing everything down to bare cinder block and even replacing the studs. Four feet would enlarge William's room that used to be my husband's office. All new electrical would be installed, a new boiler, new windows. It would take approximately two months with about four men working on the project daily. I liked this man. He was straightforward and seemed knowledgeable. I signed the contract and the work began the following week.

It was also during this period that William, his friends, my best friend and I cleaned out my mother's house. We rented trucks to bring furniture to my brother in the city and furniture to my house. I had no idea of what I was going to do with the furniture that came to my house, only for some reason, I couldn't part with many of the things. Too many things reminded me of a generation now gone. Our two-car garage was no longer William's band practice area. You could barely walk in it because it was packed with so much furniture. My living room was crammed with my dad's easy chair, her reading chair, mahogany end tables. We packed up her clothes and much of her kitchen supplies and gave them to Goodwill. We rented a dumpster and started pitching old paint cans, years of National Geographic magazines, and outdated financial records.

While I was busy with my mother's affairs, my best friend's renovations on her house were complete and she had signed the contract to put her house on the market. Everything was changing, once again.

SPRING – SUMMER 2009

In June, the moving van and movers were parked outside Dorothy's home, waiting for the thunder, lightning and rain to abate. It was a gully washer and persisted for more than an hour. While they were waiting, she and I, with the puppies in tow, made a last tour of the house she had lived in for the past twenty-nine years. I could only imagine the thoughts and feelings swirling through her head as we climbed the stairs to the second floor and inspected the four corner bedrooms. Then we climbed to the third floor, now a warm, inviting office with oak ceiling fans and huge skylights. There was not a trace of where the beams on the crane caved in the roof six months ago.

Once the movers began taking the furniture out of her house and stowing it in the very long moving van, I returned to my house. I entered into my new Mediterranean kitchen with my puppy. Yes, during the basement renovation, I had been in IKEA buying a CD bookcase for the basement, and had walked through the kitchen section. I stopped in front of a kitchen with plain white cupboards and beautiful light gray and blue tiles on the walls. I stood there for quite a while until a sales representative approached me. I inquired the price and decided that this would complete my renovations of our home. I decided then and there to gut my kitchen. When the contractors had finished the basement, they renovated the kitchen. I loved the stonework on the kitchen walls. It reminded me of Greece and I thought *we need to return. We need to bring gramma and granddad back and let them fly into the Aegean whitecaps.* I poured myself a cup of coffee and went over to the den and turned on the computer. I checked my email and saw several, but I didn't open them.

I thought *gramma and granddad need their freedom in the Aegean. How? I don't know. Sailing. Sailing is the only way. They would love it. They would love being set free together in the sea, off the stern near sunset. What about the charter company my husband used years ago in the British Virgin Islands? He captained the boat. It was a reputable charter company. Investigate them. I can't captain a boat in the Aegean. I haven't sailed for years. It's like riding a bicycle. It's something you never forget. You need to hire a skipper. A skipper? You've rented ministers. You can rent a skipper. There is something wrong with it. Renting ministers and renting captains is a violation. A violation against what? I don't know. It just is. It is a violation against something vital. You need to know your minister. You need to know your captain. Why? Why do you need to know them? Because you trust them. You trust your minister with your spirit and you trust your captain with your body. If you don't know them, you can't trust them.*

I researched companies that specialized in crewed sailing charters in the Aegean and found a company based in New Hampshire. I read every word on the website and called. A young woman answered and we began an instant rapport. We discussed various charter companies, their pros and cons and then she mentioned the one my husband had used twelve years ago in the British Virgin Islands. My husband had been impressed with how well they maintained their boats. The young woman and I began to discuss details. Realizing that the summer was upon us, I inquired as to the rates in the fall. She mentioned that October was especially wonderful because most of the tourists had left the islands, but the weather was still warm, the winds good, and the water warm. She reserved a boat on the island of Syros for the second week of October that would accommodate four passengers and one captain. I told her that I would confirm with her tomorrow. I needed to discuss this with my three children. Hanging up, I thought *if we can pull this off and we can all be together to send gramma and granddad into the Aegean– life doesn't get better than this.*

That night, when Rebecca came home from work, I called to William who was playing badminton in the side yard. I told him that I needed to talk with him and his sister. I had something serious to discuss with them. Frowning, he told his friend that he would be back in a few minutes and came inside to the kitchen table. All of us sitting, I disclosed my proposed plans. They both beamed. William said even though he would begin the university in the city in the fall, he knew one week off wouldn't detract from his studies. This was a once in a lifetime experience. I smiled and thanked him. I turned toward Rebecca who had remained quiet and looked at her inquisitively.

She slowly said, "I'd like to very much, but what do you think about you and me traveling through Greece for two weeks before the sailing week. I have three weeks of vacation that I can use."

Stunned, I thought *she and I have come full circle since 2003. She bolted right after her father died. She had hated me. She didn't want to have anything to do with the family and now, she is asking me to travel with her to a place she knows I consider sacred.*

I smiled. "I have never heard a better question. And I know the best answer. Yes, Yes and Yes."

I told them that I would call Heather in California and ask her to come.

I knew the phone call to Heather would have its challenges. After searching for employment for the past five months, she had recently been hired, and taking time off might be a problem. I also knew that she was reluctant to go sailing. During some of our sailing vacations on Cape Cod, she had experienced situations that scared her. She had been young and impressionable and had never forgotten them. Later that night, I called her and while she told me that she thought it the right thing to do, she could not take the time off from work. She reiterated that she had just begun her job and besides, the love of her life had just moved in with her. After hanging up the phone, I smiled as I remembered how strong the pull of new love is.

The next day, I confirmed with the young woman from the charter company the dates, the boat, and the island, and wrote a check for the deposit. I turned toward investigating the other sites Rebecca wanted to travel to during the two weeks before the cruise. We were going to pull this off. We were going to set them free in the Aegean.

FALL 2009

October 2009: Athens, Greece. Seven years ago, I traveled here with Rebecca. It was in a different lifetime. Now both of us live different lives, but we're traveling in simpatico. We hailed a taxi from the airport to our hotel off Syntagma Square on a side alley with many coffee shops and much pedestrian traffic. We checked in and rode the elevator to our little room on the seventh floor. There was a very small balcony where you could view the people scurrying to and from on the side street below.

I laid my bag on the floor and unzipped the long zipper. I wanted to make sure gramma and granddad made it safely. I peered inside and saw a huge white notice with blue official lettering from the Airport Security stating that this bag had been inspected due to suspicious contents. I saw gramma in her cylindrical container and granddad in his large rectangular plastic box. I laughed and thought *who would have thought you suspicious?*

My carefully packed clothes were scattered in disarray, but I didn't care. Gramma and granddad made it to Greece. That's what was important. While I had been inspecting my bag, my daughter was on the phone with her good friend whom she had first met at her girls boarding school when she was a sophomore. Her friend had been to our house many times during those years, but now she had graduated from college and was working in Athens. Her grandmother had lived in Athens and since passing away, her granddaughter lived in her grandmother's apartment.

Rebecca informed me that we would meet her for dinner around eight in the evening. I was glad. Being in the middle of the afternoon, I suggested we head over to the Plaka to see what's changed and view our girl's temple on the rock. This had been the longest stretch of time that I had been away from Greece, but my feet knew exactly where to take us. We meandered up the side streets of the Plaka and glanced at all the shops selling the same things that they had always sold and then we rounded the bend and stopped. There she was, jettisoning up to the blue sky, so majestically, as if saying, "Nothing, not your smog, not Venetian dynamite, not your wars, nothing will be able to destroy me. I will watch over my polis forever."

Rebecca and I held each other's hands and just stared. We walked slowly toward the south entrance of the Acropolis, paid the entrance fee and began the climb. We strolled through the Propylaea, which was still being restored, and slowly along the long north side of the Parthenon to arrive at her entrance on the east side. Iktinos and Kallikrates, her architects, insisted that each person take in the beauty slowly by making the spectator walk the length of the northern side of the temple until you reached the entrance. My daughter and I took our seats on some rocks in the sun and gazed at her entrance. I pointed to the holes above the pancake Doric columns where Alexander the Great had nailed his victims' shields when he overtook the city. Even his arrogance couldn't deter one from still standing in awe of Athena's beauty, twenty-three hundred years later.

I thought *back to when I was here with Heather and glimpsed the Parthenon from the Plaka and wondered "who was she?" Who was Athena, the armed maiden, valiant and untouchable virgin? Birthed from Zeus's head without a mother just as Jesus was birthed without a father, this woman through her organizational wisdom showed man how to live in an ethical world. The cultivated olive tree was her gift to her polis, not the wild olive grove. Poseidon sired the horse, but she bridled it. Poseidon excited the waves. Athena built the first ship. Hermes multiplied his flock of sheep. Athena taught the women how to weave wool. She was Achilles' staunchest advocate in the Iliad when he grasped for his sword in the quarrel with Agamemnon. She stood behind him and grabbed him by the hair. To the others, she remained invisible, but Achilles recognized the goddess. She counseled him to check his rage, lightly saying the words, 'if you will follow me,' and Achilles obeyed without question. I remember reading somewhere that whenever difficulties disappear and the impossible becomes possible, Athena is present. Maybe she is the one guiding me with my bird feathers.*

We stayed several hours and the air became chilly. We needed to get back to the hotel to shower and change before meeting my daughter's friend.

We met her friend on a street corner. When she approached us, she hugged me, kissed me on each cheek and commented how much I had changed. I tried to remember the last time I saw her and all I could remember was during the winter after my husband died. We were celebrating my daughter's birthday with her friend at a restaurant my husband had loved. I remembered being angry and upset. It had been a terrible dinner and I was glad that today, that memory was in a different lifetime. She hugged my daughter tightly and we set off down Ermou to Psiri where she knew of a fantastic restaurant. I let the two of them talk and get caught up as I walked behind.

When we came to the restaurant it was completely filled, but the owner, seeing our friend immediately went back inside. In less than a minute, two men carried a table out with another man following with three chairs. They smiled at us and squeezed this table in among the existing crowd. They could have worked in New York City with their space management skills. Sitting down, after much discussion with the waiter, our friend ordered several appetizers, the main courses and wine.

The girls were in their mid-twenties and discussed their respective career choices and where they saw their careers taking them. The conversation moved to men and my daughter beamed, talking about a young man whom she met last May in a yoga class. Her friend wanted to know how serious she thought this relationship would become. My daughter didn't know what the future held with this man, but at the present, it was wonderful. They spoke about having babies, the pros and cons. They were worried as to the impact babies would have on their careers, as it was still an imbalanced world when it came to sharing the responsibilities between men and women.

Rebecca leaned toward me and asked, "Did you regret giving up your career after my brother was born?"

I had been drinking my wine, watching the street life, letting my mind wander, drifting back and forth to their conversation.

Startled by her question, I reentered their conversation.

"No, no, I didn't regret it. I wanted to give a hundred percent to being a mother. I was grateful I had the opportunity and didn't have to work. I didn't really think what a mother was or how a mother should behave back then. You were new babes, clean slates. You didn't care if I wore makeup, dressed elegantly or wore my comfy jeans with holes in the knees. You allowed me to be me. You, three, loved me for being me. You embraced my passions and I embraced yours: swimming, art, fencing, Latin, physics, rising before dawn so you could see the sunrise.

I nudged Rebecca, "Remember that? Watching the sunrise from the bridge as it climbed over the city? We stood midspan watching the red dawn as the sun slowly ascended over the buildings in Harlem? How many kids would want to travel to Greece year after year in search of remote archeological sites, listening to their mother pontificate? I had the privilege of knowing, on a daily basis, firsthand, three wonderful people. I don't think I would have known them as well, loved them as much for all their idiosyncrasies if I hadn't spent the amount of time with them. I don't think I would have ever felt or known such unconditional love."

I looked at both of them and wondered if any of what I had just said made sense to them. I was not sure it would have made sense to me at their age. Rebecca leaned over and kissed my cheek. I smiled. We ordered dessert and coffee and I paid the bill. The girls were off to her friend's apartment and I was going back to the hotel. We hugged and I reminded Rebecca that we had an early start, driving up to Delphi tomorrow. She nodded and they set off. Walking back to the hotel, I thought *Wow! You're alone. You don't have to go back to the hotel if you don't want to. You can do anything you want. Wow! Well, what do you want to do? I want to listen to live music and have a nightcap. Okay, then. Let's go. Psiri has a good nightlife. Let's explore.*

And that's exactly what I did.

The next morning we drove seamlessly out of Athens and embarked on the drive up to Delphi. When we arrived, we stayed in the hotel that we had always stayed in. As we drove into town, I commented how on the previous trip, Heather and I had driven around the town in a circle four times before finding the road to the hotel. Rebecca stared at me with raised eyebrows. She said that the directions were very simple. We must have been preoccupied.

When we checked in and found our room, Rebecca, with her photographic memory, explained this was the same room we had stayed in when she was in seventh grade. The grandparents had stayed in the next room over, and from that balcony gramma had heard the sheep bells in the mountains.

We decided to head to the site, as it was just before noon and by this time tomorrow we would be on a plane to Chania, Crete. There was no time to waste. It was an overcast, gray afternoon and we grabbed our jackets and set out. I drove down the hill and we parked, almost in the same place as four years ago. This time, our car was squeezed in between tour buses. I scanned up to the site and saw many, many, many tourists, but I saw no one above the Temple of Apollo. As we walked along the street to the entrance, I saw one tour guide who was speaking English and asked her why no one was above the temple. She informed us that due to massive falling rocks, the site beyond the temple was unsafe. Gaia was upset with something. We climbed and were jostled and bumped by the tourists, all speaking loudly in various languages. We couldn't even see any of the treasuries through the crowds of tourists.

Rebecca and I realized that we were not going to be able to witness the navel of the universe without hordes of human beings. I suggested that we take a coffee at the little cafe on the way to Athena's temples below. She agreed and we descended, disappointedly. As we entered the one room cafe, we listened to melodic, soothing Greek music and Rebecca asked the elderly gentleman the name of the musicians. He only spoke Greek. Through sign language, by pointing to the CD player and to her ear and to her smile, he understood and opened a drawer. He took out a CD and my daughter wrote down the name of the musician and recording label. She thanked him and we took our coffee, with warm milk in a small pitcher, on a tray outside to the porch with a spectacular view of the valley.

As we relaxed, sipping our coffee, I thought *since she has returned from India, during the entire year and a half that she has been home, we have never taken the time to just sit, sit and do nothing but enjoy each other's company.* It was a peaceful afternoon and I remarked that if we didn't see Delphi this time round, it would be here for us next round. The afternoon was perfect, just the way it was. She looked down and pointed to two small kittens by her feet. I took the warm milk and poured it into my saucer and placed the saucer on the floor. The kitties slurped and purred at the same time.

We gave up on Delphi with all the tourists and tour buses and turned our attention toward Chania. We had never been there before and were excited for a new adventure on Crete. Rebecca couldn't wait to hike the Samarian Gorge. I was not as excited, mainly because I was warding off a cold. I refused to succumb to a virus like I had in Jamaica. We landed at the airport and took a taxi to our hotel. I had a feeling that I had landed on a tropical island with many palm trees swaying in the warm, salt air breeze. Our hotel was off a side street of the bustling old city and we climbed the small circular staircase to our room. There was a small anteroom as you entered with the bathroom off of it. Then through another door was a large room with a double bed. Further through shuttered doors was a small balcony overlooking a square. At the top of the square was a huge Greek Orthodox church.

It was late in the day and we were both famished. We left our room and went in search of dinner. Restaurants lined the semicircle harbor and we meandered, looking at the various menus. Rebecca selected a restaurant that had the best vegetarian dishes, as she and her new boyfriend were staunch vegetarians. We sat and ordered and she began to talk of her job with the enormous responsibilities, but enormous salary. She talked of her desire to take the software she used as a consultant and bring it into the realm of education. She wanted to help our educational system. She described in detail the various horrifying situations that exist in the inner cities and how she wanted to develop software that would help not only the teachers, but the students and their parents. She said the software must be inclusive to all of three groups of people. So many times, the schools left the parents out of the circle and this led to a collapse of communication. Maybe some parents were too busy with work, but if all the information were online and could be accessed at any time, then maybe this would be a way of communicating effectively with everyone.

I was impressed, not just with her sincere passion to help kids overcome disadvantages, but also with how well she articulated herself. She had become a professional, intelligent woman with a passion and I thought *on this trip, I will have the time to listen, to understand what's important to her, to begin to know who she's become and is becoming. I have not had this opportunity since her father died.* After dinner, we strolled along the side streets, window-shopping. Some of the stores reminded us of the Plaka, but then there were others that were unique to Chania.

The next morning, we took the public bus to the gorge and descended the bus's stairs into the chilly mountain air. I coughed and found a tissue to blow my nose, which was red and raw at this point. With our water bottles, some apples and crackers, we began our trek. Rebecca assured me the hike would only take a few hours and we would be resting by siesta time. As we hiked down the path, I noticed a sign reading, "Walk quickly. Falling Rocks." I said, "Right. I don't think walking quickly is the answer. I think not being here is the answer."

I had to admit that the geological formations were spectacular. The mother earth goddess displayed her incredible creations. After several hours, we stopped for lunch and my daughter saw that I was dragging. She reassured me we had only about two hours more to hike. I told her that it was not a problem. In reality, I would have loved to have taken a nap right about then. I felt my forehead burn with a small fever. After three more hours of steady decline and marveling at the height of the gorge, Rebecca halted and looked up to the towering cliffs and said, "You can almost see the centaurs galloping through the terrain. I'm a believer in them now."

I gazed up to the cliffs and smiled and thought *the apple doesn't fall too far from the tree. I've made her eccentric just like me.* We came to a small picnic area with a map displaying with a red dot where we were. I stared at it in dismay. We were only midway down the gorge after six hours of hiking. I reminded her that the last boat to Chania left at eight in the evening. There was nothing to do, but walk and enjoy, in a more rapid manner. We continued our journey and arrived at the water just before the last boat. We had taken our time, more time than most people, but we were glad we did. We enjoyed our time being in the mother earth's gorge.

───────◆◆───────

If you've ever been to Greece, you know rule number one is flexibility. One needs to be flexible and it doesn't hurt to have patience. This is a place where things can change at a drop of a hat, including ferry schedules and flights. It all depends. I'm not sure what it depends on, it just depends – perhaps on the way the wind blows. These abrupt changes can create havoc with your carefully prepared itinerary and time line. These sudden disruptions can unnerve you and set you scrambling.

───────◆◆───────

From the hotel, I called Olympic Air to confirm our flight in two days to Syros and was informed it had been canceled. I told Rebecca that we needed to find a travel agent and inquire as to the ferry schedules to Syros. We set out and walked from the old section of Chania into the modern city. Several travel agencies lined the street and we entered the first one. We were told that there were no direct ferries to Syros. We could take a ferry to Mykonos tomorrow and the following day take another one to Syros. That would get us to Syros the day before we were to board the sailboat.

While it sounded perfect, we wanted another day in Chania. We had planned on renting a car and touring the western section of Crete. I, especially, wanted to see the geography and villages. In the back of my mind, I knew that someday I wanted to end up living on this island. I had never seen western Crete. And besides, the ferry left from Heraklion at eight in the morning and Heraklion was about an hour east of Chania. We informed the woman behind the counter that we would think about it and left.

Undeterred, we entered the second travel agency. Perhaps the ferry schedules would have changed by the time we entered the second travel agency. This was our hope. The woman at the second travel agency told us the same thing and the understanding slowly set in that we were not to see western Crete. We should book the ferry. We noticed the increasing number of tourists in the same situation and were told that Olympic had cancelled all flights for that day.

I asked the travel agent how were we to be in Heraklion by eight in the morning. There were no buses that early. We would have to take a cab. The woman pointed to the taxi queue across the street. We would have to negotiate with one of the drivers to drive us, leaving at six in the morning to be assured of making the ferry. If we didn't make the ferry, there were no other alternatives to get to Syros by the time we were to board the sailboat. We bought the ferry tickets and crossed the street to the taxi line.

Fortunately, one driver spoke broken English and we tried our best to communicate. As was typical, after he understood that we needed a cab from our hotel to the ferry in Heraklion, he congregated with several other taxi drivers and they all discussed this.

The Greeks, especially the men, preferred to discuss everything in great detail and this takes time, sometimes a lot of time. This was where patience was not a virtue, but a real necessity if you wanted to get to Heraklion by seven-thirty tomorrow morning.

Rebecca and I sat on a bench and waited.

I thought *do not think about not getting to Syros and not boarding the sailboat. Do not think of not being able to give gramma and granddad their freedom in the Aegean. Try hard. I am, but my success is minimal. This is the purpose of the trip. This is the purpose of chartering this expensive boat and it looks like it is now dependent on these Greek taxi drivers standing in a circle discussing a cab ride from Chania to Heraklion at six in the morning tomorrow.*

Rebecca saw the distress in my face. I told her I knew that there was nothing we could do, but wait. Finally, the man who spoke some English sauntered over and pointed to a man. He told us that man did not speak any English, but he would pick us up at our hotel and drive us for fifty euros. I thanked him. Rebecca beamed. Everything was going to be okay, but I thought *of western Crete.*

Driving in the early morning, before the sun had risen along the north coast road, the dark mountains to our right and the Aegean Sea to our left, we huddled together in the backseat of the cab in the chilly morning air. I constantly looked at my watch. Once we arrived in Heraklion, the man drove to the main pier, but the ferry was not there. I pulled out the ferry tickets from my bag and showed the driver the name of the ferryboat. I knew it was in English, but I was hoping against hope that he would recognize the name and know the pier. He stopped and asked a person on the pier. I thanked god he was a man who actually asked for directions. He turned to me and smiled and I smiled back and looked at my watch. It was seven-thirty. He drove off the pier and back onto the main road, which took us into Heraklion. He was driving fast and I thought *the reason one sees so many shrines of dead people on the hairpin turns is because of these driving habits.* We arrived at a pier and I took a deep breath.

There was a huge, red ferry tied to the pier with people boarding. It was seven-forty-five. I quickly paid the driver and hopped out with our bags. We joined the crowd, climbed the stairs into the ferry and located our seats. I plopped down and pulled my sweatshirt hood over my head. I was going to try to relax and sleep. When the ferry docked in Mykonos, we descended into the bright daylight and saw many proprietors with placards, advertising their rooms to rent. We saw one lady whom Rebecca had a good feeling about. We decided to go with her. We piled in her van and on the way to her rooms, we spoke of the politics, as the National Elections were taking place soon. She said that it would take years before Greece would be able to climb out of her crisis. It didn't matter who was in power. It would take years. Rebecca and I looked at each other and nodded. We understood that it could take years to climb out of a crisis.

The next afternoon, we landed on the Cycladic Island of Syros. Neither of us had been to this island before and when the ferry docked, a bustling, large, almost industrial city was in front of us. The port was lined with nineteenth century neoclassical and Venetian buildings. I had read that this used to be the principal port of Greece in the eighteen hundreds and one could still see the vestiges. We were surprised at her size and the largeness of her harbor and the hills. Huge shipyards were to the left and I thought *how my dad would have enjoyed this. I smiled. He is with us.* We took a taxi up the congested hill to near our hotel. The taxi couldn't drive us to the door since the hotel was down several marble pedestrian walkways. Pedestrian walkways traversed this large hill, which was almost a mountain. Cars were not an option, only feet. We walked to the entrance of the hotel and I stopped and pointed to its name "Omiros" by the door.

Rebecca looked at me bewildered. I said, "The name of the hotel is Homer in English. We are staying with Homer tonight."

She smiled. We entered into a small reception area with one wooden desk and an elderly Greek gentleman. I looked around. This must have been built in the city's heyday, about 1850. I asked the gentlemen about his mansion and he explained that it was one hundred and seventy years old. It had been formerly the home of Georgios Vitalis, a prominent Greek sculptor.

I complimented him on its magnificence. We signed the guestbook and he led us to a large marble circular staircase with a black iron banister. We climbed, with our luggage bouncing up one stair at a time. The gentleman opened our door with a massive, iron key. Standing in the doorway, I was struck. The ceiling in our room was twenty feet high. There was one double bed in the center of the room with two windows whose height must have been six feet. He left us. My daughter and I were stunned at the classic grace and elegance.

She asked, "How did you find this place? It's amazing!"

I shrugged my shoulders. It was late in the afternoon and we wanted to explore this port city, as this would be our only chance. We descended many, many, many marble stairs to the port and began to acquire our bearings. We strolled up and down streets. There were streets with vegetable vendors, locals selling their wares, butchers, bakeries and then we came to a stretch of cosmopolitan jewelry shops. It was endless and we marveled at it all.

Rebecca tugged on my elbow and pointed to my watch. She needed to return to the hotel as she had a scheduled call with her boyfriend. I was not exactly sure how to get back amidst all the winding pedestrian walkways as the evening sky descended. After losing our direction several times, after asking several people where Omiros was and after much walking uphill, downhill, we located the hotel. Back in our room, I poured myself a glass of wine and walked down the stairs to the stone wall in front of the hotel, wishing to give my daughter privacy while talking to her boyfriend.

As I walked out the front door, I felt the warm, moist evening breeze. Sitting down on the stone wall, I placed my wine glass next to me and thought *we have finally made it. Gramma and granddad will finally have their freedom together. All we need is William, who is scheduled to arrive tomorrow, and then we sail. How will the sail be? What type of sailboat? What about the captain? This disturbs me. Something isn't right about hiring a captain to sail with us. I have never rented a captain.*

I have never sailed with a stranger. Right, I've only sailed with friends, and not just friends, I've only sailed with good friends. You're in the Aegean. You don't have friends here. This is not a place you have ever sailed. I know, but something still is wrong. It will be perfect. This is the purpose of the trip.

Tired, I lay down on the stone wall and gazed up to the night sky, my eyes riveted to the prominence of the orange-yellow glow of the full moon. Her round shape majestically filled the sky, diminishing the brightness of the stars. She pulled my eyes towards her and then it happened. I swear to god, it happened. I heard a voice. The voice said just one thing, "Stay here." I thought *I've never heard a voice before. Whose voice it is? Wondering if I would hear this voice again. I closed my eyes and tried to understand what voice I had just heard. Did you really hear a voice? Yes, I distinctly heard her. It is not my imagination. I do not do things like this. My imagination does not play tricks on me. I heard a voice. I did.*

Unsettled, I took my wine and climbed the circular stairs to our room and tapped on the door. Beaming, Rebecca opened it. She had finished her conversation with her boyfriend. She exuded happiness and love. I told her about the voice.

She said quite seriously, "You should listen to the voice. You are lucky. You listened. You weren't scared to hear the voice. Pay attention."

I smiled and went into the bathroom to change for bed. Falling asleep that night, I kept remembering the voice. It was firm, imperative, strong. There was no doubt in the voice.

The next morning we ate breakfast in the formal dining room. Our breakfast was served on beautiful china with real silverware. We were the only guests in the large room. The elderly gentlemen walked over to a table and put on a CD and all of a sudden, we were treated to Ella Fitzgerald singing "They Can't Take That Away From Me." Both Rebecca and I stared at each other; both of us remembered gramma's favorite song. We both felt something and neither of us knew how to define it.

We ate in silence. We finished our breakfast and I couldn't stop remembering the full moon last night and the voice.

As we packed our bags, ready to check out, my cell phone rang. It was William. He had made it to Athens, but his afternoon flight had been cancelled. He was out all last night, partying with Rebecca's friend. The only reason he woke up, he told me, was that there had been a thunderstorm and the thunder woke him up. He informed me that there was a ferry that gets in at ten tonight. I implored him to please, please be on it. We would meet him at the ferry dock. We wouldn't sail without him. He promised and we hung up. I thought *Zeus with his mighty thunderbolt is still alive. Thank you for getting my son out of bed. Thank you.*

We took a taxi to the small harbor on the other side of the island where the boat was moored. When we reached the town, we found the charter company's office and reviewed the contract with a young woman. She assured us our captain was extremely skilled. We consolidated our gear into smaller bags that we would take aboard and left the rest of our traveling gear in the office. Gramma and granddad in their respective containers sat beside our gear to bring on the boat. A man walked in and the woman introduced us to our captain. He was a tall man with broad shoulders and curly hair cascading to his shoulders, his face weather beaten with piercing eyes. He glanced at us and then to the floor at the cylindrical and rectangular container with a puzzled look. We introduced ourselves to each other and he pointed to the containers next to our gear. I told them that they were the ashes of my mother and father. I could tell that he was surprised and I thought *you sail the boat. These are my parents, my parents who loved the Greek land and the Aegean. My parents who want to be set free together, sailing. This is why we are here.*

During the day, we bought provisions for the boat and secured them in the small galley. Afterwards, we took a taxi back into the main port city to wait for the ferry in hopes that a young man we knew would walk off the ferry gangway. Rebecca bided her time by taking pictures and I sat by the port and hoped he would be on the ferry. I reassured myself that he had been traveling internationally since he was six years old, but somehow this didn't bolster my confidence that he would be on the ferry.

We walked the streets and window-shopped. It was Saturday night and the atmosphere was lively, but I didn't have the carefree attitude that I did in Psiri. I wanted the ferry to dock and for William to walk out. This trip had taken so much planning, so much effort, it couldn't derail now. Rebecca grabbed my arm and pointed. The massive ferry was entering the harbor. We made our way over to its dock. As we approached the ferry dock, we saw passengers disembarking, but through the night air, I didn't make out my son. Then Rebecca screamed his name. A tall blond haired guy carrying a duffle bag walked toward us.

We ran up to him and both of us threw our arms around him. He looked at us and thought we had completely lost it.

He said, "What, you didn't think I would make it?" He laughed.

We walked towards our prearranged taxi, arms encircling arms, with grinning smiles. We were going to actually pull this off. Once we returned to the small harbor, we went to the taverna where the captain had told us to meet him. William was hungry and now I was capable of eating, too. Now that the three of us were together.

The next morning, the captain boarded the boat and we set sail for a small island, Siphnos. Light winds from the north prevailed and the engine was left running. I understood the value of an engine on a sailboat, but I have also always hated them. The sound, the smell, the use of diesel, and the vibrations bothered me. I headed up to the bow, as I was emotionally exhausted. We had made it and I wanted to relax. I was dozing when Rebecca crawled up to the bow and sat down next to me. She took my hand and held it. She whispered into my ear that the captain had just put on a CD in the sound system, "It Had To Be You." This was Granddad's favorite that he played on the piano for his wife. I smiled and closed my eyes and thought *back to yesterday's morning breakfast's at the hotel Omiros as my daughter sang:*

> *It had to be you*
> *I wandered around, and then finally found somebody who*
> *Could make me be true, make me feel blue*
> *Just to be glad, just to be sad*
> *Thinking of you*
> *Some others I've seen, might never be mean,*
> *Might never be cross or try to be boss*
> *But they wouldn't do*
> *For nobody else, gave me a thrill*
> *With all your faults, I love you still*
> *It had to be you, wonderful you*
> *It had to be you*

When we sailed into the small port of Sifnos, the captain skillfully slid the boat to the pier. I thought *sailing is quite different here and that one day, just one day, I will sail solo here and I will give myself my own sailing test*. William was exhausted, but he sallied forth and brought a bottle of wine out to the cockpit. Rebecca joined him, bringing cheese and crackers. This was the time to acquaint ourselves with the captain and vice versa. Maybe we would no longer consider him a stranger after this evening. I considered sailing to be one of those sacred activities one should only do with friends, good friends. I had recovered from my exhaustion due to my four hour siesta on the bow, but I could see the jet lag and fatigue in my son's eyes. We drank our wine and after many clinking of the glasses, no one was feeling any pain. Rebecca asked the captain if he thought we would see any dolphins.

He replied, "Due to the high volume of ferries traveling from one island to another in the high season, the dolphins leave the area. They return in the winter months. That's when you're apt to see them in abundance."

Our conversation turned towards Greece, about the recent elections, its implications for the country, the foreboding economic crisis and the impact on the Greek people. The captain spoke with a commanding voice and a deep understanding of the foundation of his country. As the night sky descended, he said that he knew of a particularly good taverna up the road.

———◆———

Sitting after dinner, the captain adjusted his chair so that it was facing me. He leaned forward with his piercing eyes and asked me, "Where's your husband?"

My wine-soaked brain flashed back to Agios Nicholaos 2005 when the owner of the hotel asked me the same thing and I couldn't answer. Heather had answered for me then, but she wasn't here. She would have understood in a nanosecond. This guy was looking directly into my eyes and I thought *okay just say it and be done with it. Say it. My brain won't allow the words to form. Random thoughts swirl through my incoherency. Why do these guys have to ask me this? They don't need to know. What you see is what you get. Why does he want to know? It's none of his concern. Maybe my husband is on a business trip. Maybe I am divorced. My brain is screaming at the words to form. Say it. But I can't say it. I feel my face turn red and I thank god it's night.* My son and daughter were arguing over a Buddhist concept and I thought *compassion guys, help your mother over here.*

Out of nowhere, my mouth articulated very rapidly, "He's dead."

That's it. I said it. Don't. Do not ask me anything more. I don't care how long it's been. Maybe it will take me a lifetime to understand why I can't say those words. I don't know. Maybe. End of conversation. Ask the captain one of your million questions you always have. Change the subject.

Dessert came. Thank god. I tried to kick Rebecca under the table and tried to catch her eye. She didn't respond. She was engrossed in her argument with her brother. I excused myself to use the restroom. As I walked across the lane, I felt the tremble in my legs. I entered the taverna and there was man behind the bar. I asked him where the restroom was and he pointed up the stairs. I used the banister to steady myself as I climbed the stairs. I closed the restroom door and turned on the water. I cupped my hands and splashed cold water on my face until my face began to feel the coldness and then looked in the mirror.

I thought *when, when will the death drug finally rid itself from my body?* And as I was standing there with water dripping off my face, it came to me. *I get it. I remember my friend's email after cleaning up the white fluffy discharge from his mouth that cold spring day. "Anyone who has touched your heart will always be with you." And then, I remember Nagy. "It's not that the hero did not die, but that he is not dead now. He lives on the Island of the Blessed." He's living on the Island, capable of pleasure, capable of enjoying convivial feasts. It is not the death drug. It's his memory. If I say he's dead, it's as if I'm saying he's no longer living, but he is living. He is living through my memory of him. He is living. He's not dead and that's why I can't say it.*

I wiped my face and walked out of the restroom and slowly down the stairs into the taverna. I felt the eyes of the man behind the dimly lit bar on me. He asked me if I were okay, if everything were okay. I stared at him for a moment and for a moment I couldn't think of his question. I was still thinking *I get it. He's alive.* He put down the glass he was drying on the wooden bar. The sound startled me and my brain registered. "Everything is fine. Thank you."

I walked out and began to cross the street, back to our table, but my feet took me toward the pier and I walked to the end. I gazed to the Aegean night sky. I thought *the stars shine brighter here than they did in the mountains of the Sierra Nevadas. I remember thinking that those were the brightest I had ever seen. The sky is jet black with her bright shiny stars. I am only seeing the ones visible to the naked eye and I wonder what would it look like to see all the billions of stars at once, not through a telescope, but with my eyes. I would be looking at all the souls that hadn't yet reached the place where Plato's ideas live, where souls live, past the stars, past heaven.*

The next day, the captain informed us that we would sail to

Anti-Paros, a small island to the southwest of Paros. We set out on a leisurely pace, but today with good winds, the captain turned off the engine. I felt the boat, the waves and wind in their sounds with no artificial vibrations and I thought *my dad is happy.*

As Rebecca and I were below preparing lunch, both gramma and granddad got in our way. Their containers had been on the floor in the galley as this was where they were secure when the boat was underway. We brought the lunch to the cockpit and ate slowly, talking, enjoying the serenity that only sailing and the sea can yield. After lunch, I took the plates down to the galley and cleaned them in the small sink. The rectangular and cylindrical containers kept hitting my feet as the boat took another wave.

It was time. They were asking to be released. I beckoned William to the entrance of the cabin. Standing on one step of the ladder leading to the cockpit, I handed him gramma. Then, I stooped and picked up granddad and gave him to my son. I climbed up the ladder into the cockpit. I glanced at the captain who was steering the boat, looking beyond the bow. I quietly said to both my children, "It is time. Gramma and granddad are tired of being in the cabin. Neither of them would prefer being below on a sailboat. Granddad would want to go first, to make sure it is safe. That's the way he was. He took good care. He took very, very good care of his wife." Looking at both their faces, I asked, "Is it alright with you, if I let granddad sail into the Aegean?"

William immediately rejoined that he wanted to let gramma fly. I picked up the large rectangular container and made my way to the stern. Before I opened the container, I shut my eyes and thought *of how my dad had looked. He was a strong, large man with a heart of goodness and a smile which melted the angriest person. How incredibly lucky I was to have him for a father. I know he knows that he is about to be set free and will be with his love of his life. I know this is the most right thing I have ever done in my life.* I opened up the rectangular container and his crystals flew off the stern into the wind.

William took gramma's container and I thought *I don't know what he is thinking. I know my mother will be with her love of life. She will be with him. She will finally be with him again and be happy.* My son, at the stern, opened the container and gramma was in the air, floating towards the sea.

The captain startled us when he abruptly said, "Look" with his hand pointing to the bow.

We all turned toward the bow. Two dolphins swam gracefully, parallel with each other in front of the bow. Goose bumps rose on my arms as I watched these two silver dolphins with their smiles on their faces swim effortlessly past the bow and I thought *what an incredible omen.* After they disappeared out of view, my two children looked at me and I smiled.

William said, "I get it now."

He, until this time, had not been a believer in signs.

Not one person on that boat said another word until we laid anchor, several hours later, in the small, secure harbor of Anti-Paros as the evening sky turned dark with her piercing stars striking through the night air.

Once anchored, the captain made sure the boat was secure. He dismantled the inflatable pram from atop the cabin and slipped it in the water. I went below and changed from shorts into jeans and a blue long-sleeved shirt with a comfy sweatshirt. Knowing the taverna was on the beach and we would be in the pram, I left my flip-flops behind. We climbed into the pram and the captain rowed us to shore. Once the pram was aground on the beach, we climbed out and my feet felt the rocky beach.

The captain ordered a variety of Greek dishes, but none of them were appealing even as my stomach growled. I sipped my wine and tried to concentrate on the conversation at hand. After dinner, the captain suddenly left us and walked over to a group of other Greeks watching TV in the front of the taverna and sat down. I watched him and silently thanked him for allowing the three of us to be together, alone. We spoke of releasing the grandparents today and what an incredible past two days it had been with the music, the sea, and being together, the three of us. We all knew we were missing Heather. We had all wanted her to be with us. If she had been here, our family that used to be seven would be complete and be four. We spoke of how we had changed during the past seven years.

William looked into my eyes and said, "You've changed the most."

Surprised, I asked, "How?"

He quickly replied, "I don't know. But, you know. How did you change? You've become so different than you were before."

I thought *he is right. I do know that I have changed. I had to. I could not stay that person in that other life which I don't own anymore. I had to become me in this life.*

"Really? You, really, want to know my take?" They both nodded yes.

Slowly, I replied, "I think I've become more open, emotionally, spiritually, physically, sexually – to all of life and no, I don't mean just the phallus, but to all of life."

William raised his eyebrows. I continued, "Yes, sex can be ecstatic and pleasurably overwhelming, don't get me wrong. But the pleasure is not sustaining. Sustenance is found only in the spiritual realm because that is where vulnerability and faith live. To be vulnerable is not to be afraid of exposing all your strengths and frailties. It is not being afraid of shedding your skin, of releasing your old life and generating new skin. It is not being afraid of saying this is all of who I am, heart and entrails. And in turn, being able to receive love into your deepest recesses because they have now been exposed and are able to receive love. It is an understanding of the ordinariness and unknowability of death. It is always finding the silver lining, in the red cardinal, in the sound of the sails, in bird feathers and in gramma's final, silent tear. I think it is also to be grateful for the sacredness of the mother earth goddess and the life danced in balance between Apollo and Dionysos. Roethke said something like 'Those willing to be vulnerable, move among the mysteries.' And faith in the random acts of kindness, in the goodness of unconditional love, in the love of all gods. I'm not sure how, but I am sure, this faith is immortal and it will always be remembered."

"Wow!" my son exclaimed.

I smiled, "I know, but you asked. It's just my take on the last years. Maybe it's on the mark, maybe not."

Rebecca, smiled and said, "I get it. You're squarely on the mark."

Just then, the captain abruptly returned and asked if we were ready to head back to the boat. We agreed. It had been an emotionally draining day for the three of us. Before we climbed into the pram, Rebecca insisted that the girls row back. She said that it was only fair, that the captain had rowed us here. I looked over to her and said, "Really?"

"Yeah, you taught me how to row, remember?" she shot back. "It's the girls turn. Come on!"

"Okay, even though it's not equal weight distribution," I replied.

When we were all situated in the inflatable pram, Rebecca and I began to row, but instead of propelling the pram in a straight line back to the boat, our little pram rotated in circles. I started to laugh as my daughter instructed me when to pull while she paused. Our laughter prevented our arms from rowing and the pram eased slowly to a gentle stop in the middle of the Anti-Paros harbor. William, looking to the sky, exclaimed, "Look! Just look at how bright these stars are. You can see so many constellations."

We looked up and began to identify which were satellites and which were stars. Sitting in this little inflatable pram on the still, dark water, gazing up to the massive, encapsulating black sky filled with her piercing stars and satellites made everything crystal clear. I understood exactly my place in the big picture.

After a few minutes, the captain, not sharing our astonishment, took the oars and rowed with dramatic strokes back to the boat. We climbed aboard. William went below to find the binoculars so that he could scan the night sky in more detail. Rebecca headed for the bow compartment to get ready for bed. This part of the boat had become her and her brother's private area. They decided the second night to bunk in together.

Me, my private area was up on the bow, on deck underneath the stars. I grabbed my sleeping bag and comfy T-shirt and made my way up. I wiped down the deck with a towel and stretched out my sleeping bag with its head by the bow cleats. Climbing in, snuggling down, feeling its cozy warmth, I lay on my back, looking up to the night sky. I thought *of Rebecca and me rowing in circles and I chuckled. How far and different we have all come over the past seven years. Remembering what I said at dinner, I am the fortunate one. I am the one who has received the never-failing love of three incredible human beings, who have been at my side, each in their own way, each in their own time. I am grateful to them and to my bird feathers as I am to the stars overhead and to the light beyond.*

I closed my eyes and tried to sleep, but something wouldn't leave me alone. Listening to the gentle waves lapping against the hull and feeling the soft autumn breeze spread over the bow, I opened my eyes. They gravitated toward the moon directly overhead.

Did I really hear you? Was it you? Were you the voice I heard? Or were my eyes merely on you, when someone else spoke? Who spoke to me? Who are you? Why do you want me to stay here? Breathe. Breathe deeply. Sometimes, you have too many questions. Sometimes, things are just the way they are. Sometimes, you need not to ask your questions. Sometimes, you just need to be quiet and listen. Stay here.

READER'S GUIDE

In order to provide reading groups with the most thought-provoking questions, it is sometimes necessary to reveal important aspects of this novel. It is suggested that if you have not yet finished reading the complete story, you wait to read the Reader's Guide.

ILLNESS AND HEALING

1. How does the narrator handle the illnesses of her father and husband? What would you do / what have you done in similar circumstances?

2. Have you ever been seriously ill? What was most important to you at that time? Did your illness change the way you felt about people close to you?

3. Can you imagine what it might be like to be so ill as to be fully dependent on others? Was there anything in this book that made you think about terminal illness in a different way?

4. Some doctors seem more compassionate than others in this book. Discuss what kind of doctor you want when you are in need of a physician's care.

DEATH AND DYING

1. People have different reactions to a loved one who is dying. What did you discover about your own reactions when reading this book?

2. There are several descriptions of the moment of death. Compare and contrast them. How does the narrator's experience differ each time, or does it?

3. Is there any way to be prepared for death, either your own or the death of a loved one? Did you learn anything in this book that affected the way you think about death?

RELIGIOUS CEREMONIES

1. Religious ceremonies use symbolism to reflect a belief. How do the religious ceremonies in this book use symbolism? What truth or belief do the symbols reflect?

2. The narrator reacts to different religious ceremonies in different ways. How does her personal history affect the way she sees these ceremonies?

3. Have you ever chosen to leave a religious tradition?

4. Have you ever been curious about religious ceremonies different from your own? What did you learn?

5. What did you learn about ancient Greek rituals in this book? How do the old ways persist in modern religious practices? What connects the people of the ancient world with us today?

RITES OF PASSAGE

1. The narrator uses her husband's life experience to develop a rite of passage for their children. Have you ever done the same? If not, is there something of your past that you would pass on to your children or friends to remind them of you?

2. A rite of passage indicates that a person is growing from one way of being into a new way of being. When have you experienced a rite of passage – and how did it make you feel?

RELATIONSHIPS

1. Describe the women in this book. How are they similar? How are they different? How do they change?

2. Discuss the roles of Grandmother, Mother, Daughter, Sister as you see them here. How are they the same? How are they different? How do they overlap?

3. Discuss how the narrator's personal experience informs her

when dealing with her friend's loss of her husband. What has changed for the narrator? How is this helpful to her friend?

CONNECTING WITH ANIMALS

1. Have you ever confided in your dog, cat, bird, fish? How do animals comfort us?

2. Are you a dog person, a cat person, or perhaps a person who does not connect with pets? Discuss how you feel about having or not having a pet in your life.

GIFTS AND BURDENS

1. How do inheritances figure in this book? Discuss the idea of fairness as it applies to the people who receive inheritances and others who do not receive the same treatment.

2. Sometimes a gift is a burden. For example, when someone gives you a treasured vase but it is not to your own taste, you are torn between displaying it and hiding it in the closet. Describe a time when you received a gift that required something of you. How did that work out?

INCREDIBLE EXPERIENCES

1. Have you ever had an experience that you couldn't explain to anyone because it was too impossible to believe? What did you do about it?

2. Are there times when you later realized you had missed out on something because you weren't ready to accept or understand a deep experience? What happened?

GROWTH AND TRANSFORMATION

1. What is different about the narrator's description of her time in Rome from her time in Greece? What is the same? What does she learn?

2. How does the narrator change as she deals with her experiences? Talk about controlling behavior, fixing, researching, listening, and accepting. When is she more able to hear what she is being told? Is she able to let go of her need to do research? What did you learn from her story?

SYMBOLS AND METAPHORS

1. Describe the significance of:

   a. Birds and feathers

   b. Dolphins

   c. Greek temples

   d. Sailing

   e. The sea

   f. The moon

   h. Mountain roads

   i. Waiting rooms

   j. Dogs

   k. Food preparation & meals

   l. Strangers

2. Create a metaphor that describes a moment in the book when you were surprised or disappointed or angry or sad. Draw a picture of the metaphor. Explore the emotion that the picture describes. How can you transform the picture and the emotion in a positive way?

Made in the USA
Charleston, SC
21 May 2012